Andrew

The Constantine Legacy, Andrew's inaugural Jake Dillon novel was first published in 2006. Andrew's writing is a reflection of his extensive travels and inherent interest in national security and covert operations. Andrew lives in Dorset, where many of Dillon's tours take place, with his family and he is currently completing yet another novel in the series of Dillon adventure thrillers.

The Constantine Legacy

Andrew Towning

Cover photography by Jennie Franklin Photography.

ISBN: 978-1482730203

First published in the United States in 2006
Second edition published in Great Britain in 2013
Published by Andrew Towning
www.andrewtowning.co.uk

ACKNOWLEDGEMENT
For my family, Paula, Harriet and Eloise...
...with love

Chapter 1

I loosened my tie, took off my jacket and casually threw it over the back of a chair in the far corner of the small bland office. I returned here after each assignment and took comfort in the thought that it wasn't a place I had to visit very often.

I'd been on the Ferran & Cardini payroll for just over a year now. It was an investment company that didn't really have any clients or anything to invest in, which was just as well because I didn't know the first thing about that! Life was good. I got paid a large six figure retainer, and I received a cash in hand bonus after every job. I still wasn't sure which MI5 department Declan Ferran and Richard Cardini had worked for, but I wasn't complaining. This was no two-bob company, and the smart Docklands property displayed a façade of respectability and wealth.

The building, above ground level, was everything you'd expect with a spacious reception area, and lots of stainless steel and tinted glass. Even the security guards looked real.

My office and the other rooms that made up the special projects department were located four floors down. An innocent looking tradesman's entrance at the side of the building gave access to a bomb-proof elevator, which only allows you entry after you've been biometrically scanned.

Edward Levenson-Jones, LJ for short, was my immediate boss. When I gave him the report of my last assignment, he put it onto his desk like the foundation stone of the British Museum, and said. "The Partners want to introduce a couple of new ideas for tackling the issue of this large sum of money that has been pledged to those high spirited Italians you spoke to some weeks back."

"For *us* to tackle them!" I corrected.

"Well done, good to see you're still on the ball, old son. Because you'll always need to be one step ahead with this next job."

"You forget that I'm already covered in scar tissue as a result of the Partners' good ideas."

"Well, as luck would have it, this one is better than most," LJ said, ignoring my remark.

I personally saw each job as having a high risk factor to the people who were involved, and this one was definitely sounding as if it were on the fringe; but LJ, with his colourful bow ties and Panatela cigars, was my immediate boss and his decision was final.

Inside the wall safe lay a bundle of papers with the firm's crest upon it, the information no doubt extremely sensitive. He picked the papers out and quickly flicked through them.

"Anyway, the cheeky buggers have come back to us, and want the Partners to stump up the money sooner than was agreed. Apparently they want to see a sign of good will to their cause, so to speak."

"Do they now," I said sardonically, "I bet the Partners agreed immediately to that?"

LJ shot me one of his looks over the top of his glasses. "Well, funnily enough old son, a file was handed to me by one of my old pals over at MI5 two days ago, that may just tie in with all this."

"Suppose, just for one moment, that there was a way of giving the Italians what they wanted, but without it costing the firm a penny?"

6

I didn't say a word. He went on.

"Approximately three miles off the coast of Dorset there's a sunken boat by the name of the Gin Fizz, and on-board is a safe with two items inside."

"One of these items people of a criminal type, shall we say, would go to great lengths to get hold of if they knew of its existence."

He smiled, and sipped his coffee. I still said nothing. LJ continued enthusiastically, his voice upbeat.

"This boat is thirty metres down on the seabed, and as usual, the Partners are being cagey about the details. They're saying that she got into trouble and sunk. I personally think that she was scuttled. Either way, she went down, crew and all. But would you believe it, the skipper miraculously survived. Now, you may be wondering, how we know about this, and why we're getting involved? Well, the Gin Fizz happens to belong to the Cabinet Minister, Oliver Hawkworth. For obvious reasons, he doesn't want anyone to know where that boat is. That's why I now have the file, and because this may get messy, MI5 doesn't want any involvement."

"But, surely the coastguard would have picked her up on their radar?"

"The full time skipper," LJ said walking over to a tall cupboard and extracting a large scale chart, "Had been replaced with another, and he was under strict instructions to have no radio communication, whatsoever. And anyway, the Gin Fizz was fitted with a very sophisticated radar jammer."

"Hawkworth is saying that it was so he could sneak away for the occasional dirty weekend without his minders tracking him. So you see absolutely no one apart from the Partners and I know where she is at this present moment."

My boss is one of those men, who whenever he tells you about something, has to doodle or draw. On this occasion he started by tracing a line along the French coastline, which also showed the Channel Islands and the English coast.

"Now then," he said spreading the chart further over the conference table. "The information that we have, is that the Gin Fizz started her journey about here." He put a mark on the chart, near to La Rochelle on the West coast of France. "She set off at first tide and made her way up the coast to a point, somewhere about here." He marked a point just off the Normandy coast, near to Sillon de Talbert, continuing his line up towards Jersey.

"Now, somewhere between the Normandy coast and Jersey she met up with another much larger vessel and according to the skipper, who I might add, has already been extensively questioned by MI5, it was at this point a small package was transferred from an unmarked ship, over to the Gin Fizz."

"According to his report, the men on board the other vessel were all heavily armed."

"What about the nationality of this other ship?"

"Don't know. You see the ship appeared to have no markings or flags flying. But the skipper did mention that the men on board had an Asian look about them, and that the overall appearance of them and their vessel was extremely sea-worn!"

The line went on up to the Channel Islands and stopped. "Of course we can be relatively sure that this part of the voyage is correct, because it would seem that she was spotted on the way to Jersey. I had my source at the coastguard in the Channel Islands do a small favour for me, and run a check for that date and time, and sure enough the Gin Fizz had filed her course with the authorities there, and the same applied when he checked with the French."

"What did your chap at the coastguard say about the course of the Gin Fizz after she left their waters?" I asked.

LJ looked at the chart laid out before us. "Well - it all gets a bit strange at this point really," he said. It would appear that she is still tied up at Bouilly Port near St. Brelades Bay, where she's been since she docked a week ago."

He saw my puzzlement at this, even before it had arrived on my face.

"So what's the scam, if she's now lying at the bottom of the English Channel?" I asked.

"I did say you would need to be one step ahead on this one. The thought that I had was that they used two identical boats, or if you like a nautical doppelganger. The one now tied up at Bouilly Port is the clean decoy, while the other fitted with the radar jammer sailed for England, after having all the goodies transferred to her."

I got up and paced across the office, stretching my back as I went. I said, "Well this is all very intriguing LJ, and you have my undivided attention."

"But – what's so special about the contents of that safe that would merit swapping boats, the Partners' interest and indeed this department's involvement?"

LJ was one of those people who had to build up to a grand finale. "Well it's very simple really. Inside that safe are two plates of the highest quality, for counterfeiting Euro note currency, oh and a half a kilo of cocaine. The Partners told me that our friend in Government is crapping himself, this boat sinking was definitely not on the agenda. It's an absolute catastrophe for him in his position, especially as he had lent the dammed thing to one of his cronies for the weekend. So you see, the need for discretion and the utmost secrecy is vital."

"Forgive me if I've got this all wrong. But are you suggesting that we actually give the Italians counterfeit Euros to fund their fight against the Sicilian Mafia?"

"If only it were that simple," LJ said with a heavy

sigh. He took out another slim Panatela cigar and lit it.

"The idea is that we get the plates and the cocaine from the sunken boat, in order for the Partners to return them, temporarily you understand, to the person who owns them. We then get paid in sterling by Hawkworth for clearing up this mess, and as a bonus our Minister's friend produces a large sum of counterfeit currency as a little thank you, which we will then hand over to the Italians."

"Oh no!" I said. "You surely haven't agreed to stoop that low – have you?"

"What the hell do the Partners think we are down here?"

"I sometimes wonder," agreed LJ raising his eyebrows, "but I suppose the Partners have to look after certain parties, especially those that are politically sensitive."

"Don't give me their sob story, it might make me break down and cry."

LJ nodded, removed his glasses and rubbed his tired eyes with his fingertips.

"Look Jake, the Partners want us to retrieve these items. It's a way of stopping a scandal from hitting the gutter press, and the fact is, how shall I put this? Favours that can be banked, will be banked. It should last the firm for years to come, and we also get paid a handsome fee for our trouble. Another factor is that a certain member of a certain family is long overdue for retirement in Sicily. All this can be achieved without implicating the firm or costing the Generals or us a penny. Comment?"

"You mean that the Generals are going to use the 'funny money' to fund a Mafia war in Sicily, to buy weapons and then to finance their own dubious ventures afterwards?"

"Quite so," said LJ.

"Call me cynical but, there is obviously more to

this than you're telling me?"

LJ tried his impression of loosening up a little and said patiently, "Look, old son, it's like this. The boat sinking is merely coincidence and the fact that she belongs to a Cabinet Minister is just our good luck. True, it does now play a small part, in what is very much a bigger picture with the Italians. She holds a vital element - the plates - and yes you have been chosen to dive and retrieve what's inside that safe."

I said nothing.

"Look, the firm is in a very strong position," said LJ. "If the Italians do manage to create a re-organisation of control in Sicily, we as a firm stand to not only make millions out of it, but will have been, in our own small way, instrumental in changing the lives of thousands of families forever. It really is as simple as that."

"Oh, I can see how the Partners' devious minds are working. They're naturally working the firm into a position, where both of these clients will be inextricably indebted to us. While at the same time creating a flood of counterfeit currency throughout Europe. Brilliant, because this in turn will create panic and instability in the Euro as a currency. The rate will drop through the floor, which will be good news for anyone buying that currency at precisely the right time. But they're wrong."

Levenson-Jones looked up sharply, and began tapping his pen on the desk.

"You think so?" he said.

"I know so," I told him. "This Minister will be watching his back, and the Italians are tough guys. They've all been around. They're just as likely to double cross the firm if things don't go their way in Sicily. After all it was probably the Mafia who gave them their rank in the first place. Then the Partners will be all about urgent emails, all the way back down to us when the shit hits the fan."

We sat in silence for a few minutes; LJ sat there with his lower lip jutted forward, tapping it with his pen. In between this he said "Umm" five times.

After a few minutes of this, he got up out of his chair and began to pace, not wanting eye contact with me as he spoke.

"I want to tell you something. Two days ago, when I first got wind of this, I spoke to an old friend and colleague of yours, Carter over at Military Intelligence. I believe you worked with him when you were there. He told me that he knew of only fifty people in this country, who had the expertise and knowledge to carry off an assignment of this type, discreetly. He said that there were only five who could do it undetected. Carter said that you would be his unconditional choice."

"Was he drunk at the time?" I said.

"Perhaps," said LJ, who considered anyone with talent, as dubious.

"But the Partners might wish to reconsider their options if they knew that you were against it."

"Don't hold your breath," I told him. "The Partners will never pass up a opportunity of making money and acquiring favours from the Government. They're probably up in the atrium now gorging themselves on self-congratulation."

* * *

I was right. Within twenty-four hours, I had an email confirming the Dorset assignment. This was to be the first stage of a two-part operation.

As LJ had said when I voiced my doubts, "But there is no one else for this job, old son. Firstly, you lived in Dorset for many years and know your way around the local coastline. Secondly, you speak four languages fluently with the correct syntax, and your considerable army intelligence training, which I might add, will be crucial to the success of the job." And last of all, he threw in, "Oh, and you're a qualified wreck diver, of course."

Chapter 2

London: 3.45pm – Friday

Friday afternoon and the drive down to Dorset started frustratingly slowly.

The roads around the city were at bursting point; people dashing frenetically in all directions to start their weekends. But once the M25 was in the Mercedes' rear view mirror, I relaxed a little, increasing the volume of the music beating out as I flew down the M3, onto the M27 and west towards Bournemouth. Penetrating drizzle had been escaping from the low cloud since I joined the motorway at Southampton; the glow from the dash clock showed 5.30pm. Half an hour later I was on the outskirts of Bournemouth, nearing my destination - a rented house situated on the Sandbanks peninsula near to Poole.

This exclusive and enchanting area of Dorset is surrounded by ocean with only one road in and out. There are far reaching views out to sea and along the white sand beaches in either direction. The house that the firm had taken on a short lease had direct water frontage with its own mooring and boathouse. The property itself was large enough to accommodate four to five people comfortably. A private drive was entered via high security electric gates, under the watchful eye of a CCTV camera.

I pulled up and pushed the intercom button. A man's voice almost immediately boomed at me through the speaker, gruffly asking me to identify myself. Looking up and smiling at the camera, I said; "Really, Rumple, we only spoke ten minutes ago, do we have to go through this every time we work together?"

"You know the procedure sir. For all I know you could be an impostor. The rules are there for a reason."

After the week I'd just been through, I gave in easily. "Oh, very well, Mr Rumple, you win."

Rumple eventually opened the gates and let me into the drive. I could see two of the firm's very special field operatives standing at the front door, waiting to greet me. We had worked together on numerous occasions over the years; their talent and expertise was invaluable as they had a knack for blending in virtually anywhere without attracting attention. In reality they were both highly trained and well organised professionals, who for many years had been employed by the Government on various deep cover surveillance assignments. I parked the Mercedes inside one of the double garages. Greeted them both, and was immediately shown up to my room. I always travel light, so unpacking took all of a few minutes. After a refreshing shower and a change of clothes I went downstairs, where Mrs Rumple had prepared a culinary feast as was customary whenever we worked together and there was an excellent full-bodied red wine to wash it down.

After dinner, I had a look around and was briefed on the progress that they had made since arriving at the house on the Thursday morning. As I expected, every detail was being attended to, all of the equipment that I had requested was already neatly arranged in the second garage awaiting my inspection. All that remained was for me to see the boat and to take a look at the general area the next day.

On the Saturday morning, after breakfast Rumple took me down to the boathouse to take a look at the craft that was going to take the team to the Gin Fizz. "Well, I'm very impressed, Rumple. But how did you manage to get hold of a Phantom at such short notice?"

Rumple, as I knew, was an expert in anything

nautical. That was one of the reasons LJ had specifically chosen him for this assignment. "Oh, is that what it is, sir?" He said giving me a sideways glance. "This craft was already in here. The fax that we received shortly after we arrived just said to tell you that it's fitted with the same bit of kit as the other boat; I presume you know what that means sir?"

"Yes, I do know what that means, Rumple. Who sent the fax, by the way?"

"I believe it was Mr Levenson-Jones, sir."

It was our good fortune that the boathouse had been built with sufficient room down one side to enable indoor loading and unloading of equipment comfortably, without anyone being able to watch from land or sea. Doors had been fitted at both ends making entry and exit very easy, which for us was a good thing as we were going to be using it at night. The next two hours were taken up cruising along the coast to get my bearings. I did, with a scornful glare from Rumple, indulge myself a little and put the forty six foot cruiser through her paces. I familiarised myself with the array of hi-tech navigation and communications equipment on board. I discreetly checked out the radar-jamming device, while Rumple was at the helm on our way out to look at the area over the dive site.

We refuelled and, on arriving back at the boathouse, carefully checked and stowed all of the diving equipment.

"Any problem obtaining that other piece of equipment?" I asked Rumple.

"No sir, although Mr Levenson-Jones did say that the owners would like it back undamaged, if that was at all possible sir. I've stowed it safely in the forward rack, as you requested."

"Thank you, Rumple, just checking."

Saturday afternoon and most of the evening was spent calculating times, tides, distances and speed of all the various stages. As with all successful assignments sound planning is crucial, and due to the potentially hazardous nature of this one, particular care was being taken. The fact was that when the other member of my team arrived at the house on Tuesday, everything had to be in place and ready to go. We'd finished up by midnight and I said goodnight to Rumple, informing him that I had to be back in London by Sunday lunchtime.

* * *

Sandbanks: 10.00am - Sunday

There were blue skies and sunshine in Dorset, a sharp thunderstorm on the M3 and then bright sunshine again as I came off the motorway. I glanced in my mirror, then switched on the radio. Up towards and over Putney Bridge, onto the New Kings Road just as another thunderstorm clattered above. Students walking and talking on their mobile phones, girls showing off the latest fashion in tattoos and belly button piercing. Right towards the Thames and then first on the left into Studdridge Street. Just before the end, left again and back towards the New Kings Road.

Now I was sure. The black Ford Mondeo was following me. I turned left back onto the New Kings Road and then right, accelerating the Mercedes past Parsons Green Underground to the junction, and then right onto the Fulham Road. I pulled up by the entrance to the Fulham Broadway underground. The Mondeo came past me slowly as I searched the glove compartment for a non-existent pad and pen. I watched out of the corner of my eye until it stopped perhaps twenty metres up the road, then I quickly cut across the road and headed towards the Kings Road. This left the black Mondeo facing the wrong way up the Fulham Road. Now to see how good they really were.

I drove on past fashionable Victorian terraces behind which designer homes crouched, pretending to be traditional English houses. I stopped. I reached over to the passenger seat for my holdall, locked the car and walked back up the road I had just driven down to Tatiana's house. Number 14 had wooden slatted blinds at the front windows and a narrow hallway that seemed never to end. I let myself in.

Music playing provided a soft background sound while Tats floated around the kitchen fixing a large pot of freshly ground coffee. I stood and watched her from the kitchen doorway. She was wearing tight-fitting stonewashed jeans and a revealing top; her tan had not faded and the hair that hung across her forehead was still golden from the St Barts sunshine. She looked up. She was calm, her eyes as bright as sapphires.

She said, "So, did you straighten out the Rumples?"

"You make me sound like some sort of analyst," I said, smiling.

She moved across to me. Her kiss was sweet and lingering and through my shirt, I could feel her breasts lightly brushing against me.

I said in barely a whisper, "Hello, stranger."

She poured the coffee into colourful art-pottery mugs. "You were followed here, you know."

"I don't think so," I said casually.

"Why do you always do that?"

"Do what?"

"You know exactly what. You go all nonchalant and macho."

"OK relax. I know I was followed by a black Ford Mondeo, possibly all the way back from Bournemouth, certainly from the M3. I've no idea who it could be, perhaps it's my tailor."

"Pay him," said Tats. She stood well back from

the window still looking down at the street. "He could be from the finance company; he has a base ball bat in his hand."

"Very funny."

"You are popular today, aren't you? There are two more men across the road in a Porsche Boxster. Um, that car is rather gorgeous."

"You are joking, of course."

"Come and see for yourself."

I walked over to the window. There it was, a Porsche of brilliant metallic blue, suitably grimy enough to have done a fast trip up the motorway. It was parked at an awkward angle behind a BMW estate about twenty metres up the road. On the pavement two aggressive looking men in dark suits were smoking cigarettes and one was talking on a mobile phone. I found my sport binoculars in the bottom of my holdall and focused on them and the car carefully.

I said, "Well, they certainly aren't working for any Government department we know of, judging from the cut of their suits and the car they're driving."

Taking the binoculars from me, Tats went over to one of the tall narrow windows.

"They appear to be getting back into the Porsche." She turned back to me.

"And they look like professionals, whoever they are."

"I was just thinking the same, but what are they doing following me around London on a Sunday afternoon?"

Tats put down the binoculars and poured out the coffee in silence.

"Go on," I said, "Why I am I being chaperoned do you think, or could there be a connection between those two outside and this Gin Fizz project we are just about to start working on?"

Tats handed me the mug of black coffee. I took a sip. "Umm – Colombian blend."

"You like the Colombian blend, don't you?"

"Depends on what mood I'm in," I said.

"So what are you going to do?"

"Well, I'm in the mood, so I'm going to drink it, of course."

"No, silly, about those men outside."

"I'm going to find out who the hell they are."

"And how exactly are you going to do that?" Tats asked.

"Well, I thought I would go out of the back door, run down the alley and around the block, I'll then come at them from the other side of the road. As I approach them on the passenger side I'll pull my automatic from its holster and smash the side window with the butt. At the same time I'll shout instructions at them to get out of the car with their hands high in the air. Got it?"

Tats looked at me wide eyed. "It's really not had a good effect on you, that trip to the seaside, has it?"

"Or perhaps I'll try Vince Sharp, he's bound to be in this weekend." I used my mobile phone to ring the firm's switchboard. The number I was using didn't officially exist, courtesy of a favour called in by the Partners from one of their pals at the Home Office. While waiting to connect I asked Tats what my pass code was for the current project.

"Why is it that you can't remember a simple word?" she said tersely, continuing to look out of the window.

But before I could even comment, she answered for me.

"No, don't say it. It's because you have much more important things on your mind and it all seems a bit trivial to you, doesn't it? But, due to the very clandestine nature of the department that you occasionally work for, the firm has to have that added security; you know that as well as I do. The word that you're racking your brain for, by the way is Tomcat". She said. "Most appropriate, if you ask me," she added with a smile.

"Tomcat," I said quickly to the voice at the other end, and was immediately connected to the special operations co-ordinator, Vince Sharp.

"Vince," I said, "it's Jake."

"What an unexpected pleasure, and on a Sunday? It must be important."

"What can I do for you?"

By this point in the conversation, voice recognition had been completed, with the recorder and scrambler running as standard procedure.

"I've gone and grown two tails, Vince."

"I'm sorry to hear that old chap?" I could hear Vince tapping away furiously at his keyboard.

"According to our data, we have no known reason for your current problem, but I'll check with a specialist down the road; give me a description of both, will you."

I gave Vince the two car registration numbers along with details of make and colour just in case the plates were fake. I waited while he typed in the information and then read it all back to me.

"Thanks, Vince, ring me back will you, I'm at Tats' place here in London."

"Give me ten minutes, I need to make a phone call and more importantly make myself a nice cup of tea," he said jovially.

Tats poured me a second cup of coffee and produced a large fruitcake.

"What is that?" I said in mock horror.

"Don't be cruel, you know that mummy likes to bake, anyway it's your duty to eat a slice and say how nice it was next time you see her. I must say, you are careless sometimes, telling Vince where you are, you don't know, someone could have been eavesdropping."

I said, "True - but highly unlikely. The software that we use for telephone scrambling is the most sophisticated on the market and with a chap like Vince sitting there well, need I say more?"

The phone rang; it was Vince, asking me for the pass word. "Tomcat, what have you got for me?" I asked.

"OK, you really do have a couple of tails, don't you? The black one I've traced back to a security company in Hertfordshire. It's a regular, used on the whole by the Government, my guess is that I'll find that this one has cropped up a few times before. I'll have to ferret around a little deeper tomorrow morning though."

I said quickly. "Try this Minister in particular, along with any dubious acquaintances he may have." I gave Vince the name and left it at that.

"What about the Porsche, why has that one appeared?"

"Well, I've drawn a blank at present with that one, but I reckon it's connected to the assignment that you're about to start. I'll have to come back to you when I know more, but why do you think the Mondeo is connected to this job?"

"Call it a gut feeling. Anyway, thanks for checking these out for me, especially on a Sunday; I really appreciate it Vince." I hung up.

"What did he say?" Tats asked.

"He confirmed what I thought. That maybe, just maybe, the reason those cars are following me is because of the Gin Fizz. Any movement outside while I've been on the phone?"

"No, nothing, but hang on, the guy in the black Mondeo is walking up to the two in the Porsche and is now talking to them."

I walked over to the window. Peering through my binoculars, I could see that the two men in the Porsche were both speaking on their phones. The chap from the black Ford was standing with his hands deep in the pockets of his shabby check jacket. The men got out of the car and all three were talking on the pavement. Soon the two got back into the Porsche and drove away, but the black Ford remained outside.

Tats and I spent the rest of Sunday afternoon waiting for Vince to call back.

In between, she washed her hair and I read the Sunday Times from front to back. The TV was on, but I wasn't watching; some sort of fly on the wall programme was coming to an end when my mobile phone rang.

"The Porsche belongs to an acquaintance of our Minister, Oliver Hawkworth." I said into the phone before he could speak.

"Uncanny," said Vince. "How did you know?"

"Well I've been sitting here pondering;" I said. "I should have thought of it before. Friend Hawkworth has obviously got into bed with whoever really owns the contents of his safe on board the 'Gin Fizz'. Whoever that is, owns the blue Porsche, I'd guess."

Vince said. "Good thinking chap. My source has come back with a confirmed owner for that blue Porsche. It belongs to a Robert Flackyard from Dorset."

"What else have you managed to find out about him, anything or nothing?"

"What, at such short notice, give me a chance." Vince said congenially.

"But according to the tabloid info that I've been able to locate on the Internet, Flackyard likes to live life right on the edge, shall we say. At fifty-eight years of age, he owns a string of night clubs on the South Coast, as well as being a successful property developer. The only other thing that I can tell you from these articles is that there has been some speculation about how he conducts his business dealings. But, one thing's for sure, he most definitely enjoys a playboy lifestyle around the globe. There is also a definite link between him and our ministerial friend. They have been photographed together at various functions on more than one occasion, but I'll have to speak to someone tomorrow morning and request a detailed file on him. I'll mark it urgent shall I?"

"Urgent is definitely good, Vince. We have to know who we are really dealing with and why the interest in me. See what official information you can dig up; use the Partners to encourage the process. In the meantime, can you make sure that L.J. is brought up to speed when he arrives first thing in the morning. Oh and Vince, well done." I hung up just as Tats walked into the room swathed in a large white towel, having showered.

"What did he say?" she asked.

"It's as I thought, the black Ford belongs to a firm who are almost certainly working for our Minister, but Vince has to dig a bit deeper tomorrow. As for the Porsche, well I must admit that one is a surprise. It's registered to a Robert Flackyard from Bournemouth, a wealthy entrepreneur and playboy. I think that firstly, he is almost certainly linked with Hawkworth; and secondly, if that is the case, then he is the owner of the counterfeiting plates and cocaine on board the Gin Fizz, but that's only a guess."

"You say Robert Flackyard, that name rings a bell. I'm sure that a Mr R. Flackyard came to see one of the Partners last week."

"Do you know who he saw?" I asked.

"No, it was an appointment that one of them made and then posted on the electronic diary. They sometimes do that when they're working late, but there's nothing unusual about it. They do it all the time."

"I want you to check both Partners' personal diaries for last week the minute you get in tomorrow. I want to know which one of them saw this character and why."

Tats made a face at me and continued to paint a fingernail deep red. I put down my coffee cup, and walked over to where she was stood.

"My nails are still wet," she said, feigning protest and holding her arms high above her head, adding. "Jake, you mustn't."

The towel slid easily to the floor ending up in a heap around her feet.

Chapter 3

Sunday eventually returned to something resembling normality. As evening approached the skies opened up for another thunderstorm, the man in the shabby check jacket and black Ford Mondeo decided enough was enough and left. Tatiana and I decided to eat out at a new Thai restaurant that had recently opened locally.

Monday: 7.30am

Monday was a clear bright morning at the end of May that warned you summer was set to pounce. I logged on to the firm's secure server to receive my emails. A letter from the Rumples had been re-routed to me with confirmation that everything was in place and waiting for my arrival on the Tuesday. The only other in my mailbox was from LJ, instructing me to report at the office 9.30am sharp for his usual pep talk prior to an assignment. I nicked my chin while shaving and bled like I'd sprung a leak. I changed into another shirt. Arriving at the firm's wharf side offices, I found LJ in a quiet rage because I had made him late for the Partners' operational assignments meeting that takes place in that rather strange glass pyramid shaped room on the roof of the building the second Monday of each month.

It was a terrible day and it hadn't even begun yet. LJ went through all the rigmarole of my new assignment: code words and priorities for communicating with him as well as the other members of the team based in London.

"I don't know how she did it? But Tatiana has

worked her charm on the Partners, and actually got them to agree to give you extra funding on this assignment. So please don't let her, or them, down. I've suggested to all parties concerned, that it might be useful if you deal with Tatiana at all times."

"After all, she does have the Partners' authority, should you have to go outside of your brief. You'll remember, that after South America last year they said they would never indulge you again with extra funding."

"Big deal," I said, eyeing the papers on his desk. "I had no options left open to me on that assignment, as you well know. Had I not paid off the local Police Commissioner I would probably still be rotting in a cell over there."

"Anyway, they're saving a bundle this time by reducing the size of my team to four people, including myself."

"The nature of this assignment, old son, is such that the fewer people are involved, the better. Anyway, don't be so touchy about that unfortunate incident, it could have happened to any of us." To inflict extra pain LJ always gave a little smirk when referring to the South American incident.

"All right," I said, "but you don't have to be so bloody gloating about it."

LJ turned over the next paper on his desk. "Equipment."

He was looking at me over the tops of his glasses; I could see that a lecture was coming, so before he could read on, I interrupted.

"Yes, the matter of equipment. Are you aware the Partners have insisted that I am to personally insure all special equipment on this assignment?"

"Have they any idea how much that is going to cost me."

"You do have a reputation, old son. I'm fully

aware of the insurance, of course, but unfortunately the accountants have reported back to the Partners."

"The fact is that last year alone, you destroyed and mislaid over two hundred thousand pounds worth of equipment. Admittedly, your assignments do tend to be, how shall we say, a little more arduous than those of the others. But you really must be more careful. Most of this kit is loaned to us by Her Majesty's Government."

"That's as it may be. But who the hell in there right mind would insure equipment of this nature?"

LJ produced a document from a pile of papers, pushing it across the desk to me.

"If you could read the declaration, sign and date it, I will take care of the rest for you. Cover will start as of midnight."

I signed and dated all the relevant boxes. "I suppose I should've known."

I said with a nod. "There's one other thing, while we are on the subject of equipment. I really do feel I should have a weapon, say a handgun."

There was a long silence, broken only by the sound of LJ snapping his pencil.

"Handgun?" he said. "Are you going out of your mind, old son?"

"Just a thought, boys and their toys, you know," I said.

"Quite so, old son," LJ said, "but they really are nasty, noisy, dangerous toys. How would you feel if you pinched your finger in the mechanism or something?"

I picked up the copy of insurance along with the inventory of equipment to be used on the assignment and walked over to the door.

"Mr and Mrs Rumple will expect you tomorrow at 7.30am sharp," he said from behind his desk; "I would appreciate it if you would have the new European Network blueprint finished and emailed to me before you leave, and…"

He removed his glasses and started to polish them very carefully. "That Glock 10mm automatic you have that I'm not supposed to know about. Please don't take it with you, old son, we don't want any accidents, now do we?"

"As if I would," I said over my shoulder, as I closed the door behind me.

That day I completed my report for LJ on the new European Network. The idea was to have people in positions of usefulness feeding information back to the firm's headquarters in London.

All of them would be switchboard and computer operators, personal assistants or telecom repair technicians working in embassies, foreign government departments and stock exchanges. It meant setting up a recruitment consultancy abroad, which would specialise in this type of personnel. As well as describing the new idea, my report had to outline the operational side, i.e. planning, communications and procedures to ensure that anyone who was detected could not lead to anyone else. The structure for sending messages up and down the network had to ensure that no contact was made between sender and receiver. As far as the Partners were concerned the most important factor of the report was the balance sheet, how much was it going to cost and how much estimated extra revenue it would bring in.

Tats finished typing the report by 6.30 p.m. I checked it through and then emailed it to LJ as well as taking two hard copies and backup disks, one to put in the firm's strong room and the other for my safekeeping. I had only one other thing to do before we left, and that was to memorise my communications priority codes for my present assignment.

The firm's switchboard is manned twenty four hours a day. Our department however has an automated system, which can be entered only by using our mobile phones and a series of touch-tone codes. The link is made via a satellite and filters the call through a random route of countries to any person, department or overseas office that you wish to speak to within Ferran & Cardini International. The call is then monitored, scrambled, and recorded; anyone trying to intercept or bug the call has a digital impulse spike sent down the line to destroy the phone or equipment being used.

We left discreetly by our own side entrance and walked quietly by the river.

Tatiana told me which Partner had seen Robert Flackyard the previous week, but could ascertain no further information about why. I asked her not to copy the new Network report to the Partners just yet and suggested an excuse that she could give them. I knew LJ would not approach anyone with the report until he had spoken to me in person on my return from the assignment.

Chapter 4

As I approached my destination the early morning air pressed its damp nose against the Mercedes windscreen. Ocean sand and water were thrashing together in endless permutations, and three miles out in the depths beyond was the wreck of the Gin Fizz that had brought me here.

For this assignment Rumple had thought of everything, including the other team member, Charlie McIntyre. LJ had relented and given in to his request to have him on board, on the grounds that as only the best would do, the minister could foot the bill. At twenty-nine years of age Charlie was a first rate wreck diver and extremely talented with a knife and explosives.

Ten minutes after I had arrived at the rented house, an old beaten-up VW beetle camper came to a halt at the gates. Driving it was a youngish male, with unruly fair-hair. He got out of the bright yellow Volkswagen, walked up to the intercom and pressed the button.

Rumple answered almost immediately, his gruff voice booming. "Hello – state your name and business." The voice at the other end was well educated and articulate. The monitor screen showed a tanned face with classic good looks, and an effervescent smile. Charlie McIntyre's piercing blue eyes looked straight into the lens of the CCTV camera.

"Good to have on board again, Charlie," I said, as he stepped out of the old van into the brilliant sunshine.

Charlie came over and gave me a big brotherly hug, we shook hands and I knew what was coming. His grip was solid, like a vice, and the pressure made my knuckles go white. But, as was customary, I returned the gesture with equal enthusiasm. His grip had strengthened since the last time we had worked together and I thought for a split second that I was going to have to give in. Which meant, that for the first time ever, I would have to buy him a very large drink at the local bar. Thankfully Charlie had never bested me.

"One of these days, I'll do for you, Jake Dillon."

"In your dreams, Charlie boy. But we really must get out of this dreadful custom of trying to crush each others' fingers every time we meet." Mr and Mrs Rumple just looked on in utter disbelief.

"Anyway, how's your shoulder after your last assignment?"

"One hundred per cent now, thanks. Would you believe it though, I only finished the blasted physiotherapy about a month ago." Lowering his voice conspiratorially, so that the Rumples couldn't overhear, he went on. "But there was an up side to ripping my shoulder. As a bonus. This rather lovely therapist called Julia insists that I keep going back on a regular basis for what she calls a personal fitness assessment."

"Like I said, it's good to have you on board for this one, Charlie."

After a spot of breakfast on the terrace we had coffee followed by Mrs Rumple going out and Rumple checking the Phantom and equipment down at the boathouse.

Charlie and I went over the plan for the dive. The gate monitor showed a woman looking up at the camera.

"Anyone else coming to play, Jake? Asked Charlie. "Only there is one very attractive female at the gate, just about to push the intercom."

"No, I've got all the team here. What does she look like?"

"Well – let's see now, mid thirties, dark hair, tall, I'd say about five nine to five ten, full lips and curves where they should be. Oh, and an extremely well tailored linen suit, with not much underneath – perhaps?"

"Very funny, let me see." The buzzer from the intercom came alive.

"Hello, can I help you?" I said in a clipped tone.

"Yes, my name is Fiona Price and I'd like to see Mr Jake Dillon."

Her accent had the faintest of Scottish brogue.

"There is no Mr Dillon here, are you quite sure you have the right address?"

"Quite sure, thank you. Mr Levenson-Jones of Ferran & Cardini in London gave it to me personally. It's very important that I speak to Mr Dillon and give him this message."

"Did Mr Levenson-Jones give you anything else to give to Mr Dillon?" I asked.

"Mr Dillon, I will play your little game for as long as you wish. The word that you require apparently is Tomcat. Now can we carry on this conversation inside, please. Preferably before you dive this evening."

"OK, Miss Price, we have to be careful and there's no need to use a loud hailer to tell everyone in the neighbourhood, why we are here." The electric gates slid back silently, closing automatically a minute later.

Fiona parked next to Charlie's old VW. I let her into the coolness of the tiled hallway. Enough light filtered through the draped voile for me to take stock of Miss Fiona Price. Immediately I noticed that her skin was smooth with not a blemish to mar her beauty.

"Miss Price, sorry about that cloak and dagger stuff just now. Let me introduce Myself. I am Jake Dillon and this is my associate Charlie McIntyre."

"Mr Dillon, I'll come straight to the point. I work for the British Government and I have been seconded to Ferran & Cardini in a technical capacity just for this project. I have also been fully briefed about you and your assignment - the Gin Fizz."

"OK, Miss Price," I said, "So you know all about me and the Gin Fizz."

"What's your message? You can speak in front of Mr McIntyre."

She handed me an envelope with the firm's official crest on it, and spoke very rapidly. "I'm a scuba-diver with wreck investigation experience and my brief is to retrieve the logbook from the boat, and to assist you and Mr McIntyre, as and where necessary. I have my own equipment in the car..."

I slowed her to a standstill with my eyes. "I'm sure you do, Miss Price," I said.

I glanced over at Charlie, who was running his hand through his hair and smiling as usual. I said nothing; instead I turned and walked over to the window, ripping open the envelope. The message inside was simple. LJ's instruction was to co-operate but be extremely wary of Miss Price. Looking over the bay, I took my time to turn and face her again.

"Please sit down," I said coldly, "and listen carefully. If you think you're coming on a rip roaring little fun-jaunt, I'd think again."

"I'm a qualified open water diver, Mr Dillon, with experience in wreck diving."

"You'll find my expert knowledge for this job invaluable."

"I will, will I?" I said. "Well, I don't know what you call 'expert', but one of my men has spent several years as a royal naval diver. Let me tell you, Miss Price, he once saved the lives of an entire nuclear submarine crew by diving one hundred and fifty feet in sub zero temperatures to cut away a WW2 mine that had decided to hitch a lift. Not to mention the time when the Argentinian forces invaded the Falkland Islands. Along with two others, he managed to diffuse mines laid by the invaders while the Argentinian Navy threw every grenade they could find into the harbour. They only stopped after an hour because they calculated that no one could be alive down there after that much pounding. Then he and his fellow SBS team members swam up under one of their supply ships and fixed three large charges to it, that scattered corned beef all the way back to their mainland."

"By the way, he did this while you were still at university – Miss Price." I walked over to the window. The view was magnificent and very calming.

With my back to her, I said, "You'd better go and get your equipment. Please take it to Mr Rumple down at the boathouse."

Charlie made some quiet remarks about Miss Price's bright-green wetsuit, but it was much more professional than I feared it might be. I made a mental note to call an old friend at Special Branch later that day.

Rumple, Charlie, Miss Price and I had a conference. Rumple gave each one of us a file containing copies of various charts together with photographs and information showing us the position and way the Gin Fizz was lying.

"When were these images taken Rumple?" I asked.

"Yesterday morning, sir."

I carefully studied Rumple's images. The Gin Fizz was lying on the sea floor at a forty-five degree angle.

"According to Miss Price and LJ's message, our Government Minister and the owner of that boat is keen to get the log from the Gin Fizz. That is – if the Captain didn't dump it overboard before she went down," I added casually.

Before anyone could interrupt, I carried on, "I assume you have been told where to locate the log book when you get inside the craft. We can't afford the luxury of you wasting time rummaging around down there."

"And if the captain did lob it over the side?" Charlie added.

"In that case, finding it depends on how far the boat travelled between the log being thrown over and sinking and if my equipment will detect such a small flat object, which will likely be submerged in the silt." The gold ring on Fiona's finger flashed in the bright sunlight, "I suspect the underwater currents are strong as well."

Then Charlie asked Rumple about tidal movement at surface, absolute slack-water times and slack-water duration, and they discussed ways of setting out a diving timetable in order to use those facts to our advantage.

Everything said and done, I told everyone to relax for the rest of the day and said we'd have another briefing that evening, before we dived.

As the weather was unusually warm for the time of year, I decided to sit on the sand and think. The sea was kicking idly at the beach. Miss Price was nearly inside a black swimsuit, and Charlie was showing off with handstands, which were not impressing her one little bit. I asked Rumple to swim out to sea with the lovely lady from the ministry and let me know what sort of endurance she had.

"Go out about, let's say fifty metres, and come in again. Don't hurry her, but let her know you're watching her."

"Yes, I understand sir," said Rumple, and went to tell Miss Price.

I watched them run across the soft damp sand, lengthening the curved imprints to the water's edge. Rumple, although in his early fifties was as fit as any man half his age.

Charlie came up wanting to talk about the assignment. He paused, carefully designing a sentence that wouldn't sound impertinent. "Why doesn't this Minister go through official channels? Even if there is something dodgy about this boat, he could have used one of their spook departments to salvage and retrieve it for him, couldn't he?"

"The whole thing stinks, Charlie. To tell you the truth, I have an awful feeling that we are sitting out here bleating like a goat in a tiger trap. That message Miss Price brought about the logbook. It just doesn't ring true." I told Charlie about me being followed by the two cars. How one of them had been traced back to a security firm that our ministerial friend had hired and how an international playboy, Robert Flackyard, owned the other car from Bournemouth and that I thought they were all connected. "And what about this Fiona Price character?" I finished. "Why is she here and what is her real brief?"

As I said it, Rumple and Miss Price came out of the water. Rumple was tanned dark-brown and moving like he'd just stepped out of a shower. He wasn't even out of breath. Miss Price had her mouth open and was gulping deep draughts of air, throwing her head back and running an open hand through her hair. They walked slowly up to where Charlie and I were sitting, Miss Price waited for words of praise.

"How do you feel, Miss Price?" I asked casually.

She was still gulping for breath. "O.K, thank you Mr Dillon... absolutely first rate."

"Then I would like you to go out about twenty metres – but this time, please swim underwater there and back. Break surface only when you have to - I do not want to see a train of foam and bubbles. Should you experience any problems tell Rumple immediately. I'm not carrying dead heroes, I prefer live cowards. And Rumple stay close."

"What is the purpose of this, Mr Dillon?" she asked defiantly, standing with hands on hips in front of me.

"The purpose – well now, Miss Price." I kept my

voice casual. "The purpose of this is to ascertain whether or not you are fit enough to dive with us tonight." I got up and started back up the beach.

"Charlie and I are going up to that café to watch you and count the number of times you come up for air. Oh, and another thing, Miss Price you're not in London, you know, so please try and look like an English holiday maker..."

I continued up the beach with my back to them... "That is to say, miserable." Rumple knew me all too well, but Miss Price could not see the smile that was across my face as she stormed down the beach.

"Do you think you're being a little hard on Miss Price, Jake?" Charlie asked. We walked up the steps to the café.

"Probably," I said. "But I'll give her credit, she's got spirit and determination." We sat and watched in silence and then Charlie said. "You may be worrying for nothing, you know. It might just be as easy and straight forward as it seems."

I didn't think so.

Chapter 5

Darkness brought its own welcome cloak to hide us with. The next green wave lapped at the boathouse, Charlie opened the heavy double doors, tied them back and then effortlessly leaped aboard onto the dive platform.

Rumple saw to the forward and aft lines. I gently eased the Phantom out into the harbour, both of her powerful inboard diesel engines gurgling, waiting to be unleashed. The water foamed at the stern and we headed out into the English Channel as the twin screws bit the sea. Once we were in open water I gave Rumple the helm and went down to the cabin. The jamming device that had been fitted was hidden from view in a locker, but the red activate light glowed faintly in the dark. I switched on the sonar and radar and went back up to Rumple. "I've activated both the sonar and radar, so keep an eye on them both especially as we approach the dive site. I'll be below with the others, so if you need me, just holler."

Rumple nodded his OK. "The radar also has a viewing monitor below, sir."

"You'll find it in a concealed dropdown compartment over the dining area."

"Thank you, Rumple." I then called Charlie and Miss Price to join me below for a final briefing. Afterwards, I took Rumple up a hot chocolate, for which he was extremely grateful.

We were heading steadily westward, keeping close to the shore, the green black sea rolled gently beneath us, only to meet with a violent foaming end as it hissed and crashed onto the white rocks. Rumple pointed out how each individual rock or formation that we were passing has its dangers and its name. We saw Old Harry Rocks, Dancing Ledge, but I knew the most dangerous rocks were the ones that are completely covered at high water.

Those enormous flat slabs of stone around Dancing Ledge were where many a small vessel had been smashed to smithereens.

I watched the two screens intently for a few minutes. Charlie was on the aft deck smoking one of the cheroots he favoured. Miss Price was also there, but she was huddled in the corner under layers of clothing and a large waterproof jacket. Rumple had turned the sleek craft ninety degrees away from the shoreline; we were now heading straight out to sea towards the Gin Fizz.

We started to pull on our wet suits and arrange the equipment to hand.

Rumple called down as he swung the boat round in a large arc. "We've missed it, I'm afraid. I'm going round and across again. I could have put a marker buoy down yesterday but..."

"No, you did right Rumple," I told him. "Let's keep it discreet."

Charlie was keeping an eye on both screens yelling out as we passed over the wreck. Rumple killed the engines and then immediately reversed the thrust, bringing the forty-six foot craft to a stop. With the engines idling, the automatic anchor winch cut in splashing overboard and Rumple let it go until the multi prongs snagged on the bottom.

Miss Price adjusted her air-bottles. Under the wetsuit, her profile showed a slender, fit body tone. I tapped her arm.

"I don't want you down there until we've retrieved what it is we've come here for, do I make myself clear?"

"Perfectly clear Mr Dillon, I'll stay on deck with

Mr Rumple. But please remember my own orders are perfectly clear too. That logbook must return to London with me, or questions will be asked."

I turned to Charlie, who was listening, "Check the anchor line first thing when you descend. Mr Rumple - Miss Price is under your personal supervision, she goes down only when and if you say."

"Very well, sir."

"Oh, and Rumple any sign of trouble break out the little toy in the forward rack and alert us immediately on the comm. please."

"Very well sir, understood. Good luck down there."

Charlie eased his feet into the large fins, pulled his facemask into place and carefully put one leg over the side of the dive platform. In spite of the sunshine during the day, the English Channel is always cold, whatever the time of year. Charlie grimaced behind his mask, then he gently dropped overboard, waters surging over his shoulders, and he was instantly gone in the darkness of the water.

Rumple hit a switch and the entire bottom of the boat lit up. For an instant, I could make out Charlie's blue wetsuit as he swam towards the anchor chain and then down into the darkness. His lean silhouette shattered into a dozen blue moving patches as he sank, and a gush of white bubbles ripped to the surface. In parts of the Caribbean one can see well over one hundred feet but we were armed with just a few feet of visibility at most.

Charlie had quickly gone.

The sea was making background music; our boat was handed from wave to wave like a hospital patient between specialists. At its highest peak I could just see the lights of the cross channel ferry making its way over the horizon towards Poole. Miss Price tried to light a cigarette, but the gusting wind and movement foiled her each time until she flicked the long white shape away.

The weather was coming in fast from the West. Rumple came down towards me and by the look on his face it was not good news.

"The weather's closing in, the Met Office is warning of a force eight blowing up, and by this swell I would say we only have limited time here."

From the corner of my eye I caught Miss Price waving her arms at us frantically and shouting something, but her words were carried away on the wind. She pointed at the anchor chain which was juggling up and down, dark blue patterns danced in the powerful lights under the boat and then glued themselves into one shape as Charlie's blue rubber head broke the surface.

He swam round to the stern and grabbed hold of the dive platform rail. He unstrapped the big torch from his wrist and passed it into the boat. He removed his dark blue fins under water and threw those into the boat. They landed with a wet thud. Then he grasped the rail with both of his gloved hands. With one great heave he came unstuck from the wave-tops and toppled onto the dive platform. Rumple had the Thermos flask of hot sloe gin ready, and Charlie emptied the metal container in one gulp and held it out for a refill. Blood was trickling down the outside of the wetsuit from a deep cut on his right hand. Rumple produced antiseptic from the boat's first aid box and dabbed at it with cotton wool. Charlie stamped around the deck with pain as the antiseptic hit his bloodstream and the dark coloured liquid ran off his fingers.

After that we all went into the cabin, and Charlie went off to get out of his wetsuit. He took a hot shower and changed into a pair of casual cargo pants, an old rugby shirt and dark blue fleece before returning to where we all sat listening to the Met report on the radio. He turned to me and said, "It's pretty bad down there, the bottom is just a maelstrom, visibility is zero."

He said there was no point in Miss Price or I diving tonight, and lit a cheroot.

Rumple went up to the helm and spun the engines and wound in the anchor.

Disappointment showed on all our faces. We were going to have to return and try again the next day. Weather permitting.

* * *

Wednesday: 9.30am

After breakfast Charlie set up the laptop computer for his presentation, connecting this to the large cinema screen that came with the house. A secure line video link was also established to LJ's office in London to enable him to get a live OPs report showing the position and angle at which the Gin Fizz was lying.

"A factor we were not aware of is that the wreck is perched on the edge of a rock sided trench. There is what I judge to be a six-knot current pressing the hull into a vertical formation..."

Charlie was always on firmer ground when dealing with reports like this. He made arrow marks across the screen.

"The Gin Fizz is approximately forty foot in length, and she has a broad beam, which makes her a good-sized boat. But all this..." On his side view of the craft Charlie now drew a line along the middle of the virtual image and indicated the area forward of the main cabin area and below his line, "...is filled with what looks like small packages, possibly explosives. They're floating all over the place inside this main area. To go inside the boat in that storm would, I felt, have been almost certain suicide. But, the hull looks intact, as is the deck areas and control cabin. There are no bodies down there either which, even with the strong currents, I feel is very odd. But I suppose they could have been swept away?" I noticed that the cut on the back of Charlie's hand was bleeding again.

I leaned over to him and said quietly, "Why don't you let Mrs Rumple take a look at that hand of yours? She's very proficient with a needle, you know."

"LJ, can you hear all of this." I said.

"Loud and clear, Jake. Dammed strange all these packages floating about though, I'll get on to our friend at the ministry and find out why the hell we were not advised about this. I was certainly not told about them being on board. I've heard and seen enough for the time being. Either Tatiana or I will call you back later with an update on the situation. Charlie thank you for this information, you're all doing a good job."

He broke the connection, but Charlie continued: "The boat is lying at a slight angle, just as Mr Rumples' photographs showed. As I've already said, it's lucky for us that she is intact. But where the current has dragged it around; some of the deck areas have some extremely sharp and jagged projections, as I found out to my cost. The way in is straightforward enough as we can go through the main cabin hatch. But there is one potentially hazardous problem. If she has been rolled around the ocean floor in that storm last night, her hull may have been crushed or she may now be upside down in the trench. We'll find out later, when we dive back down to her."

Chapter 6

Wednesday: 2pm

We decided to dive during daylight hours. Charlie and I went down first, and found the Gin Fizz in the position she had been the night before. Charlie worked methodically, checking her entire structure for any signs of further damage. Using our comm, we kept in touch with Rumple on the surface.

We soon came to the decision that pussyfooting around and being cautious wouldn't do, especially with the potential hazards waiting to greet us.

Charlie went in through the main cabin hatch and I followed moments later.

On entering the boat, the packages that Charlie had seen through the portholes the night before were everywhere, floating like inert jellyfish. I gently pulled one towards me, for a closer examination; it felt like Semtex, but I couldn't be sure through the coarse material covering it. "I'm taking this one up to the boat for a closer look," I said, my voice sounded metallic through the microphone.

* * *

On deck Rumple and Miss Price looked on as I took my knife and proceeded to carefully cut away the wax covered material that sealed whatever was inside. I unfolded layer after layer until the contents were displayed. No one spoke for a full minute, as we took in what was laid out before us. Miss Price was the first to speak, in just above a whisper. "Well, Mr Rumple, since we've not been blown into space, would it be safe to assume that it's not a highly volatile explosive? So, what is it?"

"That, Miss Price," Rumple said matter of factly, "if I'm not mistaken, is raw opium. Once this dark brown chunk is processed in a lab and 'cut' ready for distribution onto the streets as heroin, I'd guess this pack would be worth approximately a million pounds. But that is only a guess, you understand."

"I would say that was a fairly accurate guess, Rumple. There are probably fifty of these inside the main cabin area. I think someone has some explaining to do back in London." I looked up. "Don't you Miss Price?"

The three of us spent the next half-hour bringing the waxy packages up to the surface where Rumple stowed them safely in lockers out of sight. After this was completed, I located the safe. LJ's information about where it was positioned and the entry codes were correct. Fortunately for me it had a backup battery power source. I punched in the numeric code but nothing happened. I took off one of my gloves, tried again and this time my bare fingers carefully tapped in the numbers correctly. I could hear the lock mechanism click into place.

Pulling at the door, a large bubble of air escaped as I strained it open and water gushed inside. I shone my torch in. We had been told there were two flattish packages wrapped in what looked like black velvet. I assumed these were the counterfeit plates - together with two small white brick-shaped parcels. The cocaine packs were both in clear waterproof bags, everything was present and correct, so I placed all the items into the clear zip top bag that I had with me and hooked it on to my belt.

The only other item tucked right at the back of the safe was the boat logbook. Looking around I made sure that the others had gone back up to the surface, and then pushed it carefully inside my wetsuit for safe keeping, and a little light bedtime reading later.

As I pulled myself through the hatch into open water, Charlie and Miss Price reappeared over my left shoulder. Over the comm I told Charlie that everything we'd come for was accounted for.

"What about the log book?" Miss Price broke in.

"Well, it wasn't in the safe, and I've had a thorough look round the entire boat, but it doesn't appear to be here. Be my guest take a look for yourself – you have exactly ten minutes."

She slipped through the hatch and inside the boat.

We had one last thing to do, and that was to get rid of the existence of the Gin Fizz. Charlie started packing the charges on to the hull as Miss Price swam back out, searching the surrounding area.

"What are you doing?" She asked.

Charlie was first to respond. "Our instructions are quite explicit Fiona. We have to blow it, once we have what we came for."

"But I don't have the logbook." The panic in her eyes and edginess to her voice said it all. "I must have that logbook. London will not be happy if I don't take it back with me."

"Miss Price," I said, "we have looked inside and out, as you have. We do not have the time to mess about further, so would you please surface now."

We watched her ascend, and then turned and continued to place the charges over the deck area. "By having the charges on the deck as well as the hull," said Charlie, "we should be able to create a blast that will generate the minimum disruption on the surface, although there will still be a fair bit of spray. Or that's the theory, anyway."

"If you say so," I replied.

We broke the surface and I passed the clear bag up to Rumple, who took it from me, disappearing below. He carefully placed the contents in an aluminium briefcase. I changed into a pair of khaki trousers and an open neck shirt, going back up on deck where the others were congregated in the cockpit. Miss Price was obviously not happy at the thought of having to return to London without the logbook.

Ignoring her I went straight over to Charlie, "What's the maximum range on the Detonator?" I asked.

"About half a mile, in these conditions," he replied.

"Good, that should be far enough away from the explosion not to attract too much attention from any other craft that may happen along."

It was four thirty by the time we had stowed all the equipment away. The sun was still shining, clouds were flitting around it like moths around a candle, and there was a bite in the air whenever the sun vanished.

In the distance, a small powerboat was coming towards us at speed.

Through the binoculars I could just make out three occupants dressed in dark clothing behind the windshield. Rumple had seen it too; he had increased our speed and altered course by a few degrees as a precaution.

They came straight at us, moving quickly over the water. Everything happened in a flash as they opened fire with machine pistols aiming for the cockpit but strafing bullets everywhere. We all slammed ourselves down on to the deck as the windows exploded into infinity above our heads. Glass shattered everywhere; air rushed through the opening with such a force, the noise was deafening. They raced past on our starboard side, emptying their magazines as they went.

"Who the hell is that?" shouted Charlie, his body pressed tight to the deck, covered in debris.

"I don't know and I don't care," I shouted. "What I said on the beach, remember – goats in a tiger trap." I looked up. "Rumple, are you all right."

He was slumped in a sitting position against the bulkhead. I carefully moved over broken glass and splintered timbers towards the helm.

Reaching up I fumbled around for the switch to activate the autopilot.

"I think I've taken a hit in my shoulder, sir."

He'd gone a ghastly shade of grey, and there was blood covering his right arm. I crawled over and took a quick look. Satisfied that it was a clean shoulder wound, I took off my shirt, ripped off a sleeve and used it as a tourniquet. "You're lucky, Rumple, the bullet seems to have gone right through; you sit here and don't move. Miss Price will look after you. Charlie, take over the helm and steer us back over the dive site, I'm pretty sure those goons will follow us. I'm going forward to even up the odds. When I give you the signal, detonate the explosives." He nodded his understanding.

The small dart-like craft turned as I was making my way to the forward rack. The crack of their machine pistols sounded from not too far away, bullets whizzing overhead, the occasional thud as one slammed into the fibreglass structure. Lying face down, I struggled with the forward hatch shackle, but eventually managed to pull out what I'd had Rumple so carefully stow on board for me. The latest toy that the MOD had to offer, on loan courtesy of a favour I had called in. The KZL300 laser is capable of blasting a hole right through a tank at a mile.

Charlie was taking us back towards the dive site. As we passed over the Gin Fizz, I brought my arm up and down again. The next second, the explosion could be heard as the other boat came up fast behind us; the upward pressure plumed seawater high in to the air.

After two seconds, full power was indicated on the laser's display. I locked the sight on to the small boat as they came around from swerving to avoid the great wall of water that had suddenly appeared in front of them. I squeezed the trigger very gently; the tiny craft burst in to a fireball as the beam hit them square amidships. There was no sound and nothing visual to warn them of what was coming.

"Inspiring!" I whispered to myself.

Our attackers, who ever they were, had died instantly. The heat generated by the laser canon and the explosion from their fuel tank that ensued had been so intense that there was nothing left on the surface. Charlie circled the area a couple of times, but there was nothing to retrieve.

"That was awesome! What the hell is it, and why is it on this boat?"

Charlie asked, his voice a little shaky. He knew my fixation with gadgets and that I had a contact at the Army's Establishment for Weapons development in Surrey.

"Um, was rather effective wasn't it," I said with a smirk. "This Charlie, is the little toy I was telling you about, I asked LJ to phone a friend of mine and ask if I could borrow it for the assignment; never thought we would be able to, not in a million years. I wanted it because it's as good underwater as it is on the surface. So that if there had been large rocks to shift out of the way down there, or blow a hole to gain access, this little beauty would have made light work for us."

In silence we cruised back towards Sandbanks and the rented house.

We arrived back at around six thirty. Mrs Rumple had been informed by radio that her sewing expertise was going to be required again the minute we docked. In her usual expedient manner and without fuss this was taken care of.

We decided to leave the waxy opium packages hidden on board the phantom for the night, but to take everything else up to the house. We secured all hatches and double locked the boathouse doors. Everyone except Rumple and Mrs Rumple would take turns in doing a guard duty, just in case any other unwanted visitors called.

* * *

Thursday: 6.00am

As usual LJ was already at his desk. I'd no doubt that he was already savouring a cup of piping hot black coffee to kick-start his metabolism for the day. I sat in front of the laptop using the built in camera and secure line video link.

"Good morning Jake, I hope you slept well after yesterday's activities."

"Can we cut the crap, please? We were ambushed; it's as simple as that."

"There is no other way of looking at it. Whoever those goons were, they had known exactly where we would be and I suspect what goodies we had just loaded on board. It could only be our client or this chap in Bournemouth, Flackyard."

"OK, old son, you may be right - but please calm down, – I've made a number of phone calls, Hawkworth categorically refutes any suggestion that the opium found on board the Gin Fizz was being trafficked for him. It's far more likely that this Robert Flackyard is behind the drugs, and that those three you sent to the bottom of the English Channel worked for him. Special Branch has confirmed that he is the subject of an ongoing investigation with regard to his various activities both here in the UK and abroad. Further more, Jake, please remember that had it been a team of let's say, five, instructed by our client, you would all be lying on slabs in a mortuary."

"Great, so we have a Cabinet Minister who has jumped into bed with a gangster instead. Who also has an appetite for dealing drugs and killing people? But where does that leave us, and where do we go from here?"

"Look, the first thing to do is for all of you to sit tight. I will arrange for the items retrieved from the safe, to be brought back to London, then the Partners can arrange the hand-over to their rightful owners. A dispatch rider will collect them this morning. Your code name will be used as the greeting."

"Understood?" I nodded at the screen.

"Good, because once that is taken care of, I can take my instructions from upstairs so that we can concentrate on the more important matters such as the Italian Generals and their Sicilian project. In the meantime, see what else you can find out locally about this chap Flackyard. If you turn up anything interesting, call me immediately, at any time of the day or night, you've got my London home number."

He broke the link and the screen went blank. At breakfast, I filled the others in on the conversation I had with LJ. I gave everyone something to do for the day ahead; the Rumples were to stay at the house to keep an eye on things. Fiona Price looked as if she was staying in Dorset and looked as if she were more than capable of visiting some of Flackyard's clubs and wine bars.

"Try and find out as much about his organisation as possible," I said, but please try to be discreet. Remember there's an active investigation on this character and his many activities."

Fiona assured me that discretion was her middle name, and that she didn't know I cared so much.

Around 11.30 am Charlie and I decided to take a look at the local 'in' place, a modern café bar by the water's edge. Highly polished chrome tables and chairs lined the marble frontage and overhead large billowy canvas blinds let shaded sunlight filter through, creating a relaxed atmosphere where life passes by and time stands still. We took a table overlooking the Bay. A waitress came over and took our drinks order. Charlie instantly struck up a rapport with the talkative girl, asking her if it were possible to have a chat with the owner. I noticed someone walking up the road from the direction of the beach. He was a muscular figure, perhaps a little overweight. His dark hair was cropped close to his skull and his chest featured more hair than his head.

A small crucifix dangled from a fine chain around his neck. He wore a baggy pair of swimming shorts and carried a towel, which he rubbed against his head as he walked. It was only the towel and shorts that marked him as a visitor, for as he approached us an attractive tanned woman came from behind the bar and waved enthusiastically at him.

He shouted, "Is that an English rose I see there?" In response the woman wrinkled her nose and pouted her mouth. As they met he kissed her on both cheeks and gave her a friendly hug. "God, you look good today, Georgina. How do you keep so young and vibrant, working this bar of yours morning, noon and night?" The woman ignored this compliment and guided the big American inside. I could see from where I was sitting, that she was whispering to him conspiratorially, flicking her eyes in our direction a number of times during their conversation. Five minutes later he came over and introduced himself.

"Caplin," he said, and extended a large hairy-backed hand to Charlie.

"Caplin?"

"Yes, Harry Caplin." He laughed. "I'm from the United States – I live in the house two doors from you. Look, that's it for me today. Say – I know we don't know each other and I'm being really presumptuous in asking, but would you fellas like to join me for lunch? That's if you've got nothing better to do."

Look I'll go back to the house and scramble into

some clothes. Let's say 12.45 at my place for drinks then eat around 1.00. It'll sure be good to have new faces to talk with. Bring your friends and swim-suits if you like." He laughed loudly and went off up the road.

Charlie was all for it, of course, he just wanted to break the monotony of sitting around waiting for further instructions from London. He said, "He's a bulldozer, that man; he's the American I mentioned."

I said, "He's seems friendly enough, but I've got a strange feeling that his offer of lunch was most definitely, not off the cuff. Something about him is not right and how did he know that we weren't alone? I'll get Rumple to check him out this afternoon."

Fiona was already back at the house when we arrived to collect our shorts.

"Back so soon Fiona? I thought you'd be gone at least until late tonight?"

"Mr Dillon, you will find my report on the table over by the fax machine."

She pointed across the room. "You should find it an interesting read. This Flackyard character is on the face of it whiter than white. But in reality he is into anything illegal, according to a young waitress with big ears and a loose tongue who I got talking to in one of his bars. He runs most of the working girls in the town, controlling them with what he calls his enforcers. These are basically paid thugs who collect the money and dish out any punishment as and when required, to keep the girls in line."

"Funnily enough, one thing she did mention was that there is a rumour going around that three of these thugs have just disappeared. Apparently Flackyard is really pissed off and very twitchy about it. He thinks they've stolen certain items of value from him that he was transporting for one of his associates and that he was supposed to deliver yesterday. She thinks that it's almost certain to be drugs. Unfortunately we were interrupted, so I left and came straight back here."

"Sounds good Fiona. I look forward to reading it. But now, we have a lunch date with a bullish American two doors away. Would you like to come?"

"Another pair of eyes and ears might prove useful."

"Sounds too good to miss. Have I got time to quickly change?"

I picked up the type written report. "Five minutes, and no more." I said looking down at the white sheet of paper in my hand and thinking how I may have judged her a little to harshly at the outset, and how well written and detailed her report was. Perhaps she could be a valuable asset to the team after all.

The three of us arrived at Harry Caplin's a little before 12.45. He lived in a magnificent mock Gothic house; the entrance hall was large and airy with a rich oak floor running throughout the ground level. The dark furniture did a heavy dance as we walked across the uneven plank flooring.

From the entrance hall one could see right through the house to where the green sea, dark clouds and stone balcony hung like a tricolour outside the back door. From the kitchen emerged the aroma of olive oil, onion, pimento, and fish. A wizened old woman of seventy something who 'did' for Harry was busy preparing salads. I could detect her feminine hand in the hydrangeas that filled the borders.

"Hi there, Sofia – this way, folks," said Harry, "Did I tell you, that I'm the only American on this peninsula?" He had fixed the patio with green plants and a parasol. From his balcony one could see across the harbour towards one of the many scattered islands.

Harry swirled his drink and looked across to one of these islands regretfully. "This place is going to be way outside my tax bracket when they finish developing this area."

"How long have you owned this house Harry?" I asked casually.

"Hell, I only rent this place, costs a fortune, but what the heck. I was lucky enough to be able to get off the treadmill, so I said to myself, Harry you'll soon be nudging fifty, and what are you? A small-time publishing exec. making seventy thou. and not much chance of pushing it past seventy-five."

"And what are you getting in return? Three weeks in Florida once a year and a ski trip to Colorado if, repeat *if*, you're lucky. So what did I do?"

There was a knock at the door, and a minute later Sofia led a man in his fifties out on to the balcony. He was thin and neurotic looking. His face, although cleanly shaven was pitted with pockmarks from his adolescence, he had fine hair that was parted down the middle, and one of his long sideburns concealed a small but noticeable scar around his ear.

"Let me do the introductions," said Harry. "This is George Ferdinand, he's a good friend of mine, from hereabouts. Hope you'll join us for lunch George? Sofia has cooked up the most wonderful dish using local fish just caught this morning."

"Thank you Harry, I'd be absolutely delighted to join you – that is, as long as your other guests don't mind?"

After we had all introduced ourselves, we sat down to eat. However, my appetite had been replaced with an overwhelming feeling of being fitted up.

This character George Ferdinand turning up out of the blue and on the off chance was just too convenient, as well as clumsy, to be believable.

My attention turned back to the meal, and Harry was quite right; Sofia had indeed cooked a magnificent feast for us. Charlie sat next to our late arrival who didn't seem to talk very much, although at every possible opportunity he did light up a cigarette and consumed copious quantities of wine throughout the meal. As she came by I congratulated Sofia in Italian on a fine lunch.

George had heard me and said in clear and fluent Italian also, that he had never thought fish could taste so superb. Harry saw me look over.

"And he speaks German, Spanish and Russian just as well as you and I speak our mother tongue, don't you, George?" He patted him affectionately on the shoulder. Charlie, Fiona and I all looked at each other. "How about one of my special cocktails to finish off this perfect afternoon" said Harry, looking over to Fiona. "Come and help me fix it up, Fiona."

They disappeared into the kitchen. George came and sat with Charlie and me by the water edge. We soon discovered that he talked only in general terms about anything, steering well clear of anything personal about himself.

The tide was turning as I watched the waves moving down on to the private beach. Each shadow darkened until one, losing its balance, toppled forward.

It tore a white hole in the green ocean and in falling brought its fellow down, and that the next until the white stuffing of the sea burst out of the lengthening gash.

Fiona and Harry emerged from the kitchen with a big tray of glasses and a jug with frosted leaves around it. As they came through the door Harry was laughing and saying, "…it's the only thing I really miss of the New York scene to be honest."

Then Miss Price said in a loud clear voice, "Come and get it – Harry has just made us the most outrageous cocktail with…" Harry broke in, his voice taking on a reprimanding tone, "Now you promise that the ingredients would remain our little secret, Fiona." His hand patted her bottom softly.

"That's an un-American activity," said Fiona.

"Oh no," said Harry, "we still got a couple of things that have to be done by hand."

George Ferdinand apologised profusely to Harry about having to leave early, telling him that he had a little business to take care of. I caught his attention for just a fraction of a second. There was something odd about the way, when under a little pressure, his eyes never stayed still, flitting in all directions. There was constant perspiration on his upper lip and forehead.

Since meeting him five hours ago my opinion hadn't changed; this man was not to be trusted.

The waves were tripping over, crashing on to and falling through the foamy, hissing remnants of their predecessors. I wondered how long before we would begin doing the same?

Chapter 7

Rumple's ruddy colour had returned to his cheeks. He was perched on a chair by the French doors that opened out to the garden, checking over and cleaning his dive equipment. Mrs Rumple looked up from her typing as we came into the room. We, however, all looked a little worse for wear after several of Harry Caplin's cocktails.

Rumple came over to me and said, "I caught a chap snooping around the front gates earlier, sir. An unsavoury character if ever I saw one. When I asked him what he thought he was doing snooping around, he said that he had an appointment to see you. To be honest, sir, I didn't believe him and challenged him further by walking down to where he was stood."

"Unfortunately, before I got to him he'd jumped into his car, wound the side window down and before driving off; he said to tell you to be at La Café, the one down by the beach, at nine o'clock sharp."

"Did he now, well I certainly didn't have any appointments today because no one knows that I'm here. Did he give his name Rumple?"

"No sir. Unfortunately he went off down the road like a shot out of a gun. But I'd recognise him alright"

"Go on then man; tell me, what did he look like?" I said impatiently.

"Well, sir, he was tall with smarmed hair parted down the middle, I'd say he was late forties, possibly early fifties. He had a thin long face and a complexion that looked like a lunar landscape on a very bad day."

I showered and put on a change of clothes. Before going back downstairs, I made sure the automatic pistol now holstered under my arm was completely concealed. Satisfied, I went down to tell the others what to do if for any reason I didn't phone in on the hour, every hour.

I pulled the Mercedes into the car park of La Café. In the far corner I spotted the blue Porsche, the registration was the same as the car that had recently followed me all the way from Bournemouth to London. Owned by Mr Robert Flackyard.

"Good evening, Mr Dillon - so good of you to join me." The voice was familiar yet the tone was now cruel and cold. His words hung in mid air, suspended on invisible wires.

I slowly turned to greet the darting eyes and sweaty face of George Ferdinand, who was sat at a small circular table overlooking the water. A handful of people were sitting at the bar talking and laughing loudly, as people do when they've had too much to drink. Otherwise the café was virtually empty.

I spoke with deliberate nonchalant slowness.

"Well, well, Mr Ferdinand - what a pleasure, we meet again so soon. Why am I not surprised to see you? Is this the little bit of business you had to take care of?" I noticed the small automatic laid on his lap partly covered by his jacket. He stroked the silenced barrel slowly up and down as if it were some sort of phallic. His eyes darted up at me and caught me looking at it.

"I have no wish to harm you Mr Dillon or your friends. I am here to escort you to Mr Flackyard's home in Canford Cliffs. He wishes to have a conversation with you, that's all. My instructions are to ensure that you arrive at his home safely and on time." He stood up, the 9mm held in his left hand covered by his jacket now draped over his arm. The barrel pointing directly at my stomach, without a word he jabbed the gun in the direction of the rear door.

As I got up to leave I said over my shoulder,

"Listen, George, the gun under the coat routine, it's a bit of a cliché, you know? Why don't you be a good boy and put it away before you hurt someone. After all, you know that you won't use that peashooter in public. There are far too many witnesses around, and it would be much simpler if you were to put it away yourself, before I have too take it away from you?" The end of the pistol barrel was sharply jabbed in the small of my back in reply.

Once outside he stopped and said. "I'm reliably informed Mr Dillon, that you are carrying an automatic pistol under your left arm. Please be so kind as to pass it to me - carefully."

I was instructed to get into the driver's seat of the Porsche. "If I don't call in on the hour, there will be an army of police at Flackyard's house within five minutes," I said.

"Please don't be so melodramatic Mr Dillon. Mr Flackyard would not be that stupid. Feel free to use your mobile phone whenever you wish," he said with a sneer. "Now if you don't mind, please drive. Our host does not like to be kept waiting."

I parked the Porsche in a secluded side road lined with cherry blossom trees on either side.

George was still waving his gun about as he told me to get out of the car.

He slowly pushed open the wrought iron gate, the hinges protesting noisily at this interruption of their slumber. Holding it open for me, he said in a lowered voice, "This is where I leave you, Mr Dillon. Please walk towards the house.

"A member of the staff will come and meet you." With that he silently left me alone at the home of Mr Robert Flackyard, entrepreneur and probably one of the biggest criminals on the South coast.

By 9.15pm the sun is well down. To the west the skyline was intensely mauve and the sun, hitting the higher storey of the white Spanish style house, made it as pink as the flowers on the rhododendrons along its walls. The last rays of the sun did a spray job on the side of Flackyard's angular face, and behind him the gold lettering from some of his exquisite first edition book collection did a glittery dance over his shoulder. The house was richly furnished and I didn't have to be asked to dinner to know that the cutlery would be only the highest quality sterling silver.

On Robert Flackyard's contemporary cherry wood desk was a porcelain-and-gold pen set, a gold letter-opener, the latest hi-tech computer flat screen and half a dozen A4 typed sheets. They weren't held down with bottle tops, either.

"I understand you to be a keen diver, Mr Dillon, an expert on wrecks in particular, I am led to believe?"

It wasn't an exact description, but it wasn't a question open to retort, either.

I said nothing. Flackyard undid the top button of his shirt and loosened his tie; he then motioned me to sit. I wondered just how much outside of the law you had to be to have a set-up like this.

"In the course of time, this coast has attracted adventurers of all sorts. Not all of them have sought recently lost treasure, and some of them have been far from successful. To the point of losing there lives."

We sat opposite each other in soft luxurious leather sofas, a low glass coffee table in the middle separating us. A man dressed in a formal black suite, white shirt and dark tie appeared in the doorway.

"Would you like tea or coffee Mr Dillon, or perhaps something a little stronger?" Flackyard asked.

"Coffee would be fine, thank you, black and strong please."

Flackyard dismissed the middle aged man and then continued. "In the case of you and your friends, however, I am of the opinion that your motives are not entirely honourable." He paused, and then said, "I'm hoping to provoke a reply, of course?"

"Of course. Your English, by the way is excellent." I said.

"How astute you are Mr Dillon. My mother was a Moscow prostitute. My father a wealthy Russian aristocrat who defected to England when I was just ten. After changing the family name I was packed off to one of the top public schools in the country and then ended up at Oxford. But you avoid my question."

I didn't reply immediately. Instead I sat in thoughtful silence for a brief moment, "I'm not sure how your ideas of honour could be expected to key in with mine. You and I are complete opposites, it would seem."

"That may be so, Mr Dillon, but the fact remains that you were sent here to retrieve items belonging to a friend of mine as well as to myself. Now, however…" His voice trailed away. The sun had disappeared over the hill now, leaving only a few fiery trees to mark its passage. Flackyard got up and went over to his desk. "The Partners have returned these items, and both my friend and I are very grateful to them for this service that they have performed with your help, of course."

As he spoke he walked slowly across to the corner of the room, the rich Persian carpet switching off the soundtrack of his footfalls. One wall was filled with books from floor to ceiling. He reached up and slid his hand into the shelf of loosely packed books and removed about six between compressed palms. In the space behind the books was a brown paper parcel about half the size of a cigar box. He returned to where I was still sitting and put it on the coffee table in front of me. I didn't touch it.

Coffee came in the only way it could travel in a house like that: in a silver pot attended by the finest china cups and saucers. On a side plate were a selection of small cakes and biscuits. Flackyard forced three of them on me in quick succession.

"I like to think that the people I conduct business with are honest and straightforward," he said as he poured the coffee. He pushed the package towards me.

"Please, Mr Dillon open it, I would appreciate your opinion."

I sipped at my coffee and he lit a Turkish cigarette. The package was quite light. Pulling apart the brown wrapping the contents soon became apparent.

"As counterfeit money goes, the standard of these Euro notes is exceptionally high, Mr Flackyard. Even the paper feels right."

"That is because the paper, Mr Dillon, is very genuine." he said triumphantly.

"Fascinating, but why are you showing me? Surely it's Declan Ferran and Richard Cardini who should be seeing these. For all you know I could be working for some sort of secret Government agency."

"That is highly unlikely, Mr Dillon," he laughed. "I have had my people check you out. You once had a brilliant Army career operating in numerous countries for the Intelligence Corps, attaining the rank of Captain. That is before you were discharged under some dubious and certainly clandestine circumstances. You then surfaced within a Whitehall department. Your job description there was to say the least a bit vague, and finally you joined Ferran & Cardini International. But that is of course only part of it, isn't it? An extension of your military career perhaps? All in all, Mr Dillon, you are shrouded by mystery and intrigue - are you not?"

So that was it, the man who had followed me that Sunday in the black Mondeo was not working for the minister as we thought, he was part of Flackyard's security team, instructed to find out about me.

"As interesting as it maybe, however, I have not had you brought here to discuss your past career, or to thank you. The other items that you found on board that boat belong to an associate of mine and he wants them back – Mr Dillon – all fifty of those small packages. I sincerely hope that no harm has come to them, and that they are safe and sound or, I am afraid you will be the one to pay the price."

"I'm sorry, but what exactly are we talking about here, Flackyard?"

He got up and went over to his desk again. "Please do not insult my intelligence. I know that you and your friends pulled up a large quantity of the finest raw opium from the Gin Fizz. Furthermore, you will ensure that they are available for collection by midday tomorrow at the latest. I sincerely hope that I'm making myself clear. You will be contacted in the morning to arrange the details of the hand over. I think that concludes our conversation, Mr Dillon."

"My driver will take you back to your own car. Oh, and please remember this; you really do not want me as your enemy." For just the briefest of moments I sensed the hatred that he felt towards me, but his self-control was impeccable, and soon there was only calm in his eyes.

Back at the house I poured myself a large vodka, and downed another before I felt anything like relaxed and before anyone had summoned the courage to ask me what I had learned to our advantage. "Flackyard knows that we have the opium, and that his associates, whoever they maybe, want it returned by midday tomorrow," I said.

"Tomorrow, Charlie, you and I both return to London. Fiona, I think it best if you also get back to whatever it is you normally do."

That night I lay awake turning over and over in my mind, how Flackyard could have known about the opium or how the mysterious George Ferdinand could have found out about my pistol. The only way that either of them could have known was if someone had told them. But who, and to what end?

Chapter 8

I woke early the next morning from a restless night's sleep, angry with myself for allowing LJ to ever get me involved with this assignment. Also, I was still wondering; who had a motive for leaking information and whether it had been one of the team in Dorset who had tipped off Flackyard, but for what reason, and what gain? These questions kept going over in my head. I used my mobile phone to call Tats who was still in bed.

"What time is it?" she said in a hazy voice.

"Just gone six o'clock. Thought I'd give you a wake up call. How are you?"

"I'd be a whole lot better if you'd have let me wake up organically, especially on a Saturday. You know I've never been good with alarm calls."

I could hear her stretch and yawn; I imagined her naked body warm from sleep under the sheet.

"How's the seaside. You must be nearly through down there, aren't you?"

"Nearly, but not quite. We have a small problem to sort out first. That's the other reason for my call, I want you to do a check on the Rumples, Charlie McIntyre, and Fiona Price. Dig as deep as you can and see if any of them have ever had any contact with Robert Flackyard, no matter how trivial, because I want to know about it. Call me back on this number as soon as you can. Oh and Tats – see you soon." I hung up, got dressed and went down to breakfast.

Outside the day was starting dull, the grey wind was breaking the points off the waves and white spray was thrashing the big rocks of the headland.

Apart from me, the only other person at the table was Charlie. My phone rang. It was LJ. "Jake, I want you to go along with whatever Flackyard wants. I have taken instructions from upstairs, the Partners feel that for the good of the bigger picture and the assistance that he is offering, you are to hand over the packages as requested."

Without acknowledging or answering I said, "Someone is leaking information to Flackyard." At this revelation, Charlie's head came up from his cornflakes.

"What do you mean, a leak? That's impossible. Everyone involved with this assignment has been thoroughly vetted."

"That may be, but last night an acquaintance of his escorted me at gun point to Flackyard's house for a little chat. He knew far too much, and as far as I'm concerned it can only be someone involved that's feeding him with information. I've not got a shred of evidence, of course." I paused to let LJ absorb this fully. "Oh, and I've asked Tatiana to run further checks, this time concentrating on any possible connections with Flackyard."

"Well, I'm dumbfounded, old son. I suppose that Flackyard could have applied pressure on someone. But if that's the case, I can see that a few phone calls need to be made. We can't have our clients getting one over on us, can we now?" His voice trailed off, lost inside his own scheming thoughts for a few moments.

"LJ, I'm not happy about handing over anything to this character until the firm has taken possession of the currency that he promised as part of the package. By the way, I've already seen a sample, and the quality is quite outstanding."

"I agree with you for once. Sit tight down there for a little while longer, will you, just while I make a few arrangements at this end, and don't let those packages out of your sight." With that he hung up.

Except for Charlie, none of the others knew about

my chat with LJ. We sat around doing nothing until Harry Caplin called to invite us to his place for coffee. We went.

"Jazz and Swing music," Harry was saying, "some of the greatest tunes of all time come from performers like Nat King Cole, Frank Sinatra and Sammy Davis Jr." An espresso coffee maker was bubbling away on the dark slate hearth and Fiona, in her bronze-coloured linen trousers, was sitting cross-legged like some special sort of Buddha. Around her were scattered the brightly coloured CD cases of all of those great entertainers and many more as well.

On the walls hung a series of contemporary paintings by local Dorset artist, Samantha Bush, along with photos of a young Harry standing with a rifle underarm, foot resting on a rock, surrounded by other men. What looked like carcasses lay before them, so obviously a good day's hunting had taken place. The words at the bottom read, Toronto, Canada October 1963.

Charlie was listening to Harry doing a quick run down on New York (Charlie had lived there for three years). I was looking at Harry's books, multi function exercise machine, and the pristine 7mm Mauser sporting rifle and its beautiful Carl Zeiss x8 telescopic sight. I looked at his collection of rocks and minerals in their fine wooden case and listened to the mellow music playing. Harry commented on each as he selected it. "This is a song about a man so infatuated with a girl that he feels compelled to tell her about his love and admiration for her. Of course, he does this because he's off to war and may never see her again." Harry said it in an impassioned and melancholy voice.

Fiona clapped her hands and on her face was the sort of smile when a woman is thinking about how the smile should look.

Harry took a bow and laughed loudly. He poured more coffee for everyone and I took mine back over to the shelves. In them he had almost every DH Lawrence novel in print, including a special edition of Lady Chatterley's Lover. There were various art books, many of them about modern artists dating from 1945 up to the present day. Tucked away on the higher shelves there were many geographical reference books concentrating mainly on southern Europe.

We made small talk over coffee and then Charlie said, "What made you come to live in Europe, Harry?"

"Well," said Harry, "I was eating tablets to sleep, pep pills to stay awake and vitamin supplements instead of proper meals. Here I drink the best Champagne all day, and what's more, it's cheaper!" Harry was lacing the coffee with French cognac. Charlie and I declined.

"Yes," he said, and took a swig from the bottle before recorking it, "there I was you see, up to my neck in credit card and mortgage debt, and worrying about what sort of season the Yankees were likely to have. How to break out of it? I knew there were jobs for Americans abroad but I was already to old for the big corporations. So one day I'm standing in a bar near Grand Central. Watching all of those sad little commuters walk by outside and thinking about how I would like to step off this farcical treadmill that I called a life, and I say to myself; what are these sharp suited executive nuts looking for that I could supply them in exchange for money? Well, what do you imagine I conclude?"

He looked at all of us in turn, his captive audience, picked up the pot and poured more coffee, enjoying the pause before answering.

"Wine." He continued. "Now that handed a laugh to every low life creep in my home town, because that kind of booze, ain't something to put your arms into like a Hugo Boss suit."

"But me and a guy named Marcus Cohen, who was an old buddy of mine from our college days, we struck it rich with a couple of deals supplying an outlet in Chicago with as much as we could lay our hands on, he then sold it on for a good profit. But after a short while we decided to cut out the guy in Chicago and sell direct to Mr Average Fella."

I walked over to the open doors that overlooked the harbour. There were occasional smacks of warm raindrops on the balcony tile-work. On the water an elegant yacht, her crew busy preparing her rigging, glided by under the power of her inboard motor. The crew spotted us watching and gave a friendly wave, as sailors often do.

* * *

It was about 11.30am

Harry was saying, "Balls to the big time wine guys, I said, I'm for the little guy every time. So we set up "wine direct inc.com.""

"Harry, you really are priceless," said Fiona. "Whatever were you selling?"

"Well, we published a one page web site called 'Wine in your cellar', see?"

"We sent promotional flyers out to restaurants, office blocks, bars and joints as well as running a few small ads here and there. We do all right – our overheads are small and what we sell is paid for in advance by credit card."

"But one day my buddy Marcus Cohen says to me, 'balls to these average guys, Harry, they're just a set of low spenders. What we need is a class angle'." He comes up with one there and then; 'Connoisseur Wine.com,' he says."

Harry Caplin walked across to the bookshelf and removed a leather folder.

"Did it work out?" Charlie asked, who was lounging back on the bright red sofa holding an empty coffee cup on his knee.

Harry flipped open a copy of Time Magazine to a full-page advertisement.

The caption read Connoisseur Wine.com is proud to present a selection of fine wines from some of Europe's most exclusive vineyards. Buy one case and receive another free of charge as an introductory offer, all beautifully and individually presented in hand-made wooden crates and chosen by a panel of famous growers, accompanied by a detailed history of each wine by Mr Harry Caplin.

Fiona started to clap her hands; Charlie and I didn't join in. Harry didn't seem to take offence.

"But," said Charlie, "how come as you live here in England?"

"Simple. I look through these books..." Harry grabbed two large reference books on wine from the shelf, "...and choose one for the ad in Time Magazine."

When these books were removed they revealed a smaller one that had fallen down the back of the row of books.

"But..." said Charlie, "...it says..." Charlie's face bloomed red in embarrassment.

I quickly plucked out the book.

"...it says there's a panel of famous wine growers!" Harry agreed with a smirk.

The small book, on closer inspection turned out to be the type reporters keep for jotting quick notes down in. The entries made at the beginning were mostly to do with detailed timetables of passenger ferries around Southern Europe.

"They choose the wine..." Harry went on. "... but I, Harry Caplin, select it." Harry laughed a great boom of a laugh and slapped his thigh with his enormous hand.

* * *

Saturday 1.00pm

That Saturday was one big long wasted day as I look back on it. We left Harry Caplin's and returned to the house, to find one of Flackyard's flunkies had phoned to inform us that the hand-over would not be taking place.

Instead, Mr Dillon was invited to call by at Mr Flackyard's this evening to collect the samples for Mr Levenson-Jones in London to inspect. Charlie and Miss Price played backgammon arguing continuously about almost everything; eventually they agreed to disagree and went off to La Café for a drink. The Rumples had gone into town.

I cursed myself for forgetting the package of counterfeit Euros the night before. A repeat visit to Flackyard's house was something I was definitely not looking forward to. On Rumple's return, we had the expenses to discuss, as he was the only one LJ trusted with the bookwork as well as being in charge of the diving.

It was when Rumple was locking the accounts backup discs in the writing desk drawer that he noticed it.

We checked, sat down and thought about it, but Rumple found broken woodwork and then there was no doubt at all. Everything was as we had left it, the sea charts, Charlie's sketches of the ocean bottom, but someone had stolen the photos that Rumple had taken of the Gin Fizz.

There is no alternative in situations like this. It wasn't something that either of us found enthralling. In fact it was a sordid little job of the sort that constitutes much of our work. Rumple and I began to search everyone's room. Apart from the usual personality insights that these searches always provide, there was only one remarkable thing. Among the several articles in Fiona's room that a young single woman in the employ of a mundane Government department shouldn't have in her possession was a small revolver and silencer, together with about twenty rounds of ammunition.

* * *

LJ had sent one of the company's helicopters down to take Charlie and me back to London. It was a fine clear night when I went out to the airport via Flackyard's house. There were lights on, and outside in the sweeping drive there was a silver Mercedes and a red Ferrari, each brand new with local plates. Further along the exclusive road under a flowering cherry tree was Harry Caplin's old black Mk1 Jaguar.

I knew that, as surely as sugar is sweet, a blue Porsche would be somewhere near by. It was. This only reinforced my suspicion, that there was more to Caplin than he was portraying, and that he had deliberately gone out of his way to introduce himself to Charlie and me, that day in La Café.

A bell jangled deep in the interior and echoed back like a laughing hyena. I rang again. Finally and to my surprise, Flackyard himself opened the door, and he passed me the package from his inside jacket pocket. It was still wrapped in brown paper and held together with clear tape. Charlie had the motor running when I got back to the Mercedes.

As we drove to the airport, we discussed the assignment and how we thought it was going in light of recent developments. Both Fiona Price and the Rumple's names cropped up in the conversation a number of times. We found our reserved parking space with ease, slotting the Mercedes in one manoeuvre. The warm night air held the aroma of aviation fuel that had been spent through hot jet engines, and as we approached the main terminal building I spotted our pilot standing over by the entrance. Once we'd scrambled aboard the sleek Bell Jet Ranger helicopter the rotors were engaged and within a minute we were airborne. Before I knew it we were skirting the Gatwick air traffic control zone. In the small cabin the instruments glowed and with a sudden leap the pilot had taken us through the low clouds. The bright lights of the city cut through the fine mist that was now shrouding London as we descended towards the heliport. My thoughts were bizarrely, where the hell was Charlie staying tonight?

Chapter 9

London 11.00pm

Levenson-Jones picked one up and held it under the banker's lamp on his desk. The note was as perfect a forgery as you're likely to get anywhere.

"Just gave you a bundle of these, did he?" said LJ. He opened a fresh packet of cigars and lit one. "Very good, he obviously took what I had to say to him seriously. This really is an excellent piece of work," he continued still holding the note to the light.

The phone rang. Zara said she'd run out of ground coffee and would instant do. It was gone midnight and LJ told her to go home and get some sleep, but she brought up the coffee for us, and her smile was like a shaft of summer sunshine. LJ handed her the forged Euro note. The paper was crisp and rustled as she turned it over in her elegant hands.

Zara studied each side of the note carefully, and looked up at me and then at LJ.

"Isn't it just as I said, Mr Levenson-Jones?"

"Yes, you were right, Zara," said LJ. "A quite exceptional forgery."

"But didn't I tell you that it would be? When that Mr Flackyard visited the Partners that time, he had a wad of these with him. I knew I was right."

So the Partners had already seen the quality of the counterfeit notes before we had even started the assignment. No wonder they were so keen to get involved.

Zara trotted off home at 1.30am and over our coffee LJ and I sat down and talked about the situation in Dorset and how the budget was going and how many days to his family holiday in Tuscany. That it all seemed a lot of expense for two weeks away, but his wife and kids liked it; then LJ suddenly said, "You never relax, Jake; it's getting you down, this job?"

It wasn't that he'd change it, if it was, he just liked to know it all.

"I can't make it fit together," I said, "and some things are too convenient."

"Convenience, dear boy, is just a state of mind," said LJ.

"It's understanding that's important. Understanding the symptoms you encounter will refer you to just one disease. You find a man with a pain in the foot and the hand and you wonder what he could possibly be suffering from with two such disparate symptoms."

"Then you find that while hitting a nail with a hammer one day he slips and whacks his hand, dropping the hammer which lands on top of his foot."

"OK," I said, "so much for ER. Now listen to my problems. First of all, why are we even talking to these nutty old retired Italian generals? Do they really think that they could possibly take over the Mafia in Sicily, and why are the Partners getting involved with such a foolhardy enterprise anyway? Because of this, I'm ordered to dive into a sunken boat that belongs to a coke sniffing member of Parliament, and who just happens to be involved with a south coast gangster, to retrieve his plates that will produce counterfeit money."

"Why? To give to the generals, and which will ultimately save the firm millions."

"So far so good, but while I am returning from Bournemouth two cars follow me up the motorway. The first, we discover is owned by a Private Investigator working for our Minister, and the other's owned by Flackyard and driven by two of his suited goons. When I ask for files to be pulled on both, what do you know they never appear…"

"They will," said LJ patiently, "It's only that Special Branch are involved on both counts. That's hampered my progress in obtaining them, that's all."

I gave him the curly lip treatment. "OK, so what about Fiona Price. Is she just a lowly employee of HMG? Or is she in reality something quite different? After all, she does sleep with a silenced pistol under her pillow?"

"I must admit I've run another check on her and she appears to have an exemplary career record; in fact it's totally without blemishes. I'd say it was almost certainly fictitious." LJ offered.

"Yes, perhaps it's too perfect, but I'm at a complete loss as to who she is working for and why she has been landed on my assignment. Oh, and I agree, her work record is completely false without a doubt, but her ability and expertise is real enough."

LJ took out a monogrammed handkerchief and lowered his nose into it, like he was going from the eighth storey window into something held by six firemen. He blew his nose loudly. "Go on," he said.

"Well, she arrives unannounced telling us that she comes with your blessing on behalf of HMG. Her instructions are to retrieve the logbook from the Gin Fizz and not to go back to London without it. But when it can't be found, she creates a song and dance about the trouble that she will be in for not locating it, but quite frankly her performance was very weak and I for one found her unconvincing. Unfortunately for her and luckily for us, I got to it before she did."

I handed LJ the logbook. "You might find this interesting bedtime reading. Another thing that was odd, when we discovered the opium," I put one of the waxy brown parcels down onto LJ's desk, "her reaction was a little too relaxed. Especially as we all thought it was explosives we were dealing with. Finally, both Charlie and I agree that she had the opportunity on a number of occasions to take the photographs of the Gin Fizz. But why? We haven't figured that one out, yet."

"Are you sure you're not blowing this all out of proportion, Jake?" LJ's tone was patronising.

"No I am not, "I said loudly. "From the very start of this assignment the elusive Oliver Hawkworth has, I feel, been manipulating all of us. Flackyard is far more devious and powerful than we've given him credit for, and I for one will be watching my back from now on."

"Ah…" LJ hesitated "… you think it's a frame up, don't you," he said thoughtfully.

"What's that suppose to mean?" I asked.

"It's an American expression that…" then he saw me grinning and he frowned.

I went on, "Then there's is this American, Harry Caplin, I can't be sure but my guts tell me that he's involved up to his fat little neck with those opium packages. But, I don't think it's with Flackyard…" My thoughts went back to the photograph of the hunting party at his house in Sandbanks. "He's got more of an international flavour this one, of that I am sure."

"So what do you conclude?" asked LJ.

"I don't conclude anything," I said, "but if I see a man waving the Stars and Stripes above his head I wonder if he's trying to tell me something about his national characteristics, and I wonder why."

"What about these photos of the boat that have gone missing?" LJ asked.

"Stolen. Whoever took them, wasted their time. They're of little consequence now, especially as the Gin Fizz no longer exists, and the photos are only general shots anyway."

"I hope for your sake that you're certain of that old son," said LJ sardonically, as he tried to touch his nose with his tongue.

"Yes, absolutely certain," I said.

"Well, that's OK then, but you must understand the Partners' point of view; they don't want to upset the status quo. There's far to much at stake. You must look at the bigger picture as they do Jake. Take off the blinkers sometimes."

"Oh, I do," I said seriously. "Well now, that's the Partners' position as a rule, isn't it? Not to upset anyone, don't upset all the good work we're doing – all that crap. Now doesn't it strike you as odd that the Partners encourage us into this set-up and tell us, mark you, not to let anyone know what we're doing off the coast of Dorset? But they are all bright smiles and winking eyes about it? They send down, this very attractive young woman, simply to help us?"

"Well, what do you want me to do about Miss Price?" LJ Said tapping his pen on the rim of his coffee cup.

"Give her back to whoever she belongs to." I replied.

"Now then, Jake," said LJ, "please be reasonable. I know that should be what we do, but it's not that simple. The Partners and even the police want her left in place for the time being, just watch what you do and say around her. What else do you want me to do?"

"Just one thing," I asked, "keep the wraps on that logbook from the Gin Fizz. Just don't say a word about it to anyone. Let's keep it between Charlie, you and me for the time being. You'll see why when you've had a chance to read it through."

"And Robert Flackyard," LJ said, just so that I knew he was agreeing to do so. (He would never promise to go against company policy in so many words.) He continued as though I hadn't mentioned the book. "The Price woman," he said, "you might as well use her talents, and we'll let whichever department she works for worry about what to do with her when this affair is over and done with. As you say, she's capable and quick thinking. You never know. You may even grow to like her."

I suppose I must have snorted as I closed the office door behind me.

Chapter 10

My converted loft apartment overlooks the river Thames in a fashionable part of town; I got back there at 7.30am after the all-night discussions with LJ. I paid the cab driver and climbed the spiral staircase to the top of the building.

I flicked on the heating control to constant, went into the kitchen and boiled a kettle. While I was waiting for the coffee to filter through I phoned Charlie, his mobile was switched off and his voice mail on. The message was simply for him to collect me at about four o'clock this afternoon. LJ had asked me to collect his car from the airport as we were going past it on the way to see a man who dealt in snippets of information that could be relevant to the Dorset assignment. LJ had left it there on his return from New York the previous day; as usual he'd had too much Champagne in business class.

I poured a generous measure of whisky into the black coffee and sipped it slowly. A night without sleep was beginning to pound my temples gently and tighten the muscles in the back of my neck. It was 8.15am I went to bed, then somewhere in the building a vacuum cleaner began its fiendish flagellation. I closed my eyes.

* * *

I looked at my watch in the darkness. The doorbell was ringing. I had slept nine hours, and now Charlie McIntyre was at the door, eager to get to grips with his evening of freedom in the big city. He had a brand new Audi TT from the firm's car pool. Only senior executives who had to go out of the city to visit clients used these. But on this occasion, as we were doing LJ an immense favour, he had authorised the vehicle for our use.

I had a shower, shaved and threw on the nearest smart casual clothes that came to hand. Charlie was eager to get back in the Audi and give it a blast down the motorway to the airport. It was a pleasure to see him handle the powerful car; his nimble hands stroked the controls as we slipped through the traffic with effortless ease and a skill he never otherwise showed. "Nowhere," said Charlie quietly as we approached another intersection, "do the English show a greater enthusiasm to queue than on motorways." He used the horn with Italian enthusiasm, indicated and moved the Audi over and out into the fast lane, accelerating with such speed that my whole body was pushed back into the leather seat and held there momentarily. Charlie moved past the queuing traffic with ice cool skill until we had left them in the rear view mirror.

When we arrived at Heathrow Airport he parked on double yellow lines just behind the taxi rank, and left the engine running. We drew matchsticks to see who would drive the Range Rover back to the office. Charlie won, so I would follow in the Audi.

It was 6.30pm, the sky had grown dark and menacing again and I felt fingers of rain tapping me on the shoulder. I gave Charlie the keys to LJ's car pointing to where he always parked; we could see the dark green Range Rover Vogue from where we were standing. I went over to the newspaper vendor at the entrance to the terminal. The headline on the board read; BUSH TO CONTINUE WAR ON TERRORISM. I bought the Times and walked back out into the drizzle.

The lights of the car park created an almost surreal scene. I could see Charlie at the far end; he opened the door of the four wheel drive vehicle got in and started the powerful 4.6 litre petrol engine, switched on the head lights and drove around the one way system to the exit. As he emerged the rain tore little gashes through the long beams.

At the top of the ramp he stopped to let the exit barrier rise. From inside the car came an intense light; each window was a white rectangle, and the driver's door opened very quickly. It was then that the blast sent me across the wet pavement like a paper cup. The explosion lifted the heavy vehicle off the ground and flipped it over like a tiddly wink.

"Get back in the car," I thought. Getting to my feet, I unconsciously rubbed my cut and bleeding hands down the front of my shirt. A current of cold air told me of a two-inch gash in my right leg. People ran past towards the burning car. The explosion had sent flames everywhere and a siren had began to sound close by. I heard one of the security guards shouting.

"Quickly, get the fire crew and medics here!" I got back into the Audi, eased it into first gear and inched out slowly from behind the row of taxis. From the car park I heard another "boom" and saw a flash as the petrol tank exploded.

I drove around the roundabout. "Other way, mate," said one of the cabbies.

The grazed palms of my hands were throbbing and the steering wheel was wet with blood and sweat. I took out my mobile phone and pressed the speed dial for the firm's unofficial number.

An armed policeman, machine gun in hand waved me on to the main road away from the airport. I made sure that I was well on my way before I made the call to the office. They answered almost immediately, asking for my personal code name.

"Go ahead Jake."

"I regret to inform you that; the dark green Range

Rover we were collecting for our colleague had developed a serious wiring fault while in the car park. Neither the car or the driver survived the shock."

"That is very sad news, Jake. How are you proceeding, please?"

"M25, I should be back indoors within an hour."

"Thank you, Jake, we will monitor the situation."

When LJ phoned me he was touchingly concerned for my safety, but remembered that he had to contact his insurance company. He said, "We can't afford to have them getting curious about how it happened before the firm has had a chance to call in a favour or two with the police."

As I drove, I remembered Charlie's effervescent smile.

Chapter 11

Monday 10.00am

I'd slept for barely four hours. The pounding inside my head reminded me that I had downed the best part of a bottle of single malt whisky with exceptional ease. It was a birthday gift from Charlie, given with ceremony, kilt and all. The memory of him standing there at the restaurant, telling me that only the Scots knew how to brew fine malt.

Tats had let herself into the apartment with her own keys, and was busy in the kitchen. I came through in my bathrobe, rubbing the sleep from my eyes and thinking that LJ had probably asked her to drop by and pamper me.

"How long have you been here?" The drum in my head beat louder with the effort of speech.

"About half an hour. You look absolutely awful. Why don't you go and freshen up, you smell like a distillery. Breakfast will be another ten minutes."

She was wearing a dark blue suit of impeccable quality, the skirt cut just the right length, to show off her firm slender legs to best effect.

I showered, dressed for the office and went back through to the kitchen.

Warm croissants straight from the oven and freshly squeezed orange juice awaited me and so did the latest news about the explosion that killed Charlie.

We sat a while, drinking coffee in silence. Tatiana broke the spell. "LJ spoke to one of his old pals at the Yard early this morning. They've established that the device used to blow the Range Rover is one favoured by professional contract killers. The detonator is of a sophisticated type, triggered by digital mobile phone or directly wired into the vehicle's electrical system. On this occasion they think it was detonated remotely by phone, indicating that the person was still within viewing distance of the vehicle. The bomb squad boys can't be sure of course, due to the extent of the damage caused, but they reckon about a kilo of explosive was used. They will be able to be more specific when they determine what type was used. One thing that's for sure though, Jake, that bomb was supposed to kill, not just maim whoever was in that car. That someone was without doubt supposed to be LJ, not Charlie."

"Why LJ, who would want him that dead do you suppose?" I said, absentmindedly breaking off a piece of croissant and dunking it into my coffee.

"Oh - I should think we could come up with at least a hundred or so names, of people that he's used and abused in his time. But seriously, Jake, certain parties think it's probably to do with either someone or possibly some assignment that he's been involved with in the past."

"By certain parties, you mean the Partners?"

"Yes, I mean the Partners."

"There is something else you need to know, nothing to do with the explosion," she said, "the blueprint for the new Network."

"What about it?" I said, tilting my head forward and frowning at her from across the dining table.

"The Partners have copies. I'm sorry to say that crusty old fart Morris Drysdale at the Foreign Office is to set up one of his famous little feasibility teams."

"Oh hells bells," I groaned. "I know what that means."

"You're well out of it," said Tats. "LJ is sitting in for you at present. They will discuss which department will co ordinate operations."

"Power," I said. "I left the army because of all the crap. LJ wasn't kidding when I joined the firm."

"Even our friends at Thames House are trying to get in on the act."

"I thought that might happen, the spooks see this as an excellent opportunity to acquire a brand new Network, gathering all sorts of intelligence, without having to do a damn thing." I got up from the table and started to pace the kitchen.

"You should know how it is by now," said Tats. "If the Partners don't make a token gesture to them, when it comes to calling in favours they would have no bargaining gambits to play with."

"As a diplomat, Tatiana, you are like a fox, cunning and resourceful. You constantly impress with your ability to placate me like a small child. Of course you are right, I should know better by now." I said, with a wry grin.

Tats gave me one of her quirky smiles, got up and said, "Hell, look at the time, I've got to go. I'll speak to you later." We kissed; and she left as quietly as she had arrived.

* * *

By the time I reached the firm, organised pandemonium had developed in the department. People everywhere, phones glued to ears, words being spoken rapidly. Computer screens were alive with text and images, eyes fixed on them. Everyone had one thing and only one thing on their minds, to find out who had killed Charlie McIntyre. The word from above was simple; one of our own had been killed. The objective was to pull in all our sources of information and see what came out at the other end.

I joined LJ and Tats in the conference room. The image that filled the end wall on the screen made my stomach turn and the colour shot of what remained of the Range Rover made the hairs on the back of my neck stand on end. The doors were completely gone and everything inside had been erased by the blast and the ensuing fire. Only the rims remained of the wheels in each corner, all of the rubber was burnt away.

The roof had been spilt through the middle and the bonnet lay twisted twenty feet away.

"Charlie knew that something wasn't right, but he couldn't put his finger on it, you know?" I said to no one in particular while staring at the large screen.

"I've been thinking about recent events. We should take a closer look at dear old loveable Harry Caplin. Something about him is definitely odd." I sat at the end of the large maple table staring at nothing in particular.

"What makes you think that he is anything other than what he says he is?" LJ asked, pompously.

"Call it a hunch," I said, ignoring his intonation.

"Um, your hunches have been my embarrassment before, Jake. Give me one good reason why I should concentrate the firm's resources in this area of investigation. When there is no evidence whatsoever to substantiate my doing so."

"For the simple reason that Charlie is laid out in pieces at the local morgue," I retorted flatly.

"Don't be smart. I'm as saddened as you, or anyone else who had the privilege to know him, could possibly be. What makes you so sure that this Harry Caplin had anything to do with the explosion? It was my car that was bombed, so whoever carried out this despicable act was obviously after me and not Charlie. Wouldn't you agree?" LJ's face had reddened and sweat trickled off his forehead.

I got up and moved to the end wall, standing with the projected image behind me.

"There is evidence," I said, pausing for effect.

"Harry Caplin, George Ferdinand and Robert Flackyard, there is some sort of link between them."

"Caplin has been seen entering Flackyard's house at all hours and frequents a number of his, how shall we say, less reputable establishments. As for George Ferdinand, well he really is rather odd, and he's exceptionally good at lying. Flackyard; he is a very serious individual, and capable of just about anything. But that is merely my own opinion, of course. As for Flackyard, what do we really know about him? Well, he is extremely wealthy; influential beyond belief, almost certainly has a Cabinet Minister in his pocket. Has been able to elude the boys in blue for many years with his own private army of lawyers, and is an international playboy. That last bit by the way, I firmly believe is nothing more than a charade, a sleight of hand, like a magician creating an illusion. Do you know what the most fascinating thing to date is?"

"Well, let me tell you. Flackyard is the only one asking for the opium to be given back, but he's not the one who owns it. It will be the drugs though that will flush the real owner out, and Charlie's murderer. Because the two are almost certainly linked, and if we're looking for reasons why he may want you dead, need I say more?"

I sat down; Tats poured me some more coffee.

"Oh, I see the pattern as far is it goes, Jake. But let's not jump to conclusions. I still feel that Flackyard would not jeopardise his position."

"Especially as he is fully aware of the Partners' power and far-reaching influence that they can wield if they need to. No, if anyone wants me dead it will be someone whom I've really upset in the past. Of that, I've got no doubt."

"But no matter, we will attend to that in due course and before I forget, I've been contacted by former general Franco Santori. He's now the elected spokesman for our group of Italians. Apparently they've sacked the two negotiators whom you met with at Ahmed's house in Cairo."

"They're saying that the agreement made in Cairo was not legal and that they want the firm to cough up a lump sum of Euros. If you recall the timing of this initial sum of funding was a sticking point in your negotiations. And I'm afraid that you're going to have to go back to Egypt sooner rather that later, old son, and sort this one out." LJ's mobile rang; excusing himself, he went outside into the corridor.

While he was out of the room Tats informed me from across the table.

"The Partners won't hand over the cash you know. Not unless they have the counterfeit Euros that Flackyard has promised them. Do you remember that time Flackyard came to see the Partners? Well he tried to wheedle his way into the action, of course he had no idea that his fake Euros were going to be used to fund another of the firm's client ventures. All the same he's not stupid and somehow, God knows how, he's got wind of something big going down. The outcome as you can imagine is that the Partners told him in their best Eton drawl, to basically crawl back under his stone and to stay there."

LJ came back into the room, looking less flustered and more composed.

"Do you really think that Flackyard or Caplin was involved in the bombing?" he asked.

"Yes I do," I said. "Caplin I'm not too sure about, but Flackyard - he definitely has a motive. That is to say, although he is extremely wealthy, he is also extremely greedy too. A man like that is always looking for the next fix to increase his fortune. My personal view is that when the Partners sent him scampering back to Bournemouth full of rejection and anger, he realised that blackmailing the powers upstairs wouldn't work, so he sent a professional to bomb your car. Why, because he is as evil as any one human being can be and because you are an easy target, unlike the Partners who are watched all the time. That explosion was a carefully planned venture have no doubt about that."

"Um, well, you'd better be right about this because I'm going to have to pull in a lot of favours. Tell me what you found out about him when you went to his home."

"Well, he obviously speaks perfect English – syntax and inflection is faultless. He dresses conservatively, always a black suit, tailored, not off the peg. I have sat opposite him at the dining table, I can tell you the caviar and Champagne are genuine."

"He was an only child; his mother was a Moscow society prostitute, and his father a wealthy Russian aristocrat who defected and came to England when Flackyard was ten. Public school educated at, Bryanston in Dorset, after which he went on to Oxford to gain an honours degree in law. That's about all I got out of him. His small talk is virtually non-existent."

We were all quiet for a moment, then Tats said softly, "I'd like to blow out the brains of whoever murdered Charlie."

"I'll forget that you spoke." LJ looked at her with eyes like steel for a moment, then said, "If you want to continue working down here you'll never even think a thing like that, let alone say it. There is no room for heroics, vendettas or associated melodrama in my very efficient department. You make your commitment, take the rough with the smooth and quietly do your job. Suppose, Jake had been full of macho heroism and gone running back to Charlie yesterday. He would have attracted undue attention from any number of reporters that inevitably hang around there. As well as having to answer a barrage of questions from some very inquisitive policemen. Act grown-up Tatiana or I'll have you frog marched out of here immediately."

"I'm sorry," she said.

"Apology accepted, but don't ever hanker after tidiness. Don't ever think or hope that the great mess of investigation that forms a large part of our work down here is suddenly going to resolve itself like the last chapter of a whodunit: I've-got-you-all-gathered-together-in-the-room-where-the-murder-was-done, kind of scene. Be thankful for odd scraps of information or tip-offs from a source. Don't desire vengeance, or think that if someone murders you tomorrow, anyone will be tracking him or her down mercilessly. They won't!"

"We'll all be strictly concerned with keeping out of the tabloid newspapers and the Police Gazette."

Tats was determined to prove what a master of her emotions she was.

"Chief Inspector Thomson at New Scotland Yard has sent over a copy of the S.O.C.O. report concerning your Range Rover. He thought it was safer to let you have hard copies rather than e-mailing it to you. Have you seen it?"

"Yes, he telephoned me earlier this morning. By the way, send him a little something by way of a thank you, for doing such a good job. There's not so much as a mention in any of the dailies."

"Of course," said Tats, "he did mention that he had his people sending emails to all the editors the minute he found out whose car had been bombed."

"Apparently there were at least six cars written off. If the S.O.C.O. people are right in reconstructing the explosion points, it's almost as if whoever did this wanted the fire to spread."

"Really? I said leaning forward. "Where were they?"

"Under the bonnet, centre of the roof, behind the rear seat, between the front seats." Her eyes had become ever so slightly red around the edge. She caught me looking at her, giving me a wan smile back.

LJ went off to compile his report for the Partners. We had agreed that I should return to the rented house in Dorset. The Rumples were still there along with Fiona Price, who, it was decided, could be of use to us for the time being. We walked through the department to my office, closing the door behind us.

Tats immediately hugged me tightly, sobbing quietly into my shoulder. I gently stroked the back of her head. "Charlie would not have known anything, you know. It really would have been instantaneous," I offered.

Blowing her nose, Tats turned and left the room.

Chapter 12

The high pitched note of a car horn ripped the afternoon air. Harry Caplin's old black Mk1 Jaguar was parked in the short stay area of Bournemouth's beautifully renovated Victorian station. I'd had to train it back from London as both of the firm's helicopters were being used to ferry the Partners and their guests to and from the races at Royal Ascot.

"Hi there, Ace, climb into the cart. I told Mr Rumple I'd pick you up. He looked as if he'd got plenty to do, making ready and fussing around that big boat of yours, and as Fiona's off shopping. So I thought I'd be neighbourly and help out."

I wondered by what process of deduction dear old Harry had latched on to the boat being made ready. Was it possible to keep anything secret from him? It made the whole job a little more dangerous. We wove our way slowly across town through heavy traffic. From my relaxed position in the passenger seat, I could view all the many frustrated, over worked people with bland faces sat behind their windscreens fighting their way home through congested roads, but in reality only heading towards pre-booked early graves.

"So what's the word on the street Harry?" I said, shifting round towards him. Perhaps I should tell LJ to prepare a cover for us in case trouble blew up. We crawled past the sea front and on up the hill towards the west cliff of the town.

"I just got some new CDs from the States, Ace.

Sammy Davis and Frank re-mixed and digitally re-mastered. Come around for drinks this evening. Get an earful of wax. Ha ha ha." We were outside the rented house by now. I thanked Harry and he squealed down the road towards his place.

Rumple let me through the gates and met me at the front door. Unfortunately for Miss Price she was the next person I saw. She was standing in the kitchen wearing a microscopic black bikini.

"Well hello Mr Dillon," she said, putting a sustained accent on the final syllable of each word.

"Cut the crap, Fiona, I'm really not in the mood." I said as I threw my bag down.

"Such skilful alliteration, Jake," she said keeping her eyes on the magazine that she was flicking through. "What or who has upset you in London and where's Charlie?"

"Charlie - is dead - murdered, Fiona." I said quietly. I was interested to see her reaction, but there was none. I went on before anyone could speak, knowing that this news would devastate the Rumples like myself they had worked with Charlie on many assignments in the past. "So, tell me, why is it too much trouble for a member of this team to come and meet me? And for the record, I really don't appreciate Harry Caplin informing me that Rumple is making the boat ready to sail."

"Making ready the boat to sail? Come now Jake, he didn't really say that, did he?"

"Not in so many words." I said. "He inferred that Rumple was fussing about and making ready the boat. What I want to know is, how he even got to know that. After all, the boat is completely concealed inside the boathouse. What else has been told to him about what we are doing and why we're here - Miss Price?"

"Now listen here, sir." Said Rumple. "He's just

done to us what he's done to you: mentioned the words 'making ready' to see what reaction he got."

"What would you prefer us to do? Take him up on it and start playing 'what's my line?'"

"I don't like it, Rumple. That man should not know about what we are doing here, that's all I'm saying."

"Well, you know, Jake, little us can't be expected to manage without you."

"You shouldn't have left us all on our own like that," Fiona said sarcastically.

I ignored her; the intonation in her voice made it quite clear that I was far safer to back off. Getting into an argument would not achieve anything, but I wanted to have the last word. "Fiona, please go and put some clothes on."

"So much naked flesh in a kitchen is completely inappropriate."

"I've had no other complaints…" she said, with a huff and moved past me through the door pausing, her nubile body brushing mine. "…so far." She said, and leaned forward as if to kiss me. "My, you are breathing heavily, Mr Dillon," she said huskily just an inch or so from my face.

"Go away, Fiona," I said, "I've got enough on my mind already." But I was breathing heavily.

"I hear you have a sexy blond tucked away in London, Jake. Is that true?"

Before I had the chance to answer her, the gate intercom buzzed. I backed away from her. It was a local car wash firm asking if we wanted a special deal on car cleaning? Rumple was about to dismiss the caller in his usual gruff voice, but I stopped him. Yes I would I said, especially as the Mercedes had been brought back from the airport in a filthy condition. So Rumple told the lad to drive in and that someone would be out in a moment.

By the time I got to him he was already unloading

buckets, sponges and all of the other paraphernalia that goes with cleaning a car. I told him what was required and started to small talk as he worked. Casually asking him if he knew Harry Caplin, the American up the road? Or Mr Flackyard the local big man? Yes he knew them both. Was trade good at present? It was all right but not like it is in the winter. Was this his only job or did he work for other firms? No, this was his only job all year round, but that he would always consider other opportunities.

Would he care to earn himself some extra income? Paid in cash of course?

After haggling a little we struck a deal and agreed that it was best if no one else knew of our temporary little agreement.

His job was simply to carry on washing the cars of Robert Flackyard and Harry Caplin as usual. To find out anything else while he was at their homes or in any of Flackyard's bars, for instance where they were going and to generally keep his ears and eyes open and to phone me with any information.

When he had finished and left, I went back inside to brief Rumple and Fiona about what had happened to Charlie and the assignment as it was now.

Chapter 13

Dinner was at 7.30pm

Mrs Rumple had cooked freshly caught local mackerel, served with a tomato salad and freshly baked crusty bread. I didn't want to get too heavy, but I suggested that Harry Caplin was far too inquisitive about what we were doing and that the assignment was at a delicate stage, because of the confiscated opium.

"Do you suspect Caplin of being in league with this character Robert Flackyard, sir?" asked Rumple.

"At this point in time, Mr Rumple, I even suspect you," I said, matter of factly.

There were no smiles and the air became tense. They all knew I was being deadly serious.

We continued to eat in silence. Then, as Mrs Rumple collected up the dishes, Fiona said, "I didn't know Harry Caplin had a luxury cruiser."

"Has he now," I said. Fiona had got up and gone into the kitchen. She called to us. "It's coming into the bay now."

We all went out on to the balcony to watch. Down below, beating a wake on the gleaming water, the big white boat cast a long shadow in the remnants of the evening sunlight. From the high wheelhouse a cap, blue, soft and nautical, peeked over the wrap-around windscreen. Harry Caplin's bronze face broke into a grin and his lips moved. Fiona put her flattened hand behind her ear and Harry shouted again, but the wind from the sea grabbed the words out of his mouth and tossed them over his shoulder. He disappeared into the inner confines of the boat, leaving the diesel motors idling with just enough power to hold her position without turning it beam-to to the swell. He reappeared holding a mobile phone to his ear, and the same time the house phone started to ring. I put it on loud speaker.

"C'mon, landlubbers," he said into the tiny flip-phone. "Get off your butts and get out here and have some fun."

"He really is the most vulgar man," said Mrs Rumple.

"Insufferable," added Rumple.

"I only said he was vulgar, I didn't say I didn't like it," replied Mrs Rumple.

Fiona lit a cigarette as the three of us went down to the dinghy. The small outboard motor spat and whined like a wasp in flight as we shot out towards the cruiser.

"Are you sure that we're safe with you Mr Caplin?" Asked Fiona flirtatiously as she stepped aboard.

"Hell, lady, how many times do I have to tell you..."

"Harry?"

"Well, I'll tell you, Fiona. These two guys are perfectly safe. You – aren't safe at all." He pushed his cap back and boomed his big laugh.

Inside the main cabin it was all fitted furniture and soft music. Nautical procedures had gone clean overboard. Along the wall were a stainless steel sink and an array of built-in appliances including a fridge. Set on the wall was a large plasma screen. We sank into luxuriously soft leather seats while Harry blended vodka martinis with ritualistic devotion.

"What's that all about, Harry?" Fiona was looking at the mural of signal flags which decorated the cabin wall.

"It's flag talk, see, you haul them..."

"Yes, Harry, I do understand the function of signal

flags. What I want to ask, is what is the meaning of these?"

"Sure, Fiona, that's what I thought you meant. They're international foreign flags, see these over here, they mean in nautical terms…" Harry leaned over close to Fiona Price… "permission granted to lay alongside." Miss Price Blushed and Harry slapped his leg and boomed his larger than life laugh.

"Oh, very nautical, Harry, I really must commit that one to memory," she said sarcastically, blushing the colour of a strawberry.

I noticed Rumple's lip curl, but whether at Caplin's suggestiveness or seamanship I couldn't tell.

"Come on up to the bridge," said Harry. The CD had finished and the next was already taking its place. Against the hull the water giggled and gurgled like a fool. I heard Miss Price says, "so this is the driver's seat?" Harry replied, "yep." I wondered how many of the jibes really bounced off of Harry and how many went deep under the skin like a chigoe, a nasty little tropical flea that likes to burrow into flesh. Frank Sinatra began to pump the cabin full of sound.

Rumple was admiring the treasure trove of electronic equipment on the bridge.

"Yes, sir," Harry said, "a powered anchor; right here." He pushed one of a series of brightly coloured buttons. There was a faint purr and I felt the big cruiser float free on the outgoing tide. "The latest inboard diesels," the big engines suddenly broke the calm of the quite bay. Harry moved the gear lever, and the twin screws engaged the water. We slid forward. Harry held the wheel in a firm proprietorial grip, bit on his large Havana cigar and beamed at us all from his high stool. "You Limeys have had the monopoly on messing about in boats long enough; here, let somebody else steer," he said, and poured us all another round of vodkas form the big iced jug with a design of dancing pirates on it.

What a strange scene we made like something out of a television advertisement all standing on the fly bridge of a boat called Star Dust.

Chapter 14

After an evening with Harry Caplin I was pleased to get back to the house.

Although it was well past midnight none of us were ready for sleep, so we sat around drinking brandy and coffee into the small hours. I heard Fiona say, "Any more coffee for you," but I was beginning to notice that Rumple wasn't worrying too much about coffee, he was hitting the brandy. The talk went on over more coffee and even more brandy Rumple told us about his father. "He wasn't happy in the water. He never took a bath always had a shower, he used to say that he might slip and drown in the water, until one day when the shower wouldn't work for some reason, my mother did manage to persuade him to have a bath. We were living in the south of France at the time. I remember it was sweltering; he got this enormous terracotta pot that was used at harvest time, he plugged up the hole in the bottom and filled it with water. He then got in, but all the time he held onto a hammer. He said that if he felt himself slipping he could smash the pot with the hammer before he drowned."

Then he told us about his diving exploits in the Falklands and drank even more brandy, generally glossing over his time in the Navy, Fiona was interested in this and they talked about techniques of diving, when the gate entry buzzer broke into the conversation.

Fiona said, "Who the hell is that at this time of night?"

"Probably just kids messing about. I'll go and see," I said, already getting up and heading for the door.

I guessed it might be the young lad, Sam, who I'd asked to keep an eye on Flackyard and Caplin. It was.

To my surprise he had written up a report on Flackyard's movements for that afternoon and evening. I thanked and paid him the agreed sum, plus a bonus for being vigilant and thorough. He walked off down the road happy and said that he would contact me again in a day or so. Fiona called from the doorway, "Who is it?"

"A couple of drunken kids, messing about, they've gone now." I replied.

We went back indoors, where Rumple was still drinking heavily.

"I saw you chatting away like lost brothers to one of them," said Fiona. "Wasn't that the kid who washed your car earlier today?"

"No, You must have drunk to much brandy Fiona, I most certainly was not talking like a lost brother to either of those two. I was actually telling that young drunk that if he didn't move I'd call the police, at which he came up to the gate and threatened me. What you actually saw was my hand around his throat and his face in the railings; I was simply advising him what a bad idea that was."

By the time we eventually got to bed the wind was blowing a gale outside, and below on the small private beach that belonged to the house, air, water and sand thrashed together.

Sometimes one could distinguish each separate wave; the roar, crash, confusion and withdrawal. Often, however, the sound became just one long howl; rocking the window panes, vibrating against the metal watering can, flapping the canvas awning, pounding into the head, filling the ears and spinning the mind into a whirl.

My room opened on to a small wooden balcony. Two miles out on the black ocean the lights of the local fishing boats were winking in the movement of the horizon. I imagined the misery of the English Channel at night, working for a meagre living. The fishermen's catches were becoming smaller and smaller, diminishing each year. I watched the black clouds move across the moon for a long time before going to bed. I tried to sleep, but the noise of the wind and the effect of the coffee kept me awake. At 4.00 am I heard a bedroom door open and then close with a click. Soft footsteps went down the bare wooden stairs.

Someone else couldn't sleep; perhaps a cup of tea would be a good idea.

The footsteps went on through to the kitchen. I heard the back door open and the footsteps outside on the sun patio. As I was climbing into some clothes I heard the hinges of the rusty gate creak open.

Looking over my bedroom balcony there was enough moonlight for me to see someone was moving down the path in the direction of the boathouse.

The figure turned, dropped off the sea wall and began to walk along the sand towards one of many groynes which separated each private beach. I went down the staircase as quickly as I could.

The wind cut me with an icy shiver and the needlepoints of spray penetrated my trousers and sweater. The metal of my pistol was cold against my hip. I decided not to use the gate; instead I eased myself through a gap between the garden wall and garage. Fifteen metres ahead of me the nocturnal stroller made no attempt to conceal himself. It was Rumple. He went to the first groyne climbed over it and continued along to the next and the next.

As he made his way along the last stretch of beach he came to the base of a wide stone staircase, which twisted up to the road above. To begin my ascent before he had completed his would be foolish. He had only to glance down to be certain of spotting me.

I gave him plenty of time to get to the top; then, keeping well to the inside of the staircase, I began to walk up.

I watched carefully for anything that if trodden on would give my presence away, although the roar of the sea would have swallowed the noise of anything less than an avalanche. I paused as I neared the top, took the automatic out of my belt, breathed in and out very slowly and moved up on to the road. If he was waiting for me, a deep lungful of air could make all the difference.

No one was waiting for me. To the right the road was completely empty as far as I could see. From the left came only the faint sound and red tail lights of an old MkI Jaguar as it turned a corner and then there was only the pandemonium of the sea. A little finger of grey cloud smudged the bright eye of the moon. It seemed as though Rumple had got a lift. Who did we know with a MKI Jaguar?

I was losing friends faster than I could replace them.

* * *

By the next morning, big droplets of rain dabbed at the grey slate windows.

The bad weather had moved in from the south west as the shipping forecast had predicted. The wind and rain gave no sign of relenting before late afternoon, so I worked on my report for LJ in the privacy of my bedroom.

Sandbanks was an area designed for the sun to shine upon, so when the rain came it looked confused, and most of all betrayed. Along the main road rain dripped from the shop awnings, and in La Café the girls whiled away their time when not serving the odd customer, by gazing out of the window across the bay and drinking cappuccino.

Mrs Rumple brought breakfast up to my room at around 10.00am. While she was there I asked how Rumple was after his brandy session.

"Well, sir. You know Rumple, brandy never affects him. He was up at the crack of dawn as usual, and out the door straight after breakfast. Something to do with a spare part for the dinghy's outboard motor. I think he said that there was nowhere local, and that the nearest stockist was in Brighton." She didn't think he would be back much before dinner.

I left it at that, not wishing to arouse any suspicion by overly questioning her. When I'd finished typing up my report I emailed it straight to LJ.

Afterwards, I decided to go down and check that the cargo we were baby-sitting was still stowed safely on the boat. When I opened the boathouse door I found Fiona wearing a swimsuit and shorts, her diving equipment lying around her bare feet.

"Going for a dive?" I asked casually.

"Why, Jake Dillon, what brings you down here? I hope you're not spying on me?"

"Now why would I want to spy on you? Unless…" Out of the corner of my eye, I caught sight of one of the lockers where Rumple had stowed the raw opium. I climbed up onto the lower rear deck of the forty-six-foot cruiser. The locker door was just slightly ajar, and the handle had been wrenched round so far that the spindle had snapped clean in half and the strike plate carefully twisted back out of the way. This gave the impression that the door was locked, but in reality it had just been pushed too. Fiona came and knelt down by my side. "You've got it wrong, you know."

"Sorry, what do mean," I replied, studying the damage to the door.

"I know you think that I've been landed on you,

and that I'm a pain in the arse that you really could have done without. But you've got me all wrong, I'm not here to spy on you, you know. I would really like it if we could be friends, Jake. As for who I work for, well, the only thing that I can tell you is that it's Her Majesty's Government, but usually behind a desk."

"I don't know, Fiona, there are many things about you that don't tally."

I slowly opened the locker door; inside everything was as it should have been. The brown wax packages were still neatly stacked liked miniature sandbags. Nothing seemed to be missing. I carried on and checked the other two compartments, finding each with their cargo intact.

"What is it that doesn't tally about me, Jake?" She asked, her voice low and husky.

I went to stand, her hand reached up for my arm. Looking down at Fiona I smiled in genuine admiration. Her face was alive and her eyes sparkling.

There was a vibrancy I hadn't noticed before. She wore a black skin-tight swimsuit and shorts. Her breasts loomed larger and her hips more slender than I had thought, her legs were long and athletic. She stood up and leaned against the cabin doorway, her pose was provocative and she moved with sensual vivacity.

"So tell me, Jake. What is it that doesn't tally?" She asked demurely. A bout of temporary shyness taking hold, as she dropped her gaze to avert any eye contact.

"It won't work, you know?"

"What won't work?" She said coyly, running a hand through her hair which shone under the lights of the boathouse.

"You know exactly what I'm talking about, Fiona?"

"I really don't know what you're talking about, Jake?"

"Okay, if that's the way you want to play it?

Perhaps you can tell me this?"

"Why does a desk bound civil servant sleep with a loaded Beretta under her pillow?" I said it with deliberate slowness, for full effect.

"What?"

"You heard me." I said.

"I really don't know what you're talking about."

"That's the second time you've lied to me, Fiona. One more, and as far as I'm concerned you can go to hell."

"It's true, what they say about you. You're an absolute bastard, aren't you?"

I simply shrugged my shoulders, and said nothing.

"Is that it, a shrug. Got nothing to say, Jake. Well, I'll tell you something, Mister. It's not polite to rummage through a girl's bedroom without an invitation." The intonation in her voice, made it perfectly clear that she was far more annoyed at herself for having been careless, leaving the gun where anybody could have found it. Than she was at me for having found it.

"So why do you have the gun, Fiona?"

"Well I'd have thought that even you could have worked that one out, Jake?"

"You've not been doing this cloak and dagger stuff long have you?" I said, adding. "And that's a really crap answer, by the way. I'm disappointed that you don't trust me. No matter what you think of me personally. My only hope is that you know how shoot the thing, and more importantly, that you know when to shoot it?"

"I can assure you, Jake, that when the time comes I know exactly what has to be done. But thank you for your concern."

"Um, I'm sure you do." I said jumping down off the boat. At the heavy double doors I paused just for a second; giving her yet another opportunity to come clean about who she worked for, before pushing one of them open, and walking out into the grey daylight.

"So what happens next, Jake?" Fiona shouted after me.

"I really don't know, Fiona. But I'm going to find out." I said over my shoulder as the door swung closed behind me.

Chapter 15

Tuesday 12.30pm

I made a call to Detective Inspector Daniel Jacobs, who was part of the Special Branch team investigating Robert Flackyard. Although not forthcoming initially, after being suitably reminded about a certain incident during our time at university together, he relented and give me what I wanted.

"So you see, Jake, Fiona Price is part of a team investigating Robert Flackyard and Harry Caplin. When we heard that your assignment was taking you to Dorset, it was too good an opportunity to miss. But it was deemed necessary at the outset to let you think that she was sent to simply help you, sorry about that. Your Mr Levenson-Jones knew, of course."

"Of course," I replied. "Forgive me, Daniel for being just a tad miffed about not knowing. It would have made my job a lot easier if someone had told me at the start of this assignment, but thank you for being honest with me now." I hung up and walked back down in the pouring rain to the boathouse. Fiona looked up as I opened the door, but carried on zipping up one of the bags containing her diving equipment.

"I think I owe you an apology," I said.

"Oh, no you don't, Jake. What I said earlier? Well, it was unforgivable, the way I spoke to you and my attitude towards you. It's me who should be apologising, not you."

"What - no, not that. Although I agree you were a little harsh calling me a bastard. Truc somc of the time, but not always. It's just that I feel professionally that we got off on the wrong foot. Look, to be truthful, Fiona, Charlie and I thought that you were sent to spy on us or something like that."

"Anyway, what with those photographs being stolen and various other things happening, it could only have been someone on the inside. Afraid I jumped to a conclusion about you that was quite clearly wrong. And for that, I'm truly sorry. You see, everyone else on this team was already known to each other, and then you arrived out of the blue. I then tried to run a check on you through the firm's database, which came up with a great big zero." Walking the length of the sleek cruiser I sat down on a pile of wooden crates that were stacked against the side of the boathouse.

Fiona walked up towards me, running her finger along the side of the boat as she went. "Look, you don't have to beat yourself up you know. I should never have agreed to go along with LJ's theory that a certain person would be getting sticky fingers on this particular assignment. He specifically asked for me, wanted me here not because of my diving experience and the logbook, I'm afraid, was just another one of his smoke screens. My father and LJ go back as long as I can remember. Dad had a phone call late one evening, asking him if he had anyone in his department or someone he knew from experience, who could act, throw a tantrum or two, was a qualified open water diver and would be able to look after themselves in any situation. Well, after a considerable amount of thought, all of ten seconds, he came up with me. But I really wasn't sent here to snoop on you or Charlie, bless him. It's Mr Rumple that LJ is concerned about."

I said with surprise. "Rumple, what exactly have you got on him?"

"So far all we know…"

"We, who exactly is we," I snapped at her. Just managing to suppress the sudden surge of anger rising inside me, as I remembered Rumple boasting once that he could detonate a bomb, while at the same time having a cup of tea a hundred miles away.

"We, are the Partners of Ferran & Cardini and in particular LJ, the Serious Drugs Squad to which I am currently seconded to, and the Whitehall department for which I actually work. Now if I may continue?" I nodded my head ever so slightly.

"As you quite rightly say, Jake, Mr Rumple is a very experienced field operative. For many years both he and Mrs Rumple along with their particular skills have been successfully used, and well paid I might add, by various intelligence agencies as well as going out on loan to other friendly Governments around the world. The CIA were always asking for them. It was decided at the highest level, however, that they were becoming too much in demand and a little too arrogant for their own good."

So the head of department at that time was instructed to retire them from active service, but to somewhere that HMG could, if they so required, call them back from. To cut a very long story short, they were pensioned off to your firm. Why, I hear you ask, because all of the Partners and in particular LJ still have an active involvement, as you are well aware, with HMG. That last bit comes under the Official Secrets Act, by the way."

"Um, well, I already knew most of that, including the last bit. But why start batting for the other team now and for what reason? Surely not just the money, would they really risk everything they have built up?" I paced up and down the side of the boathouse. Running my hands through my hair I continued. "It just doesn't make sense, I've known them for many years."

"Rumple's actions of late are so out of character.

There must be more to this than you're telling me."

I started to open the door to leave.

"Jake, please come back inside. Look, I'll tell you everything I know."

I went back to the side of the cruiser, climbed the ladder onto the deck and went into the main cabin. I poured us both a large whisky. Fiona sat down and took the glass from me, gulping back the amber coloured liquid in one hit.

I refilled her glass and sat down opposite her. "So, go on tell me the rest."

"Well, the department head that retired them was Edward Levenson-Jones." She brought her right hand up as if stopping the traffic at rush hour.

"Before you say it, yes it does get worse. The picture becomes much clearer when you know who the person is that told LJ to wield the axe on the Rumples. I'm afraid it's none other than the right honourable Oliver Hawkworth MP. So you see why certain people have become very nervous about these two becoming loose cannons and taking some sort of revenge, as well as a large payment from Flackyard. The fact is that LJ should never have succumbed to the Partners and their devious ways, it would have been much safer to keep them away from this assignment altogether. We think that Flackyard paid someone on the inside to dig around at Ferran & Cardini.

"Get to know about this, and well the rest is history, as they say."

"Hell - this whole assignment has been a shambles from the start." I finished the whisky, not knowing whether the burning inside my stomach was the anger I still felt or the alcohol. In the end, I decided that it was the whisky and that being angry was going to achieve nothing but melancholy.

"When are you returning to London?" I asked. My

mobile phone started to ring before Fiona could reply. The call was brief and to the point. The female voice at the other end purred and stated that Mr Flackyard was holding a Champagne reception and auction in aid of local charities at his home this evening and, that he would be delighted if Miss Price and I could attend, formal black tie, starting around 8.00 p.m. After accepting the invitation on behalf of us both, I hung up.

"Tonight," Fiona said. "I'll be driving up tonight, back to the rat race and a normal routine again I suppose, they'll almost certainly take me off the case now."

"Well, that last call was interesting. Flackyard is hosting a Champagne charity function this evening and has requested our company. So how about a few more days by the seaside – unless you have to rush off, that is?"

"Well let me see, I do have an appointment at 9.00am sharp tomorrow, with a really boring desk job. So what do you think?"

"You'd better phone your boss and tell him that there have been some interesting new developments with the situation down here and that your presence is still required. Don't say anything more than that, except that a full progress report will be with Ferran & Cardini by this evening. Here, use my phone, it's secure."

Fiona used my mobile phone to call her boss in London.

"Oh, by the way, you'd better unpack your diving gear again, we'll be going for a little swim later," I said as I left the boathouse.

As I stepped outside, the wind and rain gave no sign of relenting. Going straight up to my room I spent the next hour at my laptop, putting together a progress report on the developments relating to Robert Flackyard. I added that Fiona had come clean, telling me that we'd been working for the same side all the time! After emailing LJ, I saved the report to disk and erased it from the hard drive. This done I phoned Sam 'the car wash'. He answered after two or three rings with a cheerful hello, surprised that I was calling him. Where was he? At Robert Flackyard's home cleaning all of his flash cars? His boss had called him and said that he had been personally asked for, that there was going to be a glitzy party and charity auction there tonight and one of Mr Flackyard's Aston Martins would be sold off to the highest bidder. So he was to stay there all day and polish every one of them.

"OK, now listen very carefully, I want you to make a note of everyone coming and going, get their registration numbers if possible. If Caplin in particular turns up or anyone else arrives throughout the day, immediately text me their name on this number. If Flackyard leaves also let me know, and remember to write down times."

My thoughts were racing as I finished talking. What a stroke of luck that our young observer should be in exactly the right place at the right time. Or was it?

Mrs Rumple was no where to be found. A note on the kitchen notice board read, gone into town – back by 6.30pm. The time was now 2.30pm, leaving just four hours to relocate the fifty deadly opium packages.

Chapter 16

Take the English Channel on a cold and miserable day and keep a brisk wind striking across it from the Northeast. Put a luxury cruiser somewhere between the heaving waves with the swell on its starboard quarter, and into it put two crew standing clad in wetsuits when there should have been at least four.

The swell was enough to tip us down in the valleys between the waves at an alarming angle. To the Southwest I watched the coastline come into view from each wave crest. A surreal scene with clouds as black as coal, low and menacing. Brilliant shafts of sunlight, highlighting across sea and land like static and streaks of phosphorescence. These weren't ideal conditions to dive in, but at least the weather was, for our sake, keeping the sunshine sailors at home and only a handful of hardened thrill seekers out in these conditions.

I was already feeling the constriction of the tight fitting wetsuit and began to wonder whether it had been such a good idea to put it on back in the boathouse, especially as we wouldn't be diving for another half an hour? Fiona carried out the last minute checks on all of the dive equipment, and weighted down each one of the five bags containing the opium packages with lead we had found tucked in a corner of the garage. When absolutely satisfied that each one was secure, a nylon rope was used to tie them all together in a continuous chain.

Our heading was to a point about one mile out from Old Harry rocks to the wreck of a WWII German submarine, sunk during the last war. An ocean-going U-boat as I remembered was a very large piece of machinery, over six hundred tons and two hundred feet in length. Making it the ideal hiding place for the five sacks that we had to conceal, each containing ten of the small waxy bales of raw opium.

The story of the U-boat was often enthusiastically told by some of the older locals, who could recall the event. It went something along the lines of that the submarine had surfaced at night to off load a crack unit of SS commandos, a British destroyer was lying in wait and had sunk her. She went down in forty meters of water with all hands lost. Afterwards the Ministry of Defence had the bodies removed and buried in unmarked graves, in village churchyards around the Dorset countryside. The whole affair was then covered up so as not to fuel speculation about a possible German invasion. Their official notice stated that the destroyer was simply firing her guns after a routine re-fit.

I pushed a button and the anchor chain slid out from its housing and into the foaming water below. At one hundred and five feet it stopped. I left the engines ticking over to hold us in position and went down to the dive platform, where Fiona was waiting.

The howl of the wind and driving rain was deafening after the relative calm of the bridge, and even the steady drone of the large diesel engines was lost.

With each wave the boat lurched up into the air, but we somehow managed to put on our oxygen tanks, fins and masks without being swept over board.

I lowered the sacks into the water one at a time while Fiona took care of the high-powered underwater lanterns that we would need inside the U-boat.

I tapped her on the shoulder and shouted, "We have thirty minutes maximum down there. Follow me and stay close."

With that we clambered down the dive ladder on the port side, instead of going off the stern, so as to stay away from the propellers. I snapped the mouthpiece between my teeth and pulled the mask into place. The coldness of the water bit to the bone as I lowered myself in.

I jack-knifed through the opaque water. Beneath the heaving surface the sea was green and without dimension. A white explosion of microscopic bubbles raced to my feet as I swam down towards the great hulk of the submarine. Fiona swam close to my side, the powerful lamps already having to light our way as we went deeper. All was calm and soft. The water, no longer green but purple, was motionless as we swam down. To my right, Fiona was cleaving a phosphorescent wake, and as she descended I watched her turn a graceful somersault and touch her feet on the bottom with scarcely a movement of silt. My own clumsy effort at this ended with dirty clouds of silt and weed rising around my fins.

I let the sacks drop to the sea floor; Fiona handed me one of the lanterns, and as my eyes became adjusted to the purple darkness one vast portion of the seabed grew darker than the rest. The huge potbelly of the sunken submarine loomed over us. I clipped the lamp onto my tank harness and retrieved the end of the rope that coupled the sacks together. I then gave Fiona a hook-like motion with my free hand and climbed an invisible ladder on to the foredeck. We swam past the smooth convex swell of the main tanks.

Here and there sections of the original paintwork were still in remarkably good condition. In spite of the slight list it was easy to imagine that this was a fully manned U-boat of the German Kreigsmarine, resting momentarily on the bottom before resuming a war mission.

We passed around and over the conning tower, and

in the glow of our lanterns we could just make out the silhouette of the open hatch. The fuzzy glow of the lamps suddenly became sharp discs, as we dropped lightly on to the conning tower platform. The soft paintwork shed its skin under my hand, the flakes spinning upward like perverse seeds.

Holding the side of the conning-tower ladder with one hand I controlled my drop into the small oval room beneath. I shone the bright lamp around the interior. White circles flashed from the walls as the glass-faced gauges reflected the light back. My lamp shone up through to the hatch above my head, and Fiona's outline was just visible as she waited on the platform outside. I signalled her to lower the sacks down. This didn't take long as we had left them all tied together. Once the last one was inside, Fiona joined me in the cramped control room. Moving carefully we kept to the port side of the cluttered interior, passing the huge wheel of the hydroplane controls. The starboard side was choked with remnants of bedding, bunks and seaweed.

Above me, broken piping hung like strange stalactites, while the remains of chairs and wooden stools danced against the ceiling. I tried to imagine the final scene in this little space, crowded like a rush hour tube train, all those years ago. I half walked, half swam past broken crates, which a long time ago had held provisions.

My breathing became difficult. One bottle was empty. I switched to the full bottle and breathing recommenced.

Fiona's lamp was moving around in front of me through the next bulkhead door. I moved on, noticing the pressure hull – well over an inch thick and able to withstand water pressures at over five hundred feet, I tapped it and the metal vibrated with a clang. The far side of the bulkhead was the torpedo stowage compartment. It was cavernous; the floor lay some ten feet below us down a ladder. On either side was rack after rack of inert torpedoes, greasy and silver like Cuban cigar tubes. We dragged the five sacks over the railing and descended to the deck below. Since coming to rest on the seabed much silt had been washed gently through the torpedo stowage compartment by year after year of tidal activity. After a little searching, I found what I was looking for, covered in silt and weed. A few inches away from my feet was a flat, rectangular slab. The silt flurried around as I ran my gloved fingers along the edge to define its outline. Taking my knife I managed to insert the tip under one corner. Eventually it shifted and we were able to lift it all the way up.

Shining my lamp down into the black hole, I motioned to Fiona to hand me the first sack, I lowered it, then the next and the next until they were all inside the chamber secured by the rope onto a hook.

Before replacing the steel plate. I took a small magnetic charge of the type that we'd used on the Gin Fizz, and attached it to the side of the chamber.

Once it was securely in place, I armed the device by setting the switch to remote, and the next second a red light started to glow brightly through the gloom of the murky waters inside the dark access pit.

Satisfied that everything was as we'd found it. I ran a forefinger across my throat and pointed upwards. Fiona nodded and swam off back to the bulkhead. We retraced our route, going out through the conning tower hatch and over the 37mm gun platforms: the ocean seemed vast after the U-boat interior. Staying together we floated easily through the dark water, using only our feet to propel us. As we neared the surface the hull of the cruiser became visible. Our heads broke through the ocean top; wind ripped into my face like a blunt blade.

The splash of the waves broke the silence and the cold biting into my head and shoulders made me suddenly aware of how frozen my body was in spite of the thickness of the wetsuit. Fiona kept a safe distance away from the boat, which swung and lurched on its anchor chain, the engines just barely holding their own against the swell.

After one failed attempt at reaching the dive ladder, I managed to grab hold of it, just as a wave struck lifting the boat into the air. Once I was safely aboard, Fiona followed shortly afterwards.

* * *

5.00pm

The warmth inside the cabin and a large brandy were welcome after the numbing coldness outside. I felt a lot happier now that the opium was safely hidden away one mile out and one hundred and five feet down on the seabed of the English Channel. It would take us an hour to get back to the boathouse, with time to spare before either of the Rumples returned to the house, if in fact they did return?

"How long have you known that the U-boat was down there, Jake," Fiona stood next to me, a blanket wrapped around her shoulders, at the helm.

"So that's what you've been pondering about. Well it was one of the first wrecks I ever dived on, but it seems like a long time ago. You see, that particular U-boat is not favoured by sport divers as it's still got about seven live torpedoes on board and after sixty years or so they're probably a little bit unstable." I adjusted our course passing a fully laden container ship on our port side. Fiona was looking at me in disbelief, evidently horrified by the thought of having dived into a Second World War German submarine still having live explosives aboard.

"Why the hell have they never been taken off or destroyed?" she asked, nervousness and tension in her voice.

"Well, for a start the wreck doesn't officially exist – remember? It was a pure fluke that I discovered her all those years ago. But that area is not favoured by anyone, and that includes the Ministry of Defence as the current is very strong this far out in the channel. Also the sub's in quite deep water and a good mile out from the coast, and therefore it was deemed as non-dangerous by the authorities at the time."

"Anyway, one of the biggest problems was that at the end of the war the Germans were experimenting with many different types of firing mechanisms or 'triggers'. There were acoustics, magnetic and electric eye. It was not uncommon for a boat as highly developed as that to have a mixed bag of weapons on board. But we were never really in any danger, I've swum through that sub many times, and as long as you don't disturb the racks holding the torpedoes there's no chance of a detonation. Of course, that isn't the case anymore."

I held up the remote detonator in my left hand. "This is the remote control for that explosive charge down there, I'm going to re-route the command to our mobile phones. That way either of one of us can destroy the opium by simply pressing nine and then send. Understood?"

Fiona nodded and then said. "No wonder you hid the opium there, it's got to be the last place on earth that anyone would go – even if they did know about it. So what happens now Jake."

"Now – we go to a party, and *see* what happens next!"

Chapter 17

Tuesday 8.15pm

Sloping shoulders and a neck like a tree trunk. The young muscle-bound security guard eyed me up and down suspiciously as I handed him the invitation, eventually pushing open the heavy oak door for us.

Robert Flackyard's spacious and elegant entrance hall was as I remembered it from my previous visit. Simply decorated in Mediterranean style and furnished with impeccable taste, yet strangely cold and clinical, like a doctor's waiting room. We were immediately offered a glass of Champagne and shown through to the rear terrace, where a number of enormous marquees had been erected; the illuminated swimming pool was now the centrepiece.

Throughout the grounds torches had been lit and the gravel paths freshly groomed. The sound system on the stage area belts out nostalgic melodies from Flackyard's collection of early LPs. I wondered for just a brief moment whether it might be a love of swing music that Harry Caplin and Flackyard had in common. But, deep down, my guts were telling me it wasn't. Girls almost wearing flimsy nothings, flitted around the guests refilling glasses as they became empty.

I left Fiona talking to a tall blond haired banker called Jack from New York in white dinner jacket. The Dom is flowing, servants scurry and smile - the Flackyard hospitality is working its magic.

To one side of the half round stage stood the main attraction of the charity auction. An Aston Martin DB5, brilliant silver paintwork gleaming. Sam 'the car wash' was busy giving it a final dusting off and polishing the chrome. I approached the stage casually, glass in hand, as if to merely admire and examine the car prior to bidding later in the evening. Having spotted me walking towards him, the young watcher knelt down by one of the wire wheels and started rubbing the chrome spokes vigorously with his cloth. He concealed his face, so that only the back of his head was visible. He spoke quickly and to the point.

"Flackyard hasn't left the house all day. Apart from the caterers, cleaning contractors, florists and marquee people, only two other people have been allowed in. One of them was that pizza-faced weasel George Ferdinand, he got here about 2.30pm this afternoon. Stayed about twenty minutes and then left."

"Was he alone?" I asked.

"Yeah, he was alone, but he didn't look happy when he left, mind, slammed that big oak door at the front so hard I thought the whole building was going to fall down with the shock. Then he got in his car and spun gravel everywhere as he pulled off."

"Anything else?"

"Another bloke arrived around 4.15pm, never seen him before. Definitely not local, though, he was older, mid fifties, big and really fit looking. Might have been ex military. He only stayed about fifteen minutes and then left." Sam got up and walked to the rear wheel, crouching down he resumed his polishing with vigour.

"Well – elaborate," I said.

"I couldn't get a really good look at him; they've kept me away from the main house and I've been watched all day by the security guards. But I did manage to see something that may be of interest. Look, I want a bonus for staying here all day, you know, I've really stretched this car cleaning lark beyond belief."

"Why is that not a surprise? Go on."

"One of Flackyard's own security people obviously knew who this big guy was. Because as he came through the front gates he shook hands with him like an old friend. I think he was telling him that the boss was expecting him."

He pointed over to the gate in the wall which leads out on to this terrace.

"They were only talking for a minute or so and then this big bloke walks off."

"But as he did, the security guy calls after him using a nickname I think, and when the big fella replied though he had a really low gruff voice. I thought I'd heard it before somewhere, but because of the distance between me and them and all the noise going on like, I really couldn't hear what the name was or what was being said. Sorry."

One of the hired helps, with slicked down hair and a fake suntan, came striding towards us; SECURITY was written on a badge pinned to his lapel.

The conversation immediately switched to the car. Sam was informed that Mr Flackyard had given instructions for all cleaning staff to leave the premises, as the evening was about to commence. He was given an envelope and escorted to the main gates. Over the many speakers an announcement was made that the auction was about to start. I looked around for Flackyard who was conspicuous by his absence. I sat down at the nearest available table.

My thoughts though were elsewhere. Was George Ferdinand possibly skulking in the flowerbed or was he attending to a little business elsewhere?

Had Rumple really gone off the track? Who killed Charlie McIntyre? What of Harry Caplin, was he in league with Flackyard or working with Ferdinand? All of these questions kept rattling around in my mind, over and over again, never resting.

After about five painful minutes of sitting at a table with eight complete strangers who had all drunk far too much Champagne I quietly got up and walked out. On the way I looked around for Fiona, but to no avail. In the main hall Robert Flackyard was coming through a doorway from an adjacent room with two of his security people.

"Mr Jake Dillon, what a pleasure it is to have you in my home once again. I sincerely hope that you are not leaving us so early, the festivities have barely begun."

"Tell me Flackyard, why exactly did you invite me here tonight? It's surely not because I'm on your A-List of influential people to have at parties, is it?"

"Perhaps you just wanted to know where I would be this evening?" I said easily, all the time looking straight at him. The angry fire flared in his eyes, but only for a second, receding almost immediately.

A snap of his fingers and my way was barred. I was ushered through the doorway and into the room Flackyard had just that minute come out of by the same sullen faced security doorman who had seen Fiona and me in earlier in the evening. The walls were covered in books from floor to ceiling all placed carefully in fine oak bookcases.

Flackyard walked to the far end of the library and placed himself behind a large, highly polished mahogany desk. He stood for just a moment looking down as if collecting his thoughts. Sitting down he swung around and leaned back in the leather-faced captain's chair, all the time concentrating on the polished top of the desk. Not once did he look up at me. Clasping his hands as if to pray, he leaned forward putting his elbows on the mirror-like wood, the tips of his fingers just resting on his chin. After what seemed like an eternity he eventually lifted his gaze and looked straight into my eyes with piercing coldness.

"My dear, Mr Dillon, since you arrived here in Bournemouth you have been - how shall I put it - a thorn in my side. Your firm sent you here to discreetly retrieve certain sensitive items from a sunken wreck. Having achieved this, you disappoint me by still having in your possession something belonging to my associates and me…"

His voice trailed off, as another dark suited security flunky roughly pushed the door open with a hand tightly gripping a struggling Fiona Price under the arm. He blurted to his employer that he had found her snooping around inside the house. Flackyard, furious at being interrupted in this manner sharply barked the order that she be released at once. Getting up, he went round and pulled up an old 1930's leather easy chair in front of the desk, motioning her to sit.

"Miss Price, how good of you to join us, I am enchanted to meet you, and of course, by your beauty, you look so elegant this evening." He was instantly charming, with a golden voice, tainted by time but guaranteed to captivate, as long as you prefer tone to substance.

Before turning his attention back to me, he ordered the man who had just manhandled Fiona in, to get out of his sight. That done, he continued, "Now, Mr Dillon, where were we – ah yes, your meddling in my business, and the missing packages. I will come straight to the point, especially as I've guests to attend to and lots of money to raise for our charities. I asked you here this evening for one reason and one reason only. As you quite rightly guessed, I wanted to ensure that I knew exactly where you were. Unfortunately I was informed just a moment ago that my people have not found what they were sent to look for. Your rented house and the boat I'm afraid will need a little straightening out when you return."

I lurched forward towards Flackyard. The two

bodyguards who had been stood on either side of me, reacted instantly and with a professional expertise that sent me down onto my knees.

"Ah, but how very remiss of me Mr Dillon, I forgot to give you the credit you so rightly deserve. I should have known that a man of your resourcefulness and experience would move the packages. But my friend, you would be well advised not to trifle with me, I am not a man to cross. Show him, Nazir." He said to the big Egyptian stood to his right. But kept his gaze on me.

Nazir, cracked his fingers, like a bare knuckle boxer does, just before a fight. And for a split second I thought I was in deep trouble. He stood in front of me, his face completely expressionless, pulled a two-way radio from his jacket pocket and spoke very quietly into it. The Egyptian then walked in a business like manner to the other side of the room to a large sash window.

"Let him up." Flackyard ordered. "Why don't you take a look out of the window, Mr Dillon?" He said with a grin.

I stood up, straightened my jacket and bow tie and then looked over at Fiona, who shot me a nervous glance. I did my best at a reassuring look back.

"Well, the view over your courtyard is very nice, Flackyard. But what is it, that I'm supposed to be looking at?"

Nazir, once again spoke into the two-way radio. A dodge pickup truck backed into the courtyard and stopped just below the window.

"Take a good look. As Mercedes go, I'd say the one that you're looking at, would fall into the compact class. Wouldn't you, Mr Dillon."

I didn't say a word, simply turned and then walked across the room to where Fiona was sitting and stood by her side.

"I do so hope that you're not in any way under

the illusion about the lengths that the people who own that opium will go to. They want it back, Dillon. Think yourself lucky that you weren't in your car at the time they crushed it. Needless to say the next time..."

"There won't be a next time, Flackyard, and those packages, that you so badly want back. Well, they'll be kept safely on ice until you fulfil your part of the deal as agreed with my employers. Until then they stay safely hidden away. Of course you will be told when and where to retrieve them, as and when the Partners are completely satisfied that their business with you has been concluded. Once and for all. Is that clear enough for you – Mr Flackyard?"

The air in the library hung heavy with tension and cigar smoke. Only the tick-tocking of the grandfather clock standing in a far corner broke the silence, as I waited for Flackyard to reply.

"You are of course quite right, Mr Dillon," he said calmly. "I shall arrange for delivery as quickly as possible." Flackyard hadn't flinched; his hands now lay flat, palm-down on the tabletop. The calmness that he showed was a façade inside, I knew that he was seething, wanting to smash his fist into my face repeatedly for daring to confront him, especially in front of his staff.

"When you're in a position to conclude the transaction, Mr Flackyard, please contact me on this number. Oh and you owe me a new car." I placed my card in front of him, turned, smiled to myself and left with Fiona.

Chapter 18

London 2.30am - Wednesday

I drove the car that I'd hired into London with an odd feeling of melancholy.

Charlie had been murdered not more than twenty feet from where I'd been standing and Rumple had been shot in the shoulder right next to me. Not that I thought that either had been unsuccessful attempts to get at me, but diligence ensures a much longer life than bravery ever did. I decided to make a few discreet inquiries on my own private grapevine, even if it did mean ignoring LJ's rules and procedures.

The cool wind carved up the street faster than a stockbroker's Porsche, and a leather–clad rider on a Japanese super-bike came roaring past in search of co-operation in the act of suicide. Instead of going to the apartment I checked into one of those cheap, small side-street hotels that catered for travelling salesmen and persons looking for anonymity. It was all 80's floral wallpaper and dusty fake plants. I wrote the name of James Fisher into the register. The overweight Slavic night porter manning the reception desk eyed me suspiciously and asked for some form of identification.

"Can I see your work permit?" I asked bluntly.

Embarrassed by my retort, he grudgingly gave me a key and told me my room was on the third floor at the front. The gaudy floral wallpaper was obviously a job lot with bed linen to match. The room was otherwise clean but bland and poorly furnished. I threw my overnight bag on the floor, flopped down onto the bed and slept, waking with a start when my travel clock told me it was 10.40 am. I had already decided to let a few hours pass before contacting LJ. I used my mobile phone to dial an inner London number. The phone made all the correct noises associated with making a call. After a while it even rang at the other end.

"Can I speak to Simon Davenport?" I said. He was my first ear to the ground.

"This phone is very hot – be careful," said the voice at the other end and hung up. He wasn't usually a laconic man, but in his world of electronic wizardry, tapped land lines and mobiles being listened to by satellite were an everyday occurrence. I decided to ring someone else who definitely had his ear to the ground. This time I was a little more circumspect. I waited for Alex Chapman, an Australian, to speak first, then I said, "Hello, Alex."

"I recognise the voice of my old mate…" he replied.

"You do," I said before he could blab it across the phone.

"Are you having a spot of bother?" he asked.

"I don't know, Alex; am I?" I heard him laugh like a hyena at the other end.

"Let's not talk over this," he said. His paranoia about talking on telephones was legendary.

"How about that trendy café bar, what's it called, bloody hell it's got a name that plays on words. Ah, I remember, 'Java Kye' that's it, say in an hour."

"OK," I said.

Java Kye actually is slang for coffee and drinking chocolate respectively. This sophisticated small café bar in Kensington has a reputation for exquisite coffee, and from the moment you step in your senses are lifted with the aroma of freshly ground coffee beans from around the world. You fight your way through a selection of American and European newspapers with a few glossy magazines added for colour. Inside it's a fusion of what's now and memorabilia of a bygone age, stage set superbly to amuse the rich and famous. I heard someone saying, "... God, I feel like shit this morning, but I have to say what an absolutely excellent party." It was 12.30 in the afternoon.

"Espresso, please," I said. Alex's skull shone through his thinning hair over a copy of the Financial Times.

"Hello Alex," I said. He didn't look up. The girl behind the counter gave me the coffee and my change; only then did Alex murmur, "Bring any baggage with you?"

"Not that I'm aware of," I said. I'd forgotten this man was paranoid. His brief but frequent stays in prison had left him with a skilful technique in rolling cigarettes thinner than matchsticks, an obsession about being followed and a lifelong aversion to any food that wasn't healthy.

"We'll sit over there at the back so I can see who comes in." We moved towards the rear and two vacant chairs.

"Did you go round the block a couple of times to make sure?"

"Relax, will you."

"You have to play by the rules," said Alex. "Only careless fools don't have rules, and they get caught."

I thought that was pretty good coming from the man who got caught at least once a year. "Rules," I said over the top of my coffee cup. "I didn't know that you were an advocate of rules."

"Well, I am now," said Alex. "Rules, you've got to know what to do in any situation, so that you can do it before you even think about it."

"Sounds like something the psychiatrist at that last prison told you. What sort of rules are we talking about here, Alex?"

"Depends, mate. Like if you're at sea and your boat starts to sink, always jump off the high side. That's a good rule, if you should ever be in that situation."

I said, "But I'm not expecting to be at sea on a sinking boat in the near future."

"Oh no?" said Alex. He leaned forward. "Well, I wouldn't be too sure about that, mate." He gave me that conspiratorial wink of his and a little snort.

"What are you hearing then, Alex?" I always found it difficult to believe that Alex Chapman was a man who could keep a secret. He was such a transparent rogue. But he had as many secrets as any other man did. Alex was the archetype professional computer hacker and thief.

I ordered another espresso coffee for us both.

"What am I hearing?" he said, repeating my question.

"Well, I keep hearing about you and that firm you work for, all over."

"Where, for instance?"

"Well, I'm not at liberty to reveal my sources as they say, but I can state without fear of contradiction that you in particular my friend are as hot as a red chilli pepper as far as a certain person is concerned."

He paused, and I didn't press him, as he is a man who hates to be hurried.

I waited. He said. "Certain parties, let's say the whispering in the jungle, is that you are hard on the heels of something very special?"

It's important to know when to be cagey and when to admit the truth. I nodded. Alex was pleased to be right. He went on, "If you were an individual associated with the illegal buying and selling of certain types of hardware, shall we say…" He looked at me quizzically.

"Yes," I said a little doubtfully.

"So you agreed to supply a certain group of individuals overseas with this hardware, and were planning to finance it with the proceeds from the sale of packages recovered from a boat at the bottom of the English Channel, that doesn't even officially exist. Imagine then, suddenly finding out that these foreigners who had signed the perforated side of the contract were planning to pay you in funny money. And that the firm employed to dive down and recover these packages, were now holding on to them. You'd be right cut up, wouldn't you?"

"If the packages came out of this sunken boat that doesn't exist, you mean?" I said attentively. But my mind was already on this revelation about Robert Flackyard and illegal arms dealing. As I had thought he was using his party loving playboy lifestyle to take him around the globe as a cover. The association with drugs was purely to finance these deals. Alex came back into focus, saying...

"Yes, mate. The bloke involved in getting these packages out of the boat for this individual would suddenly become a spare part in a garage. If you get my meaning."

I got his meaning.

Alex said, "I wouldn't like to be quoted as to who finds you superfluous to requirements, but I hear the air in Bournemouth can be very chilly even at this time of year."

To say that I didn't like the situation would have been the understatement of the millennium. I knew that I would have to re-contact LJ very soon or he would be calling Fiona Price to find out where I was. I didn't much like the idea of Alex knowing so much about the firm's business. But he had confirmed what I had suspected from the start. There was definitely someone inside the firm leaking information about this and possibly other assignments.

At this stage I still had no idea who this person might be and nothing substantial with which to confront him or her. But that might change after I'd spoken to another old acquaintance who still walked the corridors of power.

* * *

I left Alex, walked around the corner and jumped into the first of a long line of waiting black London taxis. The jovial face of the cab driver looked back at me through the rear view mirror as he asked me where I wanted to go.

"Straight to Soho, and no sight seeing, thank you," I said. He smirked and pulled out into the traffic. I knew exactly where to find Jasper Lockhart at two-thirty in the afternoon.

A young oriental hostess wearing nothing but a thong showed me to a table near the main stage. With a smile, I was asked what I wanted to drink and informed that the next show would be starting in five minutes. On the raised circular stage, three polished chrome tubes, about two inches in diameter and attached at the base and on the ceiling, stood alone. From behind, I felt a hand on my left shoulder and the words, "What's a nice boy like you doing in a place like this."

Looking round, Jasper Lockhart's face was grinning boyishly down at me.

"Jake Dillon, you old rogue, what brings you to this salubrious establishment."

"Actually you do, Jasper." I said matter of factly. The firm dealt with him when we had to, but always one had the feeling that he was likely to walk off with your wallet if you took your eyes off him for even a minute. He gave me a friendly pat on the shoulder before starting to walk off towards the stairs leading down to what the sign said were the private dance rooms. "Come on," he said, "It's quieter down there."

He had an accent like an announcer at a country gymkhana. Professional instinct prevailed over personal feeling. I followed him downstairs, where he headed straight for one of the rooms in which a red haired girl of no more than twenty moved around the pole in time to the music, for those who craved the intimacy of a personal dance or two. I endured five minutes of the spectacle, while Jasper watched the nubile young thing rhythmically gyrate up and down and around the pole, even upside down in time to the music.

When she had finished he slipped another twenty-pound note inside her G-string, gently patting the bare cheek of her arse as he asked her if she would be working later. Apparently she would.

The downstairs bar area was much quieter. Jasper insisted on buying more drinks, although he had already been drinking heavily. He was wearing a handmade Italian suit with the jacket collar partly turned up at the back; his tie was askew, and stained with splashes of pasta sauce from lunch. He usually produced in me a feeling of amusement, but I was far from feeling like laughing today.

"Nice holiday in Bournemouth?" He was always fishing around for stub ends of information that he could peddle. He squeezed a slice of lemon into his drink, gnawed at the yellow pulp and sucked the rind.

I said, "What are you looking so happy about, have you just won the lottery?"

"Fat chance of that," he said, giving a brief laugh. He threw a peanut in the air, catching it in his mouth. His face had the chiselled features of a film star; long shiny hair swept backwards over his head and struck his collar, while an artful wave fell forward across his forehead.

"You look younger every time I see you," he said. Jasper Lockhart was a congenital liar - he told lies outside working hours.

In the world that I had left behind, forms of address among those men working together varied. There's 'sir' used by those high and mighty civil servants, who do not wish to pursue any form of relationship, the 'nickname' used by those who have never grown up. The Christian names of friends and the surname form of address among those who think they are still at university. Only men like Jasper Lockhart are called by their full name.

"What are you doing this afternoon? Fancy a little drive down to Hampshire? I've just bought myself a small country place, got a couple of the dance girls coming down with me. Make up a foursome, if you like? Back in time for last orders, what you say?"

"You are living it up," I said, "you've come a long way since 1998, haven't you, Jasper?"

In 1998, Jasper Lockhart overheard, and covertly recorded a conversation between two junior ministers in the corridors of power, which he promptly sold, to three separate tabloid newspapers for undisclosed sums. He was immediately fired from his job, threatened with a prison term for breaking the Official Secrets Act. But, nothing more came of it, except that Jasper had the last laugh on the Government at that time. In a way it was this incident that gave me the idea for the new European Network. Now Jasper made a living by hanging around and offering hospitality to foolish people with access to secret or semi-secret information.

"Yes, I live well," he said, "picked up my new Jag convertible last week, had it specially painted in the colour of my choice – you're right, life's just one long party."

At the next table a small group of advertising executives and their clients sat drinking Champagne at one hundred and fifty pounds a bottle, paid for with the generosity that only an expense account brings. Extolling the virtues of their particular strategy to generate higher sales volumes of a particular software system or something as interesting, no doubt.

Jasper took a sip of his cocktail, and crunched the bright red cherry while talking at the same time. "Could sell you a morsel of information you'd like I reckon."

"The private email address of the Prime Minister?"

"Very funny, but keep the wisecracks to yourself."

"What have you got," I said.

Looking around furtively, he said, "It's going to cost you a grand."

"Look, Jasper, just give me the sales pitch, we'll get to the estimates later."

"Well, I got a call from a certain party in Winchester the other day. This chap's a real high-class operator, only gets into very expensive houses, if you know what I mean. I've got to know all the breaking and entering boys."

"Anything they pick up unusual or official looking, I get to see very quickly."

"They know I'll pay top dollar with no frills attached. Anyway, this villain unbeknown to him is doing over a high profile Cabinet Minister's country residence, on the outskirts of Winchester, when he flips through the desk and finds a rather tasty leather desk diary. Knowing I'm a collector he passes it across to me for five hundred notes. What I'm offering you is just one page…"

I caught the attention of a hostess over Jasper Lockhart's shoulder and it amused me to see him spin round as if the boys in blue were just about to lift him out of his very expensive jacket.

I said, "A vodka lime soda and another of whatever my friend is drinking, but can you ensure that there are two pieces of lemon and at least three cherries, please."

Jasper smiled in relief and embarrassment.

He said, "Phew, for one moment…"

"Yes, you did, didn't you."

At the next table one of the ad-men said, "…but

excellent copy stateside."

"What do you think, then?" Jasper Lockhart ran his tongue round his mouth in an attempt to dislodge the particles of lemon and cherry.

"So you're still doing a bit of 'Politico black marketing' on the side," I said.

"Well, we've all got to live, haven't we?" This was a man with little or no scruples; he would even rob his old granny of her pension. Given half a chance.

"I'll want a second opinion?" I said.

"I haven't told you what's on the page yet."

"You aren't going to tell and trust, are you?" It didn't seem like him.

"You must be joking. All you're getting is just the first and last word."

"OK, what are these words?"

"The first word is 'Italian,' the last word is 'hardware'. Thought that might make you sit up and pay attention." He used a toothpick to remove a stubborn piece of lemon, from between his teeth.

"I don't get the bit about 'hardware'."

"Weapons, you moron."

"So, what about them."

"Don't take the piss, Dillon! Retired Italian Generals?"

"We don't get involved with the military, past or present." I pretended to think deeply. "There's a chap called Jerry Franklin at the U.S Embassy, here in London. More his kind of thing, I'd say."

"Listen, pal, it's got the name of your firm on the same page."

"I'm not deaf, you know," I said irritably, "I didn't write it."

"Well," said Jasper Lockhart somewhat subdued. "I'm just trying to wise you up."

"That's as may be, but still no sale."

The drinks came. In Jasper Lockhart's iced glass were three bright red cherries. Two slices of lemon and a slice of lime clung to the edge.

"Well, I didn't think they'd do that," he said in a breathless voice, and to tell you the truth, nor did I.

I said, "How big is it?" He raised his eyes to me, and only with difficulty remembered what we had been talking about. "How big?" He measured about fifteen centimetres by ten with his fingers.

"How thick?"

"About three centimetres – why?"

"Doesn't sound like a grand's worth to anyone I know."

"Hilarious, I'm only selling one page for a grand."

"You always did like a laugh," I said.

"So make me an offer then."

"Nothing. As I've already said, the firm doesn't get involved with military stuff."

Jasper Lockhart speared the cherries with a cocktail stick after chasing them around the bright pink drink.

"Look, I'll tell you what I'm prepared to do." I said. "Bring it to my address here in London at nine this evening, and please be on time. I'll have Vince Sharp, my department's special operations specialist, come along as well. But, I can tell you now, I don't think there's a flying pig's chance, that he'll be able to get the Partners interested in it. Even if he does, payment will be by the normal route, and you know how long that can take, so don't go spending it just yet."

The ad-man at the next table said, "But the market in India is enormous!" I knew that Jasper Lockhart was acquainted with our friend Oliver Hawkworth the Cabinet Minister and owner of the Gin Fizz. They had both worked at the Treasury around the same time. Either he hadn't put the connection with Ferran & Cardini together yet and was trading off the cuff, or he did know, and was playing a game of cat and mouse.

* * *

When I got back to the hotel, the plastic plants were still heavy with dust, and there was a different middle aged man sitting at the small reception desk clipping his fingernails with a pair of oversized scissors. I remembered the name I had given his Slavic friend. "Fisher," I said. He reached back without looking, unhooked my room key and cracked it down on the worn desktop without a pause in his manicure routine.

"Visita' waiting for ya'." He said with a heavy Cockney accent. He stabbed the scissors upward. "In ya' room."

I leaned forward until my face was close to his. His razor had missed parts of his face and his rancid breath smelt of stale coffee and cigarettes, with a little dash of rotten food between the teeth thrown in. "Do you always let strangers into your guests' rooms?" I asked.

He stopped what he was doing – without haste. "Yeah, when they tell me they're related or official, I do. You got a problem with that – 'ave ya'?"

I picked up my key, and began to climb the stairs two at a time. "Yeah," I heard him say again.

I went up to the third. The light was on in my room. I switched off the hall light, put the key in the door and turned it quickly.

I flung the door open wide and moved through it stooped.

Since joining the firm's special operations department, I've gone through life making sure there is no light behind me when entering a darkened area, scanning rooms for listening bugs and hidden cameras. This becomes second nature and then on one occasion it all becomes worthwhile.

However, this was not one of those occasions. Spread-eagled full length on the floral patterned bedspread was the seventeen stone weight of Vince Sharp; an old leather bush hat was parked over his face.

Chapter 19

"Steady, big man - it's only me." The words came muffled from somewhere under the bush hat and the sentence ended in a chesty cough. All of Vince Sharp's sentences ended in a cough. A hand removed the hat from his constantly jovial round face. I straightened up, feeling ever so slightly foolish.

"How did you find me, and what the hell did you tell that character with the bad case of halitosis downstairs?" I asked.

"I told him that I was your personal psychoanalyst and that I'd come to take you back to rehab." Vince stood up and produced a silver and glass hip flask, full of a fine Scottish single malt, from his coat pocket. He poured us both a drink, using the two plastic glasses from the sink in the corner of the room.

"Here's mud in your eye."

"After the revelations of today this is very welcome," I said.

I'd not found out how, but by some ingenious articulation of the finger joints, he was able to drink and smoke virtually simultaneously. He coughed, smoked and drank for a few seconds.

"Surprised I found you?" he coughed. "Astute, eh?" Some more coughing.

"Not really, you know. That young woman you've been working with in Dorset, what's her name, oh yes, Fiona Price, she phoned me this morning. I reckon she fancies you," he said with a wink and a nod. "Anyway she was asking me to cover for you should LJ start asking where you were. She let it slip that you'd come back to

London under a false name. Well, after that it was easy to get her to tell me what you were up to, and as for what name you'd use, James Fisher has raised his head twice before, so I just guessed he would again." He coughed loudly. "Perhaps you're getting a little bit old for this game, or maybe you're love sick?"

"We all are, and no, is the answer to that last jibe, Vince," I said, "we all are."

Vince nodded and continued to cough and drink, in that order.

"LJ would like to see you tomorrow morning, 8.00am prompt, that is if you've nothing better to do," he said with a grin.

"Yes, he's always so dammed polite, isn't he?" I said.

"He's all right, really," said Vince, and poured us both another. "Oh yes, and I'm to tell you that Tatiana is awaiting instructions, whatever that means."

"Perhaps you could also find the time to call her as soon as you can."

He picked up his hat and downed his drink in one smooth motion.

"Anything I can do for you?" he asked. "I'm going back to the office shortly."

"Yes, I think there is Vince." I pulled out an A4 sheet of paper from my overnight bag and gave him Robert Flackyard's personal and business email address. "Let's intercept his emails, unofficially of course".

"And phone?" asked Vince.

"Yes, let's do the lot," I said, smiling at the thought, and passed him another sheet of paper, this time with Flackyard's home address and telephone number on it. "Let's tap his phone, but be careful, he has monitoring equipment installed at the house."

"Um, bloody nuisance that, in that case we'll have to twist the arm of one of our friendly spook agencies who owe a favour or two. I can use one of their satellites and link up via my own laptop, less traceable that way. I'll see you later," he said.

I heard him coughing his way down the stairs and out into the street. I began packing my bag. Before I saw LJ the next morning, I hoped to have something up my sleeve.

Chapter 20

I got back to my apartment around six thirty. I ground coffee beans and turned up the heating. Outside, it was raining again, and lines of cars below moved slowly out of the city through a gauze of traffic fumes. The attractive thirty something woman reading the weather was worried about the amount of rainfall for the time of year, attributing it to the effects of global warming.

The laptop had to be set up and connected to the scanner in the study.

This done I left the room and locked the door behind me.

I was drinking a second cup of coffee as Tats arrived. Her lips were cold.

We rubbed noses and exchanged hellos in between kisses, then I brought her up to speed with the business in Bournemouth and Jasper Lockhart. Tats said, "Buy it," but I didn't want to do that. If I showed any interest it would reveal more than I wanted to reveal, especially to Jasper Lockhart. Tats thought I was being paranoid, but then she hadn't been in the business long enough to develop that sixth sense that I was always telling myself I had.

Jasper Lockhart sat in his new pearl blue metallic convertible Jag across the road for some time before coming to the front door. It was very professionally done. I took his overcoat and poured him a drink. For twenty minutes we sat and made small talk while waiting for Vince Sharp to arrive.

Jasper Lockhart had the diary in a sealed envelope. When I'd thought the tension had built up a little I asked him if I could look at it. He went over to his overcoat and pulled it out of a pocket, passing the envelope across the dining table, I tore the top off quickly and extracted a leather bound diary with gold edged pages. The surface was a little scuffed and it looked as if it had been well used.

Jasper Lockhart was about to open his mouth to protest, but I kept the diary shut and he kept his mouth the same way. I put it back into the envelope.

"Looks genuine to me," I said. Jasper Lockhart nodded. I turned the envelope slowly around handling it between forefinger and thumb. I got up, walked across to where the coat was hanging. I folded the torn envelope top and pushed it back into the pocket. He smiled sheepishly.

"Tats will keep you company," I said, "I'll just go and phone Vince Sharp, he's probably stuck in the traffic or still at the office." I went to the phone in the study.

It had been simple to drop the diary out of the torn end of the envelope into my lap and not very difficult to substitute a small book of approximately the same size. Luckily Jasper Lockhart's description earlier in the dance bar had been fairly accurate, but I had two variations handy had it not been.

Lifting the scanner lid I placed the open diary face down onto the glass surface. The white light went backwards and forwards numerous times. I turned each page over either side of the one Jasper Lockhart was offering me. Now everything depended upon Tats keeping our guest occupied.

She could reasonably ask him not to barge his way into my study, but if he got that envelope out of his pocket and found a well used edition of "The Traveller's Pocket Guide to France," my copying was liable to be interrupted.

* * *

148

By 10.30 the last copy was off the printer and a backup disc made. Jasper Lockhart had long since departed, with his diary back once more in his jacket pocket. I went back into the lounge. Tats had slipped her shoes off and was dozing on one of the sofas. I leaned over the wide leather arm and kissed her softly on her cheek. She woke with a start.

"You were snoring," I teased.

"I don't snore." She looked at me in the mirror.

"And you told me I was the only man on the whole planet in a position to know."

Tats ran her long fingers through her hair, dragging it high above her head.

"Do you think I should wear my hair up like this?"

"It looks great just as it is," I said

We were looking at each other in the mirror. She said, "You've put on weight, it must be all that sea air and Mrs Rumple's home cooking while you were in Bournemouth. I'll bet you haven't been to a gym in weeks?"

"You're right I haven't, not once. But now you mention it, perhaps a vigorous workout is what I need. Shall we..."

At that moment the phone rang. Tats laughed, and although I let it ring for some time I finally went to get it.

"It's probably Jasper Lockhart, he's decided to drop the price to eight hundred," said Tats. "Poor sad Jasper Lockhart".

"Thieves really must learn to cry," I said.

I answered the phone. It was Zara, who didn't mince her words.

"Mr Levenson-Jones says you're both to come here right away, something urgent has cropped up."

I looked over at Tats and said into the phone. "Give us an hour, Zara."

"I'll give you thirty minutes, and no more, Mr Dillon."

Chapter 21

By the time we arrived at the firm's wharf-side building the rain had eased off.

I placed my left-hand palm forward onto the cold black glass panel set in the wall. The heavy deadlock released with a thud confirming that my fingerprints matched with those on file. We took the stairs down to LJ's office. Things were hectic, LJ had taken his jacket off, undone his top button and loosened his tie.

"Take those files off that chair and sit down," he said. Zara poked her head round the door to ask if we would like any refreshments.

"Absolutely foul night," said LJ. "Sorry to drag you into this fracas. I've missed the Wednesday evening backgammon game at my club for the first time in nearly fourteen years."

"We must all make sacrifices," I said.

"Yes, when our masters say jump, we must jump," said LJ.

"Um, like puppets on strings" I said. Tats, shot me one of her looks.

"The New European Network plan, so it's all your doing - is it?" said LJ in mock admonition. "We now have the Partner's permission to go ahead with feasibility study" – he stared at the monitor screen in front of him – "N.E.N. feasibility study." He looked up and beamed. Behind the beam was a worried man.

"Subtle titling," I said.

"Quite," said LJ doubtfully, and then he was off into the administration - he was very good at the tactics of Partner bureaucracy – but then he has had a lot of practice.

"The Partners want to initiate four studies, Communications, Finance, Training, and Network Administration. Now we won't be able to control all of those, so what we do is this. Let our friends across the river have anything they want, in fact we'll nominate a couple of groups and lavish compliments on their suitability. Incidentally," LJ blew his nose loudly on a big white monogrammed handkerchief, "don't overdo the compliments; their controller of E.U. networks is beginning to suspect you of sarcasm."

"I'll do my best," I said.

"Yes of course you will, now; when we've got them all fired up, and they're in right up to their necks you will suggest a further study: a Compatibility Study – for co-ordination…"

"Are you as ruthless at backgammon?" I asked. "So it's exactly the same form as you allegedly used with the Americans two years ago – you ended up controlling the lot. I've often wondered how you pulled that off."

"Mum's the word, old son," said LJ, an extended forefinger tapping the side of his nose. "I'd like to try and pull it off again before I'm tumbled."

"OK," I said, "but when does all this begin?"

"Well, as it's your brainchild, so to speak, I don't see why the Partners shouldn't appoint you as head of the training study."

"I think I follow you all right, so that between the two of us we'll have the situation well in hand; but what I actually meant was, when does it begin?"

LJ looked at his monitor screen. "The first meeting is this Friday at 11.30 am, and the Partners have insisted that it be held here."

"No good for me I'm afraid, the Dorset situation is far too volatile. I need to be back there in the morning."

"Ah yes," said LJ. "I want to speak to you about

that." He sat down and typed in the command that brought up details of all current assignments. "I want you to complete your report on this assignment as soon as possible."

He kept his eyes on the screen while he talked, avoiding my gaze as he always did in these situations. I knew that this was the real reason he had hauled me over here at this ungodly hour. The New Network was just a smoke screen.

LJ swivelled uncomfortably in his chair and pushed the intercom button on his desk.

Zara answered and he said, "Operational name for the Gin Fizz Assignment?"

Zara's voice came through the speaker, "Poseidon," she said.

"How very erudite," I said to LJ. In Greek mythology, Poseidon was the chief god of the sea, brother of Zeus and Pluto who together dethroned their father Kronos and divided his realm. Poseidon took the sea as his kingdom.

LJ smiled and pushed the button on the intercom to tell Zara what I had said, then turned back to me.

"We're winding up 'Poseidon'. I'll need a full report for the Partners by the morning. That comes straight from the top."

"You must be joking," I said.

"I never joke – as you are well aware. Especially about matters concerning this department."

"That assignment is at a critical stage – as you are well aware. We still have the loose ends to tie up."

LJ tensed up. "Possibly, but you won't be required to continue, and you should remember completeness is only a state of mind."

"So is Partner interference a state of mind. If I have to I'll go back to Dorset in my own time, I'll take two weeks leave."

"Be reasonable, Jake, what is wrong here?"

I brought the wad of scanned copies from my pocket. Thirty-one pages from a private diary, stolen from Oliver Hawkworth's house in Hampshire.

Most of it written in the penmanship of busy professional men – badly.

There were cryptic dinner appointments and an almost obsessional compilation of entries regarding expenses. The reference to Italy concerned undefined sales of various pieces of machinery and numerical nomenclature of bank accounts in the Cayman Islands.

One page, however, contained something more specific.

'Tell HC' he'd written, then used some sort of cipher made up of letters and numbers on three lines, which meant nothing to me.

I'd given this coded concoction to Vince when we had arrived earlier. His computer had located the code in a matter or minutes. Now I told LJ about it.

"What this means, according to Vince Sharp, is that the hardware has been procured. Payment will be required in the sum of ten million Euros by the end of the month. The latter part of this code is something quite different, it relates specifically to me."

I waited while LJ got the full implication. He took out another cigar and lit it.

I went on, "This message has been sent to HC. I believe that this is Harry Caplin, who I know has been keeping an eye on me ever since I arrived in Dorset. Our Cabinet Minister ends the message with a warning. He says to beware of me."

"I know just how he feels," said LJ. Solemnly he removed his glasses, cleaned the lenses with his handkerchief, replaced them and read the whole thing through again. "Zara," he finally said into the intercom, "you'd better come in here right away." While we were waiting for her to arrive, LJ added.

"This whole affair, Jake its all a bit odd, isn't it? It simply doesn't fit together. I mean, why would a high profile Cabinet Minister get himself involved with someone who was under suspicion of illegally trading in weapons and class A drugs, for that matter? Hell's struth, what's the fellow thinking?"

He thought that I was bending it a bit to interpret the word 'authenticate' as 'terminate'.

LJ's department was responsible only to the Partners, and they were responsible only to Sir Lucius Stagg, former Prime Minister, and the firm's benefactor; you could see why he was being hesitant to go against their will.

Crossing swords with a member of the cabinet was not a wise thing to do even with their blessing, and this was a very powerful member of the cabinet and a client of the firm.

Finally, four cups of tea later, LJ leaned well back in his chair and said, "I'm convinced that you are quite wrong." He was staring up at the ceiling.

"Convinced," he said again.

Tats caught my eye. Zara was taking notes, "And therefore it is…" he paused, "of the utmost importance to continue with the assignment, to protect the Government and our client's position."

That's what LJ said to the corner of the ceiling, and while he said it I raised an eyebrow at Zara, who responded with the faintest smile.

I got to my feet. "Please do not take advantage, Mr Dillon," LJ said anxiously, "The Partners will only tolerate your maverick behaviour for a short while." He swivelled round to his screen again and continued with the new network plan.

"You'll overbalance one day," I heard him mumbling to the computer screen as we left. I suppose he was bored with talking to the ceiling.

Chapter 22

After dropping Tats off at her place around 3.00 am, I decided to drive across town, and unofficially find out a little more about our friend Oliver Hawkworth.

Deep down on the lower fourth floor of the Government building the air is conditioned, filtered and purified from all outside pollutants. Two armed guards; body searched and scanned me for anything concealed. A passport-sized photograph was produced inside a laminated pouch with the words VISITOR printed on it. The double steel door slid back silently and on the far side was yet another security check waiting. I asked for Mr Vass and it was five minutes before he came to sign me in.

After shaking hands he led me through a maze of corridors eerily lit with blue coloured lamps, which eventually led to a large open plan room. The unusually high ceiling was a complex grid of piping hidden behind a suspended matrix of mesh panels. Every so often water sprinklers protruded through the panels; below the false ceiling, lined up in orderly rows, were computer terminals, each with someone observing intently the information on the screen in front of them. Everyone wore a headset clipped over one ear complete with microphone.

We were standing in the middle of the 'Arena', so named by those who worked at the secret establishment of the Central Archive and Intelligence Bureau, located underground near to the Houses of Parliament. Where information received from Commercial Espionage or Government departments is collected and deciphered by the men and women sitting at the computers.

I watched as a young woman spoke into her microphone. A moment later a supervisor went over and together they checked and compared how the un-coded version compared to the original that had been received.

He or she then explained why certain items of text had been left out and why others had been inserted. Once this had been completed the supervisor keyed an authorisation code into the terminal and the original coded message was deleted. A hard copy was then printed off at one of the many printers lined up along one wall. The room held an air of expectancy, as if something big was about to happen, but strangely, there was no feeling of hurry; in fact it was a very calm place.

Adrian Vass's office was a glass-walled eyrie reached by a lift. From it, we could see the entire room. Columns of stainless steel were positioned here and there. A sobering reminder that we were deep underground.

"What, no Bournemouth rock?" asked Adrian.

"Very funny, and it's Brighton rock by the way, Bournemouth's far to posh for sticks of rock. Word soon gets around doesn't it?" I said.

"Yes, I'm afraid it does, but not much gets past us down here, you know."

Adrian smiled expectantly. His moon-like face was much too large for his short slim body, and was made even larger by his receding hairline. He motioned me into a bright red chair. "You've put on weight, you old dog," he said from the other side of his desk.

"This must be the first time you've been down to see us since Charlie McIntyre..." He didn't finish the sentence. We had both liked Charlie.

Adrian looked at me for a minute without saying a word, and then said, "Somebody put a firecracker under Levenson-Jones' Range Rover, I hear."

"Yes, we have a pretty good idea who it was – just have to prove it," I said.

"Well, you'd better watch your back. Whoever it was, is most definitely a nasty piece of work."

I said, "It was Levenson-Jones they were after, not Charlie or me."

"Famous last words. Personally, I'd wear a cast iron jockstrap for the time being if I were you."

He reached inside his blazer and pulled out a small notebook with a cheap pen pushed through the spiral ring binder down the side.

"I'd like you to tell me something and then forget that this conversation ever took place." In tacit agreement Adrian slid his pen back down the side of the notebook and placed it back in his pocket.

"What is it you want to know? Who's fiddling their expenses in Whitehall or which Junior Minister is sleeping with hookers?"

"Perhaps I'll save that for next time," I said. "What I want to…" I paused.

"Here, come into my other office, it will make you feel much more relaxed."

He pushed a button on his key-fob and a concealed door behind him slid back revealing another room, a little smaller than the one we had just come from. No listening device on earth could break through the specially formulated linings to this area. Known only as Fort Knox, it was the depository for all information received and sent by spooks and their agencies over the last fifty years. It took Adrian only a few seconds to locate the correct database and files relating to the information I wanted to see. I glanced through medical records. All information was included; height, weight, scars, birthmarks, blood group, reflexes as well as full dental records and any medical treatment received since the age of ten.

I opened up the main content of the file.

HAWKWORTH, Oliver S.R.
File renewal: six months.
Birth: Born 1950. Caucasian – British National –
UK Passport – UN Passport.
Background: Cambridge/Sandhurst   Military
Academy/Blues   and   Royals   Regiment/Member   of
Parliament. Married S. Hamilton/1 daughter – Elizabeth
– aged 18 years.
Property: London   -   Penthouse/Winchester   -
Country House/Tuscany – Small Wine Growing Estate.
Assets: Shares (disclosed) in various multi-national
Companies. Two bank accounts – one Italian and anther in
the UK. Also undisclosed deposit account in Switzerland.
Personal: Mistress (see file X9D100). Alcoholic –
has undergone rehab - five years ago (never made public)
– no relapse to date.
Interests: Boating - owner of power cruiser the 'Gin
Fizz'. Shooting – pheasant/grouse – excellent marksman.
No recorded homosexual activities.
Travels throughout Europe on behalf of the British
Government – Tuscany Villa/Italy.
He holidays with family four (4) times a year.

Chapter 23

Adrian walked across to the sheer wall of glass, thoughtfully looked down upon his minions before slowly turning back to me and answering my question.

"What's he like?" he repeated. "It's hard to say in a few words. He was made a colonel at thirty-five. Which means he is no fool? They say that when officers are up for promotion," Adrian paused, "it's probably just a load of old bollocks, but I'll tell you anyway. Officer candidates at that level are invited to a small gathering of notables in Army circles. The candidate has to endure his peers' scrutiny as well as their child like behaviour throughout the evening. Not only is he bombarded with an array of obscure questions, but they're also watching to see if for instance he drinks out of the finger bowl." I smiled and nodded.

"Oliver Hawkworth was served with some sort of Californian prune crumble just to see how he negotiated the stones. But he fooled the lot of them by swallowing every one of the little blighters. I couldn't say whether it's all true, but it's certainly in character. Nearly all of those men around that dinner table went onto become some sort of advisor to the Government. To this day they still meet up once a month for a big gut bash and a cosy chat. They're the sort of people who have devoted a lot of time and expensive training to detect the difference between a vintage bottle of Dom and Spanish sparkling wine."

"He earns around a million a year and that's only what he declares."

I whistled softly. Adrian went on, "He obviously pays tax on some of it, and very unofficially sits on six or seven boards who like to have a member of the old boy network. Hawkworth's big contribution is that he can influence affairs abroad, is tenacious and extremely charming. He has personally financed at least two successful take-over bids in South America that we know of, and is always quick to put a few hundred thousand into the hands of a discontented general. His reward is always by way of holdings in some of the region's largest and wealthiest national companies. As he is persona gratis with most of the Presidents, it really is gambling without risk."

The phone on his desk rang. "Vass." Adrian rubbed his eyes.

"Complicated wiring diagram?" He pinched the bridge of his nose. "Just run off a copy in the normal way, show the technical people before you destroy the original." He was listening intently. "Well, just show them the part that hasn't got the originator's name on it." He hung up.

"Hell's struth," he said, "they'll be asking me if they can go to the coffee machine next. Where was I?"

"I wanted to ask you about land deals," I said. "Isn't that how he's made his fortune?"

"Partly true, but his family is one of the wealthiest in England, don't forget."

Adrian lit one of his own rolled cigarettes, then spent what seemed like minutes removing shreds of tobacco from his lip.

"Hawkworth has the Midas touch where land acquisition deals are concerned. He buys a parcel of land at rock bottom price and then sells it at a premium almost immediately. Nothing clever or wrong in that, you might say, except that in every transaction the same Development Company's name crops up. Can't for the life of me, think what that is at present, but anyway, it's always very large sums of money changing hands. Some have speculated that it's nothing more than an elaborate money laundering racket, but no one can prove that, of course. Others say that it's a Member of Parliament abusing his position. But again that is only speculation. He is extremely careful to always cover his tracks. So you see, Oliver Hawkworth keeps on making vast sums of money and then some more again."

The phone rang. "Phone me back, I'm busy," Adrian barked into the mouthpiece and hung up immediately. He turned back to his monitor screen, asking: "You understand what this column is?" He tapped the screen with his pen.

"Well, I'm no expert," I said, "but I gather that these abbreviated prefixes are a record of his personal weaknesses or traits that he may have such as women, drink, membership of drinking clubs and the like."

"Absolutely spot on," said Adrian.

I pointed to the letters 'CI'. "An accessory to an illegal act," Adrian said as quick as a shot.

"Meaning something he has been prosecuted for?" I said.

"Hell, no," Adrian replied in an astounded voice.

"He's never been within a hundred metres of a law court, let alone inside one. No, for anything about which the police know anything it's another sort of prefix entirely – it's 'PL' for that."

"What about a 'BR'?"

"Bribery of a public servant."

"Let me guess, once again not prosecuted?" I said.

"No, as I told you, it had to be a 'PN' prefix if it's been made public. It would be a 'PP' if he had been accused of bribing a public servant."

"Anything for illegal selling."

"That would be a 'RT' prefix," said Adrian. Now I was beginning to understand how the system worked and I'd found the item I wanted.

* * *

The next morning I got Tats to show me the revised notes relating to the new European Network. After shredding them into a million tiny strips, we went through it all again. I thought about Oliver Hawkworth. Two items about him were still hazy. I phoned Adrian from my mobile. "That matter I spoke of earlier this morning."

"Yes?" said Adrian.

"Tell me, why was his file so conveniently to hand on your hard-drive?"

"Even you need a security clearance to pull the records of a Cabinet Minister."

"Very simple. He'd already asked for your records only the previous day."

"As you are well aware, anyone who has been or is a civil servant has a file past and present."

"Oh," I said, and heard Adrian chuckle as he hung up. Of course he could just be having a laugh. But the fact was, I wasn't laughing.

Chapter 24

The plain-clothes policeman led me along the softly carpeted corridors of power; austere men in military uniform looked quietly down from dark paintings lost in a penumbra of varnish. Mr Oliver Hawkworth MP was seated behind a vast oval mahogany table, which was polished like a guardsman's boot.

A slim mahogany clock stood discreetly against a panelled wall pacing out the silence. On Hawkworth's table a banker's lamp with a green glass shade marshalled the light on to four heaps of papers and newspaper clippings.

Only the crown of his head was visible. He continued with what he was doing, allowing me to feel embarrassed for interrupting his private study. The policeman motioned me to a hostile looking chair in front of the table.

Hawkworth ran a finger across the open book and scribbled in the margin of one of the typewritten sheets with a gold fountain pen. He turned over the corner of the page and closed the green leather cover.

"Smoke." There was no trace of query in his voice. He firmly pushed the silver box across the table with the back of his hand, put the cap on his pen and clipped it into his inside jacket pocket. He retrieved his cigarette from the ashtray in front of him, put it into his mouth, drew on it without releasing his grasp on its filter, mashed it into the ashtray with controlled violence, disembowelling the torn shreds of tobacco from the lacerated paper with his immaculately manicured nails. He brushed the ash from his jacket.

"You wished to see me?" he said.

I lifted the lid of the small silver box. I took a cigarette and lit it with a match I then blew it out and tossed it towards the ashtray, allowing the trajectory to carry it on to Hawkworth's pristine paperwork. He carefully picked it up, snapping it in two before placing it into the ashtray. I drew on the strong tobacco.

"No," I said, stripping my voice of interest, "not really."

"You are discreet – that's good." He picked up a sheet of paper, and held it under the light and quietly read from it a potted history of my career in Army Intelligence.

"I really don't know what you're talking about," I said.

"Good, good," said Hawkworth, not at all discouraged. "The report goes on; 'inclined to pursue developments beyond the call of duty. He must be made to understand that this is a dangerous failing in military intelligence work'."

"Is that what you wanted to do," I asked, "to tell me that my obsession with tying up loose ends is dangerous?"

"Not merely dangerous," said Hawkworth. He leaned forward to select another cigarette from his silver box. The light fell momentarily across his face. It was a hard bony face and it shone in the light like a marble bust of a long gone Roman Emperor. Eyebrows and hair were the palest blond and as fine as silk. He looked up. "Potentially fatal." He took a white cigarette and lit it.

"In wartime, soldiers are shot for disobeying even the smallest command," continued Hawkworth in his gravelly voice.

"Is that so, but this is the twenty first century, that law is completely outdated and quite unnecessary in today's civilised society."

"Absolute nonsense," he said flushing with anger.

"I've been informed by the Partners of Ferran & Cardini, that you are demanding the assignment concerning the Gin Fizz be continued. I would like to remind you, Mr Dillon, that your job in Dorset is now over. Your refusal to accept that is impertinence, sir, and unless you change your attitude I shall ensure that life becomes extremely difficult for you." Hawkworth drilled me with his eyes while he puffed on the cigarette firmly placed between his index and forefinger.

"No one owns me, Hawkworth. My employers pay only for services rendered. I work for them, and for the Government from time to time because I believe in what I do. But that doesn't mean that I'll be used as and when others feel like it, especially by a self-centred, egotistical multi-millionaire."

"What's more, don't give me that 'fatal' crap, because I've taken a postgraduate course in fatality."

Hawkworth blinked and leaned back into the opulence of his chair. "So," he said finally, "that's it, is it? The truth is that you think you should be as powerful as your employers, and the Government?" He rearranged his pen set.

"Power is only a state of mind," I told him. "Except if you hold a position of power, and have wealth to go with it, it seems you can get away with anything…" I left it at that.

Hawkworth leaned forward and said, "You think that because I hold shares and sit on the boards of a few companies, all of which I have disclosed to the House, I should not have a say in the control of my country?" He held up a hand in an admonishing attitude.

"You just sit there, and listen – it's my turn to lecture you. It really is simple, isn't it, Mr Dillon? You are no better than a common or garden spy. I do not impugn you or your firm's motives as to why you do what you do. But please feel free to impugn mine as a Minister.

You might say that it is my duty as an Englishman to increase prosperity for all. As it's your duty to do as your employer's command."

He paused for a moment before adding, "Without questions. Your job is to provide success at any price, by means fair or foul. Men like you, Mr Dillon, are simply implements to do things with, shadowy figures that are in the dark recesses of ordinary people's minds. Who when done with, are forgotten, quickly."

"You mean, that I'm a janitor in the wash room of state?" I asked humbly.

Hawkworth gave a cold smile. "You are a very annoying fellow, you know?"

"You sit here talking of ethics, as though you were employed to make ethical decisions. You are nothing in the scheme. You will complete your tasks as ordered: no more, no less. This is what you are paid for. There is nothing more to discuss." He leaned back in his chair again. It creaked with the shift of weight. His hand clamped around the black silk rope that hung beside the Curtain, and a moment later the policeman appeared.

"Show the gentleman out, Constable Baker," said Hawkworth.

I made no move, except to pull out of my inside pocket a number of folded sheets of paper and place them onto the mahogany table and push them across towards Hawkworth.

"What's the meaning of this?"

"These are for the man who has everything. They're pages from a diary," I Said, watching Hawkworth's face.

"They're from your diary." I watched the policeman out of the corner of my eye; he was hanging on to every word.

Perhaps he was planning to tell his Govenor!

Hawkworth flicked his tongue across his drying lips like a hungry python.

"Wait outside, Constable," he said, "I'll ring again." The policeman had withdrawn to his notebook before Hawkworth spoke again.

"Where did you get this?" he asked.

"I'll tell you," I said, and lit another of his cigarettes while Hawkworth fidgeted with his guilt feelings. This time he left the dead match where it had landed.

"I know of some pieces of hardware, or shall we call them mechanical digger parts, that go to Argentina in regular consignments. I'll tell you, those importers must be very inefficient because they have received shipments of the stuff and yet, there are no parts to be found on any shelf - anywhere! You can hardly blame them for being a little confused."

Hawkworth's cigarette lay inert in the ashtray quietly turning to ash.

"It would seem that the same applies to shipments going to India and China. Of course, it wouldn't be cricket if a company with an English M.P. as a director sold this type of thing to volatile regions of the planet. The Americans would blacklist them, but what with all this muddle in the Argentine everyone ends up extremely happy." I paused. The clock ticked on with its steady beat.

"As a way of moving gold or even possibly weapons there's nothing to beat..."

"Enough, you are making up fairy tales Mr Dillon, you are in fact, just guessing," Hawkworth said calmly.

I thought of the small diary that Jasper Lockhart had obtained from his friend the housebreaker and how he had made it so available to me. Making my subsequent guessing much easier, "You're right I'm just guessing," I agreed.

"Very well," Hawkworth said in a resigned but businesslike voice, "how much?"

"I've not come to blackmail you - Hawkworth. What I want from you, is an assurance that I can continue with my janitorial duties in Dorset without interference from the management. I'm not pursuing you. I'm not even remotely interested in doing anything beyond my brief. But I want you to remember this: I'm the person who's responsible for this assignment, not Levenson-Jones, not even the Partners of Ferran & Cardini. I'll be responsible for what happens to you, whether it's good or bad. Now be a good chap and ring your bell for Constable Baker. I'm leaving, before I throw up all over your beautiful Persian carpet."

Chapter 25

When I got to the office on Friday morning, Zara was talking with one of the other personal assistants from upstairs. Seeing me she broke off her conversation and crooked a slender finger in my direction, beckoning me to follow her into her office. It was as I expected, immaculate, not a piece of paper or file out of place. She sat down behind the curved beech desk, retrieving a file from a stack in front of her.

"You'll be pleased, I've no doubt, to hear that Poseidon is to remain active. Unofficially that is, a memo came down to LJ late yesterday from the Partners."

"Oh really, that's good," I said.

"Don't give me that 'Oh really, that's good' stuff. I know exactly what you've been up to, Jake Dillon."

"Zara, as if I…"

"That's all Jake." It seemed a little odd that Zara should ask me to step into her office just to tell me that. As I turned to leave she said, "Please try to look just a little bit surprised when LJ tells you. The poor man is tragically deluded and certainly doesn't know you as I do."

"Why thank you for those kind words, Zara," I said.

"Thank me for what, aiding and abetting his pathetic delusions?"

"Yes of course," I said, "but thanks anyway." I said as I closed the office door behind me.

Back in the department, I found Tats who had put her hair into a single French plait looking positively stunning. "You will find on your desk, twenty-two letters to sign along with copies of various memos relating to 'Poseidon' that I thought you might like sight of." Tats said.

I signed the letters and stuffed the memos into my briefcase. I stuck my head into LJ's office. He was straightening up a large oak framed picture of Winston Churchill austerely standing by a desk, hand clutching the lapel of his pin striped suit, British bulldog at his feet. The small brass plate at the bottom had the words engraved; Blood, Tears, Toil and Sweat 1874 – 1964.

Looking round LJ said, "Ah, Jake, what do you think of this?"

"Very well painted," I replied.

"Present from my son. He's very much into Winston Churchill. Each year on the great man's birthday we have a little family get together, and all guests have to have a Winston anecdote or quotation ready."

"How fascinating," I said. "I do exactly the same when I get given an assignment."

LJ slid me a narrowed glance.

He took out a cigar and lit it to ease the tension.

"You intend to pursue Poseidon?"

"I want to know why Hawkworth recently sent Harry Caplin a cheque for ten thousand pounds and why he's renting a luxury house for him by the sea?"

"You think that will explain everything?" asked LJ, still admiring the painting.

"I really don't know. Perhaps, but I'll be able to tell you that with more certainty after I've talked to a man I know in the highlands of Scotland who has been looking into Caplin's private affairs for me. As well as his bank account, all unofficially and very discreetly, of course. But I now feel that Caplin is in some way involved and possibly working for or with Hawkworth, not Flackyard as I previously thought. If that proves to be the case, then my gut feeling is that it was Caplin not Rumple whom had the explosives put in your car. But the bit I'm at a complete loss about is why, and in such a public way?"

LJ nodded. "Well, have a good trip to Scotland, I've arranged for Phil Allerton to fly you up in the helicopter." He moved the painting just a little more to the right.

Outside the sun shone between white cotton-wool clouds hanging across the sky like balloons. Traffic wardens were issuing tickets and wheel clampers were busy immobilising illegally parked motorists.

* * *

Through my headset, Phil updated me on our position, pointing out landmarks along the way. In between my thoughts were on Oliver Hawkworth. I had blocked him for the time being, but I had done it at the expense of making a very powerful enemy. It wasn't something one could do too frequently without uncomfortable consequences. Perhaps it was something one couldn't do once without uncomfortable consequences.

I really was near the end of a thin plank over a dark and very deep sea.

I wondered who of those involved with 'Poseidon' might be connected to Hawkworth and Flackyard. Who had the pictures of the Gin Fizz and who would benefit the most from obtaining them? What was George Ferdinand's real role in all of this?

After the warmth of the cockpit, the pure Highland air was exhilaratingly refreshing. Phil had put us down in the middle of a small clearing surrounded by trees. Cows in a field nearby became curious after the rotors had stopped and the noise from the engine had faded away. They hovered together in the dells where odd trees of twisted dead wood were spattered with black blots of huddled birds.

From high up on the hill a Land Rover broke the

tranquillity by sounding its horn as it careered down the narrow muddy track towards us. The driver could be seen bouncing up and down in his seat. Barely missing the gateposts on either side, the old battered green vehicle shot through the opening of the field and slewed precariously to a halt within ten feet of us.

The engine stalled and the driver's door burst open. Two large leather boots swung out onto the grass followed by their owner Angus Macgrath, who was roaring with laughter.

"Och, Jake Dillon you old rogue, it's good to see you again – alive that is," said Angus, raising his eyebrows and laughing loudly. I introduced Phil, but forgot to mention to him that this enormous bald headed Scotsman had a handshake like a grizzly bear.

"Now then, we'd better get going, we've got that hill to negotiate before we get to my croft."

Phil said that he'd stay with the helicopter, and that we should be back in the air within a couple of hours.

* * *

Past the trees and on up the hill, the going was treacherous as the Land Rover's powerful diesel engine turned all four wheels through the sticky mud of the track. The higher we got the more barren the landscape; the moor land was bleak and wind-scoured. Through the mist Angus pointed a finger at a crooked castle, the ruins of which had stunted trees growing inside, hunchbacked against the wind.

It suited Angus to live alone like a hermit, but for his computers, numerous gadgets and satellite dish all powered by a large diesel generator. His small crofter's house had been greatly improved and was clean and tidy. As we opened the heavy oak door of the stone building the draught made the fire flare. There was an oil lamp on a small round table, and its soft green light glowing up onto the ceiling flickered with the sudden rush of cold air. A soot-caked kettle hissed with boiling water. Angus went over and carefully lifted the dented metal container off its hook over the fire, filling a large china teapot to the brim before replacing it.

Seated in front of the fire, we quietly let the heat thaw us for a minute while we sipped the sweet dark liquid. Angus rapidly sank his scalding tea and threw another log on to the flames. Finally, he lit a filthy old pipe and said, "You got my report by email okay then?"

"Picked it up this morning, it was fine," I said, "but I decided it was far safer to come up to this Godforsaken place you call home and see you personally - if you know what I mean. My problem, Angus is that I know very little about the intricacies of manufacturing and distributing of class A drugs."

"Ah," he said, "well, you've come to the right place laddie, and as luck would have it, I've just finished a wee job for the CIA. They had me, unofficially, delve into the personal files and many bank accounts of a former KGB enforcer, who is now residing in London of all places, is no where sacred anymore? Anyway, I found the trail that leads to his fortune, which I've no doubt was made from the illicit profits of trafficking heroin all over the world."

"And – did you?" I prompted him.

"Och, I have to live, Jake, you know me too well - and there was so much money, just sitting there, it seemed rude not to redistribute some of it in my direction."

"Was, and redistribute in your direction?" I repeated.

"Well - he won't miss it and he certainly won't be able to trace where it went," said Angus, laughing loudly. "Och, but don't you go worrying, now, the Swiss are still very discreet, even by today's standards."

Chapter 26

"So, Jake, you want to know about class A drugs, do you," said Angus. "Well now, as you already know there are many different types of hard drugs out there. But if I'm not mistaken, the kind that you're interested in grows naturally and can then be changed in a laboratory. Opium or cocaine, both originate from plants – which is it to be then."

"Tell me about opium," I said.

The kettle had been singing for two minutes and he turned the wick of the oil lamp up a little to give him more light to make the tea. I wielded the long brass toasting fork and put the butter nearer to the fire to soften it. Outside the wind howled and moaned around the small windows, and I thought of Phil sitting in the cold cockpit of the helicopter. "Opium," said Angus as he warmed the teapot.

"Difficult to grow, therefore sought after. The basis of narcotic smuggling grows anywhere up to a latitude of fifty-six degrees. The Oriental poppy or the common poppy is of no interest to the drug cartels, because only the P.S.L. (the Papaver Somniferum Linnaeus) gives opium. They are sown in May for the August crop, and in August for the April crop."

"It's like painting the Golden Gate Bridge," I said.

"Oh yes, it's definitely year round employment," said Angus, spearing another crumpet onto his fork and holding it over the flames of the roaring fire. "To get it... You want to know?"

"Of course, that's what I'm here for."

"Little incisions are cut into the green capsules or

pods of the poppy before the seeds ripen. White latex appears and you wait ten to fifteen hours for the latex to harden and turn brown. The evening they do this you can smell the aroma for miles around."

"So then what happens to the latex?"

"Well, then it's either packed in its raw state or shipped off to a lab for processing into heroin or "smack" or whatever other name it's being given these days. This ends up as a brownish powder, which is then sold on to dealers who usually dilute or "cut" it with other substances, like sugar or quinine, to make it as white as snow."

"Angus, I'm a little confused about the various strains of poppy?"

"Well, yes it is confusing, when you've got poppies ranging from white to purple-black, but I really couldn't tell you at this point in time which strain is currently the best." Angus poured the tea and I buttered another crumpet.

"Where is it grown? You haven't said where."

"Afghanistan is one of the world trading centres. This year alone they've harvested more than 4000 tons of opium, making them the world's No 1 producer. I'll put that into perspective for you, laddie. That's around a US$1.4 billion gross income. The Taliban are not fussy about who they sell it to, either, and both the Russian and Sicilian Mafia take regular shipments, with most of it ending up in the US. I believe that around 60% of all heroin in America is imported and distributed by the Sicilian Mafia and exported direct from Afghanistan. Other areas heavily involved in opium production are the Yunnan and Kwangsi areas in Taiwan, still definitely hot, as are Thailand, Laos, and North Korea, to name but a few. The Americans have a huge problem on their hands because as their intelligence shows there are certain governments in and around those regions who support the trafficking to simply undermine the U.S. The cartels like to move it that way, because that's where it commands the highest price. Mind you, this is a worldwide industry and I've only been talking about illegal cultivation. Many countries produce and process their own legal quantities as well, you know."

"For the medical industry, I presume."

"Aye, that's right. Pass me another crumpet will you. See, the latex from the P.S.L. poppy isn't much good as it is. It has to be made into morphine base, and then that has to be made into diacetyl-morphine. Which is more commonly known as heroin or 'H' depending in which circles you move in."

"So, how big do these laboratories need to be?"

"The lab doesn't need to be that big, but the drainage is usually the problem. There is a tremendous amount of acetic acid to get rid of. If you use the public drainage system it's likely to attract some rather unwanted attention. However, if you could pump it straight out into the sea – well that's probably as good as it gets. You do know what acetic acid is like?"

"It's great on fish & chips?"

"Aye, that's right. Vinegar - salt - fish and chips - och, you're torturing me, you wee Sassenach, the nearest chip shop is about seventy miles away from here."

We talked a while longer, eating more crumpets and drinking strong black tea.

By the time we stepped outside the sky was awash with orange, scarlet and crimson hues as the old red eye stepped over the edge of the horizon.

The damp highland mist was starting to drop its cloak around us as we careered back down the hill to an impatient Phil Allerton and his helicopter.

On the flight back down to London, I thought about my talk with Angus and about the information he'd managed to get for me on Harry Caplin and Oliver

Hawkworth, now safely tucked away inside my briefcase.

So, the waxy packages that we found on board of the Gin Fizz were on their way to a laboratory for processing. When I'd handed over the logbook, I had also given LJ one of the packages to be analysed; he'd put it straight into a specially adapted secure compartment in his car. Now I was beginning to understand why so many explosives had been placed throughout the Range Rover.

Someone was determined to destroy the evidence that was inside the glove box. I should have remembered that he'd told me he was going to the lab personally on his return from New York. Whoever was responsible for detonating that bomb not only wanted to destroy the evidence but also wanted the driver dead.

Everything seemed to point back to Dorset and 'Poseidon'.

* * *

Tatiana met me at the heliport. She was driving a Mercedes SLK convertible from the firm's car pool.

"What is it you do to the car fleet director, that he loans you a car reserved for Partners' use only?"

"You have a disgusting mind." She gave me a girlish smile.

"No kidding, how do you get him to trust you with one of these? I've never managed to get into one of these cars when it's parked, let alone moving."

"When he sees me enter the car park he sends one of the security guards to make sure I don't get too near to any of his precious toys."

"Well, I'll tell you. I compliment him about the efficiency of his department and how all of the cars look amazingly clean, always. It's something you've never heard about, but among cultured people compliments are all the rage, you should try them sometime."

"Ouch, your talons are sharp today, but point taken," I said.

Chapter 27

Under the porch of the elegant Georgian building hung an old lantern, its brass work burnished to an illegible sheen. Inside the entrance a vast fireplace, the coals long gone out, now had a magnificent display of white and yellow lilies set in a tall vase of blue glass. Behind a circular reception desk sat a uniformed security guard, who checked our names off against his list and issued us both with visitor identity passes. There were two senior officers from Special Branch, a face from MI6, and one from Interpol there when we arrived; we all shook hands after a Constable on the door was persuaded to allow us in.

The large square room overlooking the walled garden at the rear, had been set up for conference use. There was a large wall mounted plasma screen and an array of equipment required for giving a presentation using computer technology. Vince Sharp was along for the ride, busy plugging cables into the back of his silver multi-media notebook.

The first minute was satire at its best. The young Italian police officer wearing plain clothes had put the camera down on a large rock and inadvertently left it recording while he took a leak behind a large tree, and then to his dismay grappled with the zipper of his fly, which had got stuck.

But the serious stuff was very well done. The sleek black Mercedes threaded its way over the cobblestone road, stopped and an older man in his late fifties climbed out. The tall upright figure walked up a flight of steps and disappeared into the darkness of the mausoleum.

Another shot, same man, medium close-up moving across camera. He turned towards the camera. Our photographer had probably complained that he was blocking the view, for Robert Flackyard walked a little more quickly out of frame. There were fifteen minutes of film centred on Flackyard. He was the same imperious figure of a man who had given me an envelope full of counterfeit currency on a night that seemed so long ago. Without warning the screen went blank.

The two policemen got to their feet, but Tatiana asked them to stay a moment longer to see something else. A still picture flashed on the screen. It was a black and white snapshot. A group of men all dressed in city suits were sat and standing face on to the camera, heads erect, arms folded.

Tats said, "This photograph was taken at a formal function inside Whitehall in 1979. Chief Superintendent Craven sorted it out for us." I nodded to the policeman across the room. Tatiana went on, "Chief Superintendent Craven is second from the right, back row. He was an inspector at the time this photograph was taken. At the end of the front row there is a young man, who at the time was working at the Russian Embassy, here in London."

"Yes," I said.

Vince enlarged part of the picture showing the young man, so that the big close up filled the screen. Tats went over and pulled down a clear over-screen and with a special marker pen drew in a new hairline, added a pair of glasses and darkened the eye sockets.

"OK," I said. It was Robert Flackyard as a young man. The man sitting next to him was unmistakably Oliver Hawkworth in full military uniform.

* * *

DECORATED SOLDIER
FACES COURT MARSHALL
FOR ACTS OF DISHONORABLE CONDUCT

The 1981 press cuttings that Tats had copied from the firm's extensive tabloid archive database were neatly laid out on my desk. The cuttings accompanied a file on a certain individual whose personal details I wanted to look at more closely. Out of all the information contained in the medical, psychiatric and career records, here it was, the clincher:

George Thomas Ferlind

- *Male - White - Dark straight hair*
- *Complexion - Facial scarring due to chronic teenage acne*
- *Distinguishing marks - Small scar around left ear*
- *Eyes - Blue. Height - 6' 0"*
- *Weight - 12 stone 10lb*
- *Temperament - Excitable*
- *IQ - Very high*

This was the sinister George Ferdinand. Tats had used her contact at the Ministry of Defence to search for soldiers with a rank of sergeant or above who were serving in the same regiment as Oliver Hawkworth around the years 1979-1982 with names sounding like George Ferdinand. The database had come across one name similar to that of George Ferdinand – George Thomas Ferlind.

So Georgie boy was trained in explosives and was a qualified open water diver, had served in the Falklands, and was accused of and dishonourably discharged for bringing his regiment in to disrepute. So how had he escaped going to prison and a very long sentence? I remembered the story that Rumple had told that evening at the rented house in Dorset, of his exploits in the Falklands and how he was used to handling explosives.

Chapter 28

To wake up to the sound of the sea rolling lethargically onto the beach and the sun streaming through the window is to be in heaven. I lay in that misty half-way place between sleep and consciousness, pulling the cover up to my chin not wanting to advance into the reality of wide-awake. The sound of passing boats and distant voices trickled into my awareness; I heard cars passing on the road outside, the birds singing in the trees and the squawk of cats exchanging blows and fur. I got out of bed, stretching as I walked across the room to throw open the French windows.

The sun beat down onto the wooden balcony. As I stepped outside the seagulls slid down the offshore wind, disappearing momentarily into the water for their breakfast.

Fiona was fixing coffee and toast, holding the front of her loose-fitting silk pyjama top closed. I was particularly pleased that a large proportion of the coffee making was a two handed job. She was five feet ten inches tall and every inch a woman, as the light from the window showed off so effectively.

The death of Charlie McIntyre had put a completely different perspective on the whole assignment. Each day I'd had Fiona take the boat out and dive in a different spot around the local coastline and in completely the opposite direction to where we'd hidden the opium sacks. The sole purpose was to mislead Flackyard, or whoever else might be watching us, as to where the real site might be.

After breakfast, Fiona told me that the air bottles needed recharging but that she would be only a couple of hours, unless she decided to go shopping for a new outfit, of course. "Take as long as you need to," I said. Miss Price was very pleased.

I walked along the beach, trying to reconcile the facts I had access to with the guesswork I'd made. As I look back on it I had enough information then to tell me what I wanted to know. But at that time I didn't know what I wanted to know. I was just letting my sense of direction guide me through the maze of motives.

It was quite clear to me that the charismatic Oliver Hawkworth was connected with Flackyard right up to his double chin.

But what was his involvement? George Ferdinand alias George Thomas Ferlind, was a very dangerous individual as well as a highly competent explosive expert and qualified diver. But the strangest thing was that he had served in Hawkworth's regiment. Who was he working for? Flackyard, as it appeared, or Hawkworth? Harry Caplin had received a ten thousand pound payment from Hawkworth, but why? A house by the water's edge, Harry Caplin had said, and living in Sandbanks were absolutely perfect for him. I wonder why?

Oliver Hawkworth originally denied all knowledge of the opium packages aboard his boat the Gin Fizz, but that now seemed likely to have been merely a ruse to take the attention off him. Flackyard was quick to tell me about his past, but left out that he had been a diplomatic attaché at the Russian Embassy in London for two years. Was his brief really to study the European markets and report back to Moscow, or had he been involved in more clandestine activities connected to Hawkworth?

Did Hawkworth give the order to bomb LJ's Range Rover? Had Hawkworth's past caught up with him? Perhaps he was being blackmailed by Flackyard to participate in his illegal ventures. But why? Every road pointed to Hawkworth, and it was his motives I wanted to take a much closer look at - but time was running out.

I met Fiona at a smart bistro bar in the fashionable part of town.

The main bar area with high ceilings, and contemporary décor, gave this former bank building an air of cool sophistication. The late morning sun cascaded through the long windows, and men and women dressed for the office were standing at the bar chatting over a lunchtime drink, and taking in the easy-relaxed atmosphere.

We sat for a while longer drinking coffee, discussing the developments of my trip back to London and up to the Scottish Highlands to see Angus. Over a sandwich Fiona informed me that on at least two occasions while diving, she had spotted the same powerboat stalking her. It was always the same person watching, but far enough away for Fiona not get sight of who it could be.

Outside the air was warm compared to the coolness of the solid stone building that we had just left. Fiona was going to see if she could dig up any further information on George Ferdinand. She was meeting the young girl who had been so talkative before, when she was working as a hostess in one of Flackyard's seedy clubs. Shortly after her last chat with Fiona, she had been dismissed for talking too much, and was now between jobs. Keen to tell all about Georgie boy - for the right price?

That evening, the thought of another takeaway meal was too much, so we went to a popular restaurant in Lilliput for dinner. The small intimate dining room was full to capacity with people enjoying light conversation, locally caught fish dishes and excellent house wines. The meal was cooked to perfection and the drink had a relaxing quality. So by 11.30 p.m. I was starting to feel sleepy with the effect of the wine. But then Fiona suggested a swim in the heated salt-water pool back at the house.

The water was kept at a constant temperature and moonlight shone through the clear glass roof, trickling across the water like cream in black coffee. Jazz music scalded the soft night air; Fiona's hair shone in the light and her body was phosphorescent in the clear black water. She swam near to where I was sitting on the side, and playfully splashed me before swimming off again.

"Do you ever wish that things could be different?" Fiona asked thoughtfully.

"Sometimes. Why, have you got man problems?" I replied.

"How intuitive of you. Would you believe that even in the 21st century, women still want love affairs to go on forever and ever. Why aren't we clever enough just to enjoy it on a day-to-day basis?"

"Love is merely a state of mind," I said using one of LJ's little sayings.

There was a note of cynicism in Fiona's voice. "What absolute male rubbish, it has to be more than that," she said. "Sometimes two people see each other just for an instant, perhaps walking along a pavement, and there's a rapport. It's not sex, it's not love, it's a sort of unexplainable magical fourth dimension of living. You've never seen this person before, you'll never see them again; you don't even intend to try because it doesn't really matter."

"Everything that is good, I mean, that is profound and understanding in the two of you, becomes reality at that precise moment."

"My grandmother gave me two pieces of advice when I was a boy," I said.

"Don't ever jump off a high building without a parachute or go out with a woman who keeps a diary. You are definitely starting to sound like a diary-keeper. It's time I went to bed." I said, getting up and pulling on a towelling robe around me.

"There's one thing I'd like to know," said Fiona.

My Omega watch showed two o'clock. "Why are you really so interested in Robert Flackyard - is it the opium?" Fiona asked. I must have stopped in my tracks, for she added, "If it's one of those big boy's secret, and I'm not allowed to know. well then, you really don't have to tell me if you don't want to."

I didn't rise to her baiting, but went and sat down on one of the wicker chairs at the poolside.

"What is it that you're supposed to be doing down here now? Why are you still here, Jake? You know as well as I do that if Oliver Hawkworth is found to be involved with Flackyard there will be a cover up by the Government."

"Especially if it were likely to bring any adverse publicity or disgrace on them."

"Who is it that you are so interested in, Jake? Why do get the feeling that you've got a hidden agenda"

"You sound like you have a theory," I said. "What do you think?"

"I think you're lost, I think you're pursuing yourself," she said.

She waited for a comment, but I made none.

"Are you Jake?" she persisted.

I said, "Things have happened during this assignment that have made me take a very close look at myself and what I do. The first rule in this game is to always look at the facts as laid out before you. But, for this assignment, I'm going to make an exception to that rule. I'm going to go with my gut instincts, they're usually right and have saved my life numerous times."

"Well you'd better count me in on that, Jake Dillon, because I'm not going to let you have all the fun alone."

"Look," I said. "Can't you see it, haven't you grasped it yet, that everyone is alone? We're born alone, live alone, die alone, do every fucking thing alone."

"Forgive me, but even making love is simply a way for two people to pretend they aren't alone. But they are. People in this business are even more so alone, and aching with a whole perverse bundle of insecurities and un-tellable truths turning over and over in their heads. You're groping around in the dark trying to find your way through the bureaucratic maze with a hundred people shouting different directions at you. So you grope on; grabbing handfuls of whatever comes within reach and occasionally you actually get your hands dirty. You are alone and so am I. You've got to get used to it or you'll wind up telling people that your husband doesn't understand you."

"I'm still single – remember," said Fiona. "I can tell you, darling, there will be a whole lot of men very miserable on the day that I get married."

"Really, you're so modest," I said. "Exactly how many men are you going to marry?" She glared up at me and then immediately changed the subject to Harry Caplin and his youthful spirit and wonderful larger then life personality.

"Did you know that Harry has an enormous cellar under his house?" Fiona said, as she stepped out of the pool picked up a large white towel and wrapped it around herself. "It was the other day while you were in London, he'd asked me over for drinks and was definitely trying to get me drunk."

"Anyway, after we'd polished off the second bottle of bubbly he excused himself to go and get another from the cellar. Call it curiosity or perhaps professional interest, but I decided to have a snoop around. Do you remember the oak panelling in the hallway?"

"Vaguely," I said.

"Well, there's a secret door that leads down to the cellar. Harry had left it slightly ajar. I'd got half way down the stone steps, when he turned the corner at the bottom and spotted me. He was furious when he found me there, he made a real fuss about the steps being slippery and how dangerous they were and that the cellar was off limits to everyone including Sofia his housekeeper."

Fiona ran her long fingers through her hair in an attempt to untangle it, and while she was doing this, I contemplated what she had just told me; on the beach the sea kicked the shore in delinquent spite.

"So did you get a look at this cellar, was it well stocked?" I said.

"To be honest, Jake, from where I was standing on the steps, I couldn't really see much, except for a small window and arched doorway at the end of the room. If my sense of direction is correct, though, this was almost certainly on the seaward side of the house. But the weirdest thing though was the overwhelming smell of vinegar down there. It was so strong it almost choked me."

'The problem is the vast quantities of acetic acid that you have to get rid of…'

I thought about it momentarily. Then I said, "Get dressed; we're going to take a look at Harry's enormous cellar right now."

Fiona wasn't keen to go but we went.

Chapter 29

We discarded the notion of getting to Harry Caplin's house on foot, because even at two o'clock in the morning there was the likelihood that we would be seen. Using the small inflatable dinghy from the boathouse, we paddled, kayak style, pulling on the plastic oars, cutting silently through the black water.

Darkness, along with the neighbouring jetties and moorings kept us concealed along the way and as we got closer to the rambling Gothic-style property, its sheer walls of granite looming above us through a shroud of sea mist. Gargoyles, looked down from their high perches in snarling condemnation at anyone entering their domain.

We left the small boat secured to Harry's jetty and covered the distance across the garden to the back of the garage block, staying low, our feet sinking into the freshly dug earth of the flower border. We moved around to the side of the single storey building, and crouched down to take in our surroundings.

A light was on below us at the cellar window and the sound of water gulping down a drain was loud in the night. Around us colourful hydrangea bushes lined the walls, and from the lit window came the sound of Sinatra.

I dropped down onto weather worn flagstones outside the cellar window.

I raised my head slowly above the sill. I saw the brightly-lit area at the bottom of the stone steps, which at first sight looked like any other room for storing wine. Except that tonight, the rows of racking, heavily laden with bottles, had been moved back on rollers out of the way and were now stacked against the end wall. This secret part of the room was large and well equipped with machinery and laboratory benches. A draught of hot air was coming from the heater fans.

Nearer to me an electric vacuum pump was pounding gently. Harry Caplin walked across the room; his black T-shirt was stained down the front. The smell of acetic acid was almost overwhelming.

I felt Fiona's hand on my back as she looked over my shoulder, and could hear her swallow hard to avoid throwing up on the acrid fumes. Harry went across to the small electric pulverizer and pulled the switch. The music was washed away on a tide of noise from the little electric motor. The cellar had obviously been very well sound proofed and Harry was oblivious to the din coming from the machines and pump. Outside, the sound of the sea slapping against the jetty wall and the wind was all that could be heard.

This was definitely a small morphine-processing lab: the vacuum pump, pulverizer, drying area, everything to turn morphine into heroin before it was distributed to the dealers. Harry Caplin I thought; a retired American wine distributor living his dream by the sea in England. More like creating a nightmare. He was almost certainly the go-between through which supplies travelled and were then processed. I leaned through the open window, raised my 10mm Glock automatic, and aimed with care. The small weapon spat through its silenced barrel. The only sound was the gun coughing. On impact the bullet tore open the compact disc player on a shelf above Harry's head, sending fragments of plaster and sharp plastic everywhere.

Harry cowered down by the side of the bench that he had been working at, raising his arms to protect his head. Disoriented by what had just happened he stood up very cautiously, a Walther PPK pistol in his right hand.

"Switch off the pump and the pulverizer and drop

the weapon, Harry, or I won't hesitate to shoot you," I said. For a moment he stared at me, then he did so and silence descended on the room. He placed the pistol on the bench.

"Now, Harry, walk slowly towards the door and open it."

"You must be outta..." His voice trailed off as I cocked the Glock.

"Don't say a word," I said. "I haven't forgotten that you were partly responsible for the death of Charlie McIntyre." Harry was about to speak, but decided not to. He came over to the arched door and slipped the bolts. I motioned to Fiona to go to the door, but she was already one step ahead of me and was there, gun in hand.

"OK, Harry, now back away from the door. There's a good chap. Just stay where you are, and I promise not to blow holes into you or any of your very expensive equipment..."

Harry was biding his time, waiting until I had to move away from the window, but what he hadn't allowed for was double jeopardy. Fiona pushed open the door, her gun pointed at his genitals. I joined her inside, closing and bolting the door behind me.

The three of us stood there in silence until Harry, having regained his composure, said, "Welcome to the dream factory, people."

Fiona and I stood there and said nothing.

"Who the hell are you people anyway? I know you're not cops," said Harry.

"No, were not cops, Harry. But I can call one if you like?" You could cut through the tension that had mounted inside the cellar.

"So, tell me, Harry, why did you plant a bomb under my boss's car? Was it him you were after or the opium inside the glove compartment? Or did a little bird inside Ferran & Cardini give you a call and tell you that

LJ's car was going to be moved?"

"You've got it all wrong, Ace," said Harry. He was tanned darker than the last time I'd seen him, and the skin where his watch had been was like a white bangle. His wrinkled forehead was covered in beads of sweat and he kept wetting his lips with the end of his tongue.

"What's the use of explaining," he continued. "I really thought you were an OK sort of guy, a little stiff assed at times, but OK. No hard feelings. As they say back home, Ace, when Fall comes you can always tell which trees are the evergreens!"

"Well, where you're going, Harry, it's going to be winter all year long," I said.

He looked across at me and gave a rueful smile.

He said, "Son, why is it I get the feeling that you're shouting at me from the other side of the highway when all you've got is small talk on the sidewalk. If you get my meaning." He was cold and as hard as the northern mistral winds of Southern France.

"How did you get into this racket?" I asked him quietly.

"Can I sit down?" he asked.

I nodded, but kept the automatic aimed at him.

"Look, we've all got problems, Ace," Harry said, as he sat down heavily, "and they have to be put into perspective; the trouble is that problems look big close up." Fiona got out her cigarettes and threw one to Harry along with a lighter. He took his time lighting one up.

"You don't have to play games, I know all about your enterprise here," I said.

"Yeah, so tell me Ace, what do you know?"

"What I know, is that I came here to retrieve certain items from a sunken boat off the coast of Dorset. Simple enough, wouldn't you say, Harry? But something obviously went wrong on the night she went down - didn't it? I'd guess that just before the Gin Fizz was deliberately scuttled someone or something became a problem. Your precious consignment of opium goes down with the boat. More than likely the pickup was late and the captain panicked. This must have made you very unhappy, Harry. Especially as you'd almost certainly had to pay extra to have it transferred to the Gin Fizz just off the French coast."

"I'm introduced to a certain gentleman by the name of George Ferdinand, who turns out to be an ex-soldier by the name of George Thomas Ferlind, who served in the same regiment, and at the same time as our Cabinet Minister, Oliver Hawkworth. As I see it, he is either working for Hawkworth or with you, Harry. Either way he is in a sweet position to keep an eye on Robert Flackyard and his activities down here in Dorset."

"Yeah, you are right up to a point Ace, the opium should have been picked up just before she was scuttled. The guy sent to collect it was thirty minutes late, by the time he arrived that little weasel of a captain had put the Gin Fizz on the bottom," said Harry reflectively. He nodded and suddenly began talking quickly.

"I got involved with this racket, because, well, because I needed the dough."

"I met George in a bar in London about three years ago, and I suppose we hit it off instantly because for the next two hours I went through the whole mess back home. My pal Marcus Cohen was on a tax evasion charge at the time and it looked as if he would be going to the pen for a serious amount of time."

"Well, I couldn't just let him rot in a jail. I got enough money from my first little venture with George to pay off his entire tax bill including the interest and penalties. Back then, though, it was a simple case of buying the processed stuff in, cutting it, and then selling it on to the smaller dealers outside of London. As I say, we made a huge bundle of dough in a very short space of

196

time. After about a year, we decided that there was far more money to be made by processing the raw opium and then distributing it to the guys from whom we had been buying. But to move into this league you need cash and lots of it. George felt that we needed another investor, someone who had a hard business head and who wasn't afraid to get to get their hands dirty from time to time. That's when Oliver Hawkworth got involved."

"That's all very interesting, Harry, but you can save it all for the police."

"Be smart, Jake," Harry pleaded, "go and take a look at what some nice person has paid into your bank account recently."

"Nice try, Harry," I said, "but no, I checked all of my accounts yesterday, and all monies have been accounted for."

Harry drew on the cigarette Fiona had given him and waved it gently in the air. His initial burst of nervous talking had passed and now his speech was slower and more cautious. "Listen," he said. "It won't be long before the Government, here in the UK, legalises cannabis. I know that for sure, from my buddy Oliver Hawkworth. Then the tobacco companies will move in; there'll be tastefully designed packs, sold in every corner shop and supermarket in the country. The warning on the pack will read something like; "inhaling smoke will make you seriously mellow."

I said, "But this is now, Harry, and were not talking a little dope here. I suppose, though, that people who deal serious drugs and make very large sums of money out of it are often misunderstood."

"You are such a wise guy," Harry said. "OK, so I did it for the money, and as I got it so I spent it. You know how it is with money, Ace."

"No, I don't," I said. "Tell me how it is, Harry?"

"Pick up a handful of sand and see how it slips

through your fingers before you know it. It disappears like youthfulness. Hell, Ace, I'm not getting any younger. This is my last chance at making enough dough to retire on. Believe me when I say that in this industry it's a miracle if you make it to retirement, with the type of enemies you make on the way up."

"So, Harry, is George Ferdinand one of those enemies?"

Harry grinned. "Hell Ace, I know him far to well to be a friend," he said.

I waited while he fiddled with his cigarette. I knew he'd have something to say about George.

"You think George is a really complex character, don't you? Decorated army career, ending with court marshal and to top it all a dishonourable discharge. I bet that's eating away at you, not knowing whom he's working for or whether it was him who blew up your friend. Real puzzling it must be."

Dropping the cigarette butt on the floor he stubbed it out with his shoe as he asked Fiona for another. She pushed the pack across the bench towards him, and after taking one he threw them over for me to catch. I brought the automatic up from my side, knocking the pack to the ground, cigarettes splayed over the floor. Harry apologised, making a move towards my feet to pick them up, but seeing the gun-barrel move in his direction he thought better of it and sank back into his chair. We exchanged glances; I shook my head, and Harry smiled.

"No strikes, no runs, no problems," he said.

"So, tell me how I can stop being puzzled about Ferdinand," I said.

"He's malevolent," said Harry. " Whatever form that may take, I'm against it. George has a very nasty mind. The only reason we haven't come to blows and tried to beat each other to a pulp is because I'm such an easy-going sort of slob. But he's just obsessive about everything having to be in its place and tidy, all of the time. Even the guy's appearance is impeccable. What a nut."

I nodded. I had thought that the first time I had met him, those darting eyes and profuse sweating were sure signs that dear old George was indeed fastidious about his appearance and definitely not dealing with a full deck of cards.

"Everyone's against you, Harry, and yet you are such a nice guy at heart," I said, and I smiled. I was thinking of Charlie, but I smiled at Harry.

"Round outside means a soft centre," Harry said with a wide grin.

He pointed to a cigarette near his foot. I nodded and he picked it up, lighting it from his stub. "This man isn't interested in anything other than himself, he's not an idealist or intellectual. He thinks with his muscle. Guys like George work themselves into an early grave, always scheming and scamming. Treading on toes and upsetting the wrong people, in wars they appear to be heroes and get awarded honours - or a court marshal!"

"Sometimes both. George said that he had been recommended for some sort of gallantry award at the time he'd been caught dealing smack and cocaine while on active service in a war zone."

"It was a DSO," I said.

"Well, there you are. Like I told you, no sex, no drink, and no politics, a dedicated anal retentive if ever there was one. But probably the best guy in Europe with explosives."

"The best now maybe," I said. "But before Charlie McIntyre met with his untimely end, he might have been in Charlie's league – but only in his dreams"

Harry's face tightened like a clenched fist. He said, "George would not have done that. I don't like the guy but he would never kill in cold blood, believe me."

"All right," I said, "we'll leave that for a minute. Tell me how Flackyard fits into the picture. And before you start: I'm not a policeman, Harry. My reasons for being here don't include handing you in at the nearest police station. I'm here for information: set up the facts, and then you can fade as far away from here as you like as far as I'm concerned."

Fiona rose to her feet and walked over to me.

"Fade?" she said. "Do you know what you're saying?" She moved across to the equipment like a Luddite and swept some of it to the floor with a crash of disintegrating glass and metal denting as it hit the flagstones.

I said absolutely nothing.

Harry said, "Sure he does, cutie, he's just too smart to mention it before he has all the info he wants."

Fiona froze. She said to me, "sorry," and sat down again.

"I'm not messing with you, Harry," I said, "I'll shut you down as far as the UK is concerned but I'll give you a chance to get out and away."

"That's very magnanimous of you, Ace," Harry said. He was leaning forward with his elbows resting on his knees, massaging his eyebrows and tired eyes with the tips of his large fingers. "OK, so what do you want to know?"

"Who is Robert Flackyard?" I asked.

"Boy, you're really skipping the easy ones," he said. "Robert Flackyard; people think a lot of him hereabouts. The image he promotes is that of a legitimate businessman and benefactor to many local charities. He says that a man in such a privileged position of power and wealth, as he is, should put back into the community some of what he has taken out."

"But you don't believe him?"

"The guy's a phoney, he's nothing more than a

Cossack and a crook. His kind are all the same."

"Meaning?"

"Meaning, that I've paid him a sum of ten thousand pounds a month via an offshore account for protection and an assurance that the local cops don't come a calling."

"Protection?"

"Yes, that's it. I could afford to throw him a load of dough each month, in return for a hassle free existence and because he is a major client of my little venture down here in Dorset. Unfortunately for me, it all backfired when you turned up and swiped my opium from the Gin Fizz. Flackyard tried to persuade you to give it back, but man are you a tough nut to crack, eh?"

"Don't be bitter, Harry," I said. He kneaded his soft brown face again with his huge hairy hands, and as his eyes and nose emerged from the open fingers he smiled a humourless smile.

"And Ferdinand," I said, "how did he get along with Flackyard?"

"OK. Flackyard is indifferent, as he tends to be around all people. George is just a little too creepy around him for my liking."

"Have you ever gone into a room and heard any conversations between them that perhaps you weren't supposed to hear? Any talk of hardware, for instance?"

"Well, thinking back, there were a few times when the talk just stopped when I walked in on them, but I've never overheard them actually talking."

"Never, and that's all?" I said. "Listen, Harry, we'll play it your way, if you like."

"But let me remind you that we're in a sound proofed room in the middle of the night with only the sea to keep us company. I'd like to think that we could continue our conversation in a gentlemanly manner. Or perhaps you'd prefer that I work you over a little and then string you up on that hook over there and pump your veins full of that shit you've been producing, let's say one hundred percent pure. That should send you on your way to Mars. The choice is yours Harry, you can walk out of here free, or I'll give you to the local police, and they can carry you out in a black body bag."

"Just try," Harry said.

"You've got me mixed up with all those nice guys, Harry. I will try." I said.

There was a short, sharp silence.

"Hey, Ace, I'm no smack head," said Harry. His tan had disappeared now.

"A hundred per cent pure won't just send me to Mars, it'll send me to the undertakers." He folded his arms tightly.

"Harry, you can be sure I won't kill you. Not with the first needle anyway."

"You will survive for the second dose and the others until I decide to hand you over to the authorities. By then you will be so dependent on the stuff, you will beg me to let you have a hit. You'll talk, Harry, believe me. Look upon it as sales research – hell, it's probably tax-deductible."

Harry's head sank forward and he rocked gently in his seat as he tried to wake out of the nightmare in which I existed. When he continued to speak it was in an impersonal monotone. "George Ferdinand used to work for Flackyard. George had a great respect for him. Even after we had enough money not to worry, George would continue to say 'sir' to him. George had contacts all over Europe, and they all liked him. Maybe you find that hard to believe, but it's true. George had only to whisper about something he wanted done and bingo, it was done. He has always arranged the supplies of the opium, while my end of the business was to process and sell."

"How did the opium usually arrive?" I asked.

"Always by ship, once a month. The cross channel

ferry from Cherbourg to Poole has been our regular mule, if you like, for well over a year. There is a French side to this operation. They would send a diver down at night, while the ferry was in dock, and he'd secure the opium in a specially designed watertight metal case to the hull using magnetic clamps.

"As the port authorities never check the outside of the hull below the water line this has been an extremely safe and effective way of transporting our supplies to the UK. All we had to do was listen on a short wave radio to the shipping talk and when the ferry started her approach into Poole Harbour we would dive from inside the boathouse using a powered underwater sled to get out to the ship quickly. As you are aware, only an expert diver would be able to get under the hull of a moving vessel and remove the metal case that was held on the bilge keel by the magnetic clamps."

"Who dived at this end, Harry?" I asked quietly.

"Well, at first George did, until that is recently..." He let the words hang in mid air and then went on smugly. "That is until he met up with his old chum Rumple. What a piece of luck, and how easy to get him on board. In fact it was as easy as taking candy from a kid."

"How many times did Rumple dive for you?" I asked.

"Three times," Harry said, holding up three fingers. "Go on."

"As you can now see, this house has played a vital part in what we did."

"Once the opium was back here, we would process and distribute it, all from this house. George had contacts with haulage companies all over the place."

"The drivers would be paid well for carrying in their cab a briefcase. This was full of smack on the way to the cartels up and down the country. It's as easy as that, Ace. How am I doing?"

"You're doing OK," I said. "Your boat; did George ever use that?"

"Sure, he's a far better sailor than I'll ever be, he borrowed it whenever he wanted. It was Flackyard borrowing it whenever it suited him that made me sore. I'd never trust the guy alone, I don't care if he is the local Mr Big, there's something not right about the guy."

"Tell me more about Robert Flackyard," I said.

"Flackyard drives around town in his flash chauffeur driven cars like he was a king. Thinks he owns the place. He has sent George along at night to borrow the boat like he's doing me a favour. Flackyard the wise guy. One day I get back here; he's down in the cellar, helping himself to the goodies."

"'I've gotcha red-handed,' I say, smiling like I'm joking. 'My dear Mr Caplin, I've never been caught red handed, in my entire Life.' He says – nonchalant as you like. 'So who cares?' I say. 'I do,' he says, 'and I'm the only one,' and off he drives with my smack in his pocket."

"He's in up to his neck with a few politicians both locally and in London."

"Only last week, there was a group of Japanese business tycoons over. The official reason for their visit was to strengthen trading relations. Hell, they were here to negotiate a narcotics deal with Flackyard, and to sample some of ours," Harry raised his head and said, "you're not kidding me about letting me fade away, are you? Because if I'm shooting my mouth off for nothing…"

"No," I said, "you can talk your way out as far as I'm concerned."

"Boat and all?" asked Harry.

"Boat and all, just keep talking, Harry," I said. I decided to try a bluff, to keep the momentum going. "The visitor from London," I coaxed gently, "don't forget the visitor from London, Harry."

"Oh him, pal of George's," Harry said. "Smooth

talking guy, great sense of fun."

"What's his name?"

"Jasper Lockhart," said Harry, "great sense of fun."

"Great sense of fun," I said. Now it was all falling in place. Jasper Lockhart knew George. A messenger, perhaps, or more than likely a courier? It certainly accounted for the new Jaguar convertible. Did Hawkworth tell George what to do or was it the other way round? In either case, why?

I looked around at the brightly-lit cellar: the equipment and the pile of aluminium briefcases stacked against the wall.

"Harry," I said, "I want George Ferdinand here; get him here now and you can go."

Harry sucked his cheeks in and snorted a laugh down his nose. "Hell Ace, you can get him down here as easily as I can," he said. "You don't have to kick dirt in my face." He got up slowly and walked across to the large white sink, washed his hands with soap, dried them, put on his Rolex watch and turned to face us. "You did the hero bit already. Now if you don't mind I'm out of here, gun or no gun."

"You think so," I said, but I did nothing as he walked across to the chair and picked up his jacket, and nothing as he walked down between the benches towards the door. He looked back to see what my reaction was. I put the gun back in the holster under my arm and he looked reassured.

It was then that a flash roared across the tension and echoed around the room like a frenzied shark in a pond full of goldfish. Fiona had fired her un-silenced pistol at Harry. I saw him spin around and fall forward against a large crate on the floor. I reached out to take the gun away from her. The hairs on the back of my hand parted as it went off again. The bullet thudded deep into the plaster of the wall somewhere over Harry's head.

My hand closed over the smoking barrel to drag it away from her; there was enough heat for me to instantly drop the weapon onto the floor with a crash.

I grabbed Fiona around the neck and twisted one of her arms up behind her, so that with her back to me I was able to prevent her from doing any more harm.

From behind the crate Harry's voice asked, "Has that crazy dame still got a gun, or can I come out without getting my head blown off?"

"It's OK Harry, you can come out, it's safe. Now go quickly, before I change my mind and let the lady here finish the job."

I released my grip on Fiona, who turned around quickly, beating me on the chest with clenched fists and screaming in between sobs, the tears rolling down her cheeks, "Don't let him go – he killed your friend," over and over again. She stopped to draw breath, "You just aren't human," she gulped. I held her tightly while Harry made his exit, with a big red hand clamped over the top of his arm.

Fiona sat down; finally she looked up at me. And told me that she was an undercover narcotics officer working in conjunction with other Government agencies including the serious crime squad. How I'd just about messed everything up, but it was her damaged esprit de corps she was really crying about as she sat in Harry Caplin's dream house.

"Then you knew that the smell of vinegar was acetic acid and would be coming from the processing of morphine. Why didn't you let me in on the real reason you were here?"

She blew her nose. "Because a good operator lets the professional law-enforcers spearhead his or her actions," she quoted verbatim.

At that precise moment we heard the powerful twin

diesels of Harry's boat the Star Dust start up. Moving outside, we watched as the elegant cruiser moved away from the jetty, Harry at the uppermost helm. He looked behind once, pushed the throttle levers hard forward, lifted a hand and waved. Five minutes later Harry Caplin had faded out of sight. Fiona looked up at me and smiled wanly.

* * *

It took only a few minutes to get back to our boathouse in the dinghy. But, all the way Fiona kept saying, "You've let him get away. I must call my boss."

As we were stowing the dinghy away I finally said, "Look – I don't know what they teach you in the police force, but if you think your prestige there depends on putting the handcuffs on Harry, you are quite wrong. Let him go and spread the good news among his friends. If he goes back to the States, you can be there in a matter of hours. Or you can phone your colleagues in narcotics over there and have them hold him. This is simply like a game of chess; the idea is to out manoeuvre your opponent. Not try and kill him."

This last remark hit the spot; Fiona's face flushed and she told me that I was no better than Harry Caplin was. As for hurting Harry, if it hadn't been for me getting in the way she would have killed him without any hesitation. As for my conduct, it would remain to be seen as to whether I was simply dismissed or charged with obstructing a police officer in the line of her duty.

I couldn't have Fiona contacting the authorities and attracting attention to what was going on, not just at the moment. At least not before I'd contacted LJ, cleared out the rented house and faded away myself. I began to be aware of a silence and realised that Fiona had said something. "What was that? Sorry, I was a million miles away."

"Oh, all I was saying was, that it's all so dammed confusing. I'm used to taking the job so far and then handing it over to more experienced officers to finish off. I really am in way over my head, Jake. What am I going to do?"

"Confusing," I repeated, "of course it's confusing. When you're involved like you are, undercover, rubbing shoulders with drug pushers and serious criminals, it's bound to get confusing. Look, Fiona, we really are on the same side here, the only difference is that I work for Ferran & Cardini and you work for the Government. The end result has to be the same."

"Shit, if it ever gets out that I let a key player in a major drugs ring casually walk out of his processing plant, get in his million pound powerboat and sail away into the night, I'll not only be kicked out of the force, but would almost certainly never get another job in law enforcement as long as I live. This has to end right here, Jake, make no mistake about that."

"Players like Harry Caplin, Fiona, have the type of lawyers that walk into a police station and five minutes later walk out with their client alongside them."

"What's that supposed to mean, that this case won't stand up?" said Fiona.

"It means that people as well connected as Harry and his friends would be back out on the street on bail within hours of their arrest. They have no hesitation in bribing officials or even by bringing to bear the sort of pressures that are so powerful that the law can be changed to suit the lawbreaker. But the most effective thing of all is good old-fashioned lying by old liars like Harry Caplin."

"Why, was a lot of what he said untrue?" She sat down on the deck of the Phantom.

"Definitely," I said, "but like all first-class lies it had a firm foundation of truth."

"So, what was true, then?" asked Fiona.

"Well, I'll just say this, he didn't leave me in any doubt about the way that this investigation should continue. Providing that it is tailored one hundred per cent to the convenience of Harry Caplin. Who I now believe to be one of the most manipulative individuals that I've had the misfortune to ever meet."

"I'm still no wiser, but I suppose you'll enlighten me at the appropriate time" said Fiona, jumping off the deck of the boat. "I'm going to shower and then sleep in that order," she added over her shoulder as she walked back up to the house.

Chapter 30

The email came through just as we got back to the rented house. On the small laptop screen a flashing envelope alerted me that there was one new message in my mailbox. Fiona came in and stood beside me, intrigued as to who the sender was at four in the morning.

It was from Harry. "How nice of him to write" said Fiona sarcastically.

The note read:

Sorry to leave without saying my goodbyes properly, but when you gotta go, you gotta go. I didn't know whether you were playing straight or not when you promised to let me fade. Mr Thomas is jumping around like a cat on a hot tin roof. You can bet on Fiona's sweet ass that he will want to get his hands on my lady of the sea whom I decided to leave behind and is residing just around the corner from Round Island.

What I didn't tell you is that Mr Thomas has one of the slickest blackmail set-ups of all time and I do mean of all time. If I mentioned, Constantine's list, which no one has been able to locate, listing the names of politicians and certain high ranking military types who like to do a little cocaine, hookers and smack, you'll know I ain't kidding.

Keep an eye on the lady for me, Ace. You never know your luck; you might even get to close the file on this one – GOOD FISHING! Have a nice life!

Harry

* * *

The Rumples had completely disappeared into thin air or were on the run, with every Government agency in the land looking for them. But who would they be looking for? As masters of disguise and deception, I doubted very much whether the Rumples were even in the UK anymore.

Anything that had to be done had to be done on our own. I sat down in front of the computer screen.

"What are you doing?" asked Fiona. I looked up at her, and asked her if she would mind making some very strong coffee for us both.

I typed the brief report to LJ in London, clicked the Send key and then put the laptop away. Fiona brought coffee. I told her I had sent an update of the situation to LJ, and that she could either continue the chase with me or was free to take any action she wished in respect of the drugs operation. I also reminded her that because of the Partners' association with the British Government, any mention of Ferran & Cardini or myself would be denied emphatically and that all traces of our involvement down here in Dorset would be erased from all files as a matter of course. That said, and out of the way, I stood up and went through to the kitchen.

"You're not giving me the brush off, that easily. I'm with you all the way, like I said before, Jake Dillon. We're going to finish this together, whether you like it or not."

"If that's what you want. We'll start by rowing out to Harry's boat then," I stifled a yawn, and was suddenly feeling really tired.

* * *

Fiona brought the dinghy gently alongside the hull of the Star Dust. I scrambled on to the teak laid deck in my bare feet – I didn't want to risk leaving wet footmarks across it. Fiona stepped agilely onto the ladder, and before coming aboard, kicked the dinghy away into the channel.

I watched through night vision binoculars, willing George 'Thomas' Ferdinand not to appear until we were both suitably concealed. Then I walked across the bridge looking for a place for us both to hide and wait. There was only the one stowage locker on the far side of the wheelhouse, which would just about take me. Fiona wasn't happy about getting inside the tight space and so went off below to find her own hiding space.

It was a bit tight for my size, almost coffin-like, but I jammed the blade of my diver's knife under the bottom edge of the fibreglass lid, which gave me some airflow, but not enough to dispel the smell of damp. We waited.

Half an hour later, something struck the side of the boat with a dull thud. It wasn't very seaman like and I began to wonder whether it was George.

Perhaps Harry had still been playing games and had lured me into a trap. I flushed with sudden fear at the thought of this locker really becoming a coffin.

I heard George's voice shouting at the other person in the dinghy to keep a tight hold of the rope. The dinghy was evidently drifting away. A young woman's voice, a little hysterical was telling him to take hold of the metal case. "Don't drop it in the water, you stupid bitch. The oars are all over the place; you're going to lose one of them."

George pulled hard on the rope and the small dinghy slammed into the side of the hull again. The girl clambered onto the deck and in a West Country accent, she hurled a string of expletives at George Ferdinand.

They seemed to be an age getting aboard, and then I heard George walking across the deck to the control console. There was a click as he switched on the lights over the controls. If I held my face horizontal, with my ear pressed tight against the deck, I could just see through one of the small ventilation grills at the bottom of the locker lid. My right eye had a narrow range of vision that included the top half of the person at the controls.

I could see George in profile – the pock marked face with long sideburns and the small scar around his ear. The anchor came up with a clattering and the big diesel inboard motors throbbed into life at the push of the starter button. George engaged the twin screws and I felt the water thrash under the hull.

The lights above his head threw his sunken eyes into two dark, skeletal shadows. His hands moved across the controls, articulate and smooth, while his eyes watched the beams, the compass and the rev. counters. This was the real George, a man that I'd never seen before, a very capable, professional sailor. From the seat at the controls he couldn't see the ship's clock. Every few moments he would call to the girl with him, "What time is it?" and she would tell him.

He moved the throttles as far forward as they could go and the hull began hammering against the water like a road worker's pneumatic hammer. When he was satisfied with the course, George told the woman to take the wheel and hold it steady. I heard the click as the aluminium case was unlocked. I pressed my ear closer to the wooden deck inside the locker, and this gave me a slightly wider range of vision. The woman was staring into the dark while George crouched on the floor over what looked like some sort of portable sonar equipment, to which he was connecting headphones and the cable for what looked like the underwater sounder. Then he stood up and walked to the stern of the boat, placing the coil of wire near to the lower dive platform, and his footsteps came back towards the wheelhouse.

He shouted, "Starboard – keep the bloody line steady as she goes, will you." The girl he had brought aboard was mid twenties and definitely, I thought, the same person that Fiona had interviewed, firstly at Flackyard's club and then for a second time only a few days ago.

She sat at the wheel, her hands gripping it tightly, looking straight ahead into the darkness. George was talking quickly to her about Harry making a run for it. How the bastard had cleaned out George's bank account of nearly three million pounds. George was completely at a loss as to how Harry could possibly have found out the details and passwords of the account, gained access electronically using an Internet Café access point, and then completely covered his tracks.

There was a click and the girl was bathed in reflected light as Ferdinand moved the beam of the big searchlight out across the waves. I felt the boat slow and the engine pitch drop as George brought the cruiser about a few degrees, slamming it into the swell. Outside there was the sound of water sloshing over the edge and rushing along the teak deck. The boat vibrated again as Ferdinand pushed the big throttle levers forward as far as they would go. After two or three minutes he slackened off the power and turned to port.

He shouted at the girl to use the big searchlight and to keep her eyes peeled for any rocks just below the surface of the water. We must be entering a cove, I thought. These parts of the Dorset coastline abound with both large and small inlets and coves that have been used for centuries by smugglers, and are ideal places for putting ashore without anyone seeing. George had dropped the sonar over the side, and was now listening through the headphones intently. His arm came up, flapping about and he shouted frantically at the girl to go gently around the cove again, this time in a tight arc.

Becoming more and more panicked by George's shouting, the young girl was not only trying to look out for rocks, but steer the boat as well.

Ferdinand in frustration at her slowness to respond to his orders hurled at her a string of four letter words as he snatched the wheel from her and spun it viciously, knocking her sideways onto the throttle levers in his haste to get her out of the way.

The large cruiser slid sideways, uncontrolled, the propellers screaming to get hold of the water as the deck heeled over towards the dark sea.

It was bad timing on my part that I had chosen that moment to emerge.

The locker lid flew open and I tumbled out, sprawling across the deck with the life jackets that I had been lying on. My face struck one of the uprights supporting the chart table, my arm-twisted behind me, and I heard my automatic pistol slide forward out of its holster. George got control and the deck came level.

"Get to your feet," George said, his voice menacing. I wasn't to keen to stand up just yet, especially if it meant that I was going to be knocked straight down again. On the other hand he could have just kicked the hell out of me or shot me with the ancient looking Smith & Wesson he held in his right hand, if he'd wanted to.

"Listen, George, I don't want to fight you," I said.

"I'm not going to fight you, Mr Dillon. I'm going to kill you." He didn't say it like a cold-blooded killer but like a man who, although completely mad, talks like any other calm, educated and mentally stable person.

"In that case, George, you will be making a serious mistake," I replied. But it was no use; I had read this man's army personnel file. He had fitted into civilian life so badly, building up resentment and rage against people in positions of power, so that he was a bubbling cauldron of violent behaviour just simmering under the surface, and waiting to erupt.

The girl was back at the wheel, and the boat was drifting with the swell, the engines at idle. George faced me across the bridge. "I was going to make it quick and clean by shooting you, Mr Dillon. Followed by a dignified burial at sea, of course. But I've decided to make an exception in your case."

"Especially as you have taken it upon yourself to destroy my lucrative little venture down here in Dorset. For that, I am going to take great pleasure in destroying you – blow by blow."

He moved slowly, ensuring he kept his balance. His eyes stared into mine, sizing me up, judging my probable actions. We faced each other no more than an arm length apart. He brought his hands slowly and easily upwards in front of him, fists clenched. He widened his stance and turned his shoulders very slightly.

It confirmed what I had suspected. George was a street brawler; his stance was that of a boxer, one hand and one foot slightly advanced.

Rivulets of seawater caught in the light meandered across the deck under George's feet. I brought my left arm up in front of me in a basic block, sweeping it across to the left, deflecting George's right fisted punch. I watched his eyes, he was deciding whether I was going to be a pushover. He came at me with a short left hook in the ribs, followed with a jab at my face.

His fist scraped my cheek, but my body was wide open. I ignored the pain in my side, bringing my left leg around in an arc, and the top part of my foot made contact just behind his knee.

His leg buckled with the blow. As he went down on one knee, he spun round in an attempt to kick my feet out from under me.

I stepped back quickly out of his reach. It was the correct counter but he was slow, far too slow. A man off balance thinks of nothing but getting balanced again; aggression disappears. He lunged forward, knees slightly bent, body forward, eyes keeping constant contact with mine.

My left hand blocked and gripped his right forearm as he came in for another punch, and my right fist made contact with his stomach, just under the ribcage. George doubled over, my knee smashed into his nose, bone crunched and splintered, and blood began instantly pouring onto the teak deck.

Still holding onto George's right arm, I stepped around and behind him twisting the outstretched limb up at an angle. I heard a sharp intake of breath as I applied upward pressure to the point of dislocating or breaking George's arm.

The girl turned and looked over her shoulder, her eyes like belisha beacons as Fiona Price came crashing through the open salon doorway. She moved like a cat, low and crouching until she was out in the open. Then she stood up and fired her pistol into the air.

Even at that instant George did not allow the pain to influence him. He still tried to struggle out of the hold I had him in. He was a tough man, this George Ferdinand. He fell away as I released him and sat on the floor holding what was left of his nose.

He said, "You know I could easily throw you over the side – and no one could ask any questions?"

"Of course you could, George, but there is just the possibility that I'll break your neck while you're trying or the lady over there will shoot you."

"We've got no power on that side." the young girl pointed to the starboard side. The cable from the sonar had probably wrapped itself around the screw. I retrieved my automatic, motioning George down towards the dive platform.

"Fiona, cover the girl while I attend to our friend here."

I tied George to the steps with the rope from a life buoy and went back up to the bridge. I told the girl to head back towards Poole Harbour and Sandbanks, using only the port motor. It would be a slow journey and the wind had got up, coming at us with the dawn sun. This floating gin palace was definitely not the type of boat to be in at sea with only one propeller.

"You've got nothing on me," Ferdinand shouted.

"When we hand you over to the police, or perhaps those gentle souls from drugs, you might think differently."

"There's nothing linking me to Harry Caplin or anyone else, so dream on, Dillon, and another thing, the authorities won't be holding me for too long when we get back. Once I've phoned my lawyer," said George, with a twisted sneer, his eyes flitting in all directions and beads of nervous sweat all over his face.

"Who's to say that you will get a phone call, George?" I said. "It's like this, certain parties that I know want to question you about your involvement with the distribution of class A drugs across the country. I've no doubt they will also want to know where and from whom you obtained the list that enables you to blackmail some of the countries most influential and wealthy people."

The wind howled all around us. George was getting the full force of it where I'd tied him up. The girl sat at the wheel keeping close to the coast as we made our way back to the harbour.

"Save your fantasies for your report," said Ferdinand. "You have no interest in drugs."

"No? So what am I interested in, then."

"Your only interest is in Constantine's list, the one I would have retrieved from that cove had you not gate crashed the party."

"Well done George, that's exactly right," I told him. "My brief has always been to locate the list and then to destroy it. But my colleague up there is most definitely wanting to talk to you about the drugs."

Fiona looked down at me quizzically at the mention of drugs.

"It's not there," he said, "it's gone, you'll never find it, not now – not never."

"But you admit that it has been your source of blackmailing inspiration?"

"Of course, it contains the names of some of the most powerful people in this country. It's not everyday you get the opportunity to screw those filthy rich bastards, is it now? But, I really can't recall much of it," he added for good measure.

"Let me help you remember," I said. "I'll tell you one name that was on it."

I named Hawkworth. Ferdinand said nothing. "The man that you served under in the army and whom with your friend Jasper Lockhart you decided to blackmail."

"You know about Lockhart," George's eyes filled with hate, and he flared his nostrils in a primitive show of anger. "Leave him out of it. He's all right; he was just trying to help me. He's not involved in…" George stopped talking and looked out to sea.

"He's not involved, eh?" I said, but didn't push it any further.

I sat down under the canopy on the lower deck, just above the dive platform. The nagging pain in my side told me that at least one rib was possibly fractured, maybe two.

George sat slumped on the deck, his hands tied together to the steps. His nose had started to bleed again and both eyes had started to swell. Just to add to his discomfort.

"Did your friend Flackyard give you the list or did you steal it from him?" I asked out of the blue.

George slowly looked up at me through swollen eyes before speaking.

"No," he said quietly, "Robert Flackyard is the

most honourable man I know."

"Look, George," I said, "I rarely interrupt people when they're talking; especially when they are misinterpretting 'honour' and inventing lies and half-truths, because, in fact, *they* are far more interesting than the actual truth. However, for you I'll make an exception; either you start telling the truth or I'm going to drop you over the side with your hands still tied together."

"What do you or your kind know about honour?" he said tersely.

"Honour," I said, "Sure and of course you do; you, Caplin, Hawkworth and Flackyard. An honourable bunch of thugs. Look, Ferlind" – it was the first time I had used his real name – "you're just trying to break one leg off of a centipede. Behind me is another, just like me, and behind him another. I'm a pussycat compared with some of the others who are going to descend on you in any part of the world you go. All that my boss and those in Whitehall want back is a report stating the assignment is 'closed' written in bold letters across the front of the file. Those individuals named in that list can then get on with their sordid little lives, without the fear of being blackmailed. Try and be a bit sensible. I may even tell the authorities what a helpful chap you've been. You never know, they may even cut a deal with you."

"What do you want to know?" he said.

"I don't know what's missing until I hear it, if there is anything you don't want to tell me just miss it out!"

"How very cunning," said George, "the gaps tell you more than the story in between."

"Something like that," I said, "I'm really the Chief Constable travelling undercover with a wire taped to my chest, or it could just be George, that you are a little paranoid!"

Getting up, stiff from sitting on the deck my ribs ached from where Ferdinand had whacked me. I walked to the main cabin, leaving Fiona to watch both the girl and George while I poured him a large brandy from Harry's well-stocked drinks cabinet. I released Ferdinand's left hand from the steps but left his right securely tied to the handrail, just in case he decided to jump overboard on his own. He sipped at the big glass of brandy I had given him, lost in deep thought.

He said, "Bosnia? Do you remember the news footage, the images that came out of the Kosovo conflict? Dying and wounded babies, animals and children, hundreds of dead bodies everywhere, riddled with bullets or torn apart by landmines?" He lit a cigarette, taking a hard pull of smoke into his lungs.

"Frightened, I was so bloody frightened. People like you don't understand..."

"...do you?" he said. He wanted a reply.

I said, "As long as you don't say it's because of my lack of imagination."

He went on staring out to sea and smoking. George Ferdinand nodded.

For a moment I thought he was going to smile.

"Yes, I was there. There are times you're so frightened of something that you have to make it happen sooner. I was merely someone who wanted to come to terms with my trauma. Men I had known from the army had volunteered to fight as unpaid mercenaries with the Kosovo Liberation Army."

"So I went to join Slobodan Milosevic's Serbian force as a highly paid mercenary, just to be different. They posted me to a small elite unit inside Kosovo which was carrying out assassinations against their own Serbian police officials and Albanian collaborators. Why? I hear you ask. Very simple really. To discredit the Kosovar Albanians, who at the time were part of a peaceful movement. Caplin thought I was working with the Liberation Army."

"He liked it that way so I never disillusioned him."

"How long were you with the Serbs?" I said.

"Long enough. It was just like an exercise really, we'd be told which police official or collaborator to hit. All we had to do was follow him around, see where he went, plant a bomb somewhere convenient and using a remote detonator, execute him. Bombing was always the preferred method, as it always gained maximum shock horror reactions. It made it a nice impersonal fight for me. No close up view of who you were hitting. No one trying to hit you. The best bit was being paid thousands of pounds by the Serbs to actually go out and kill Serbs. Ironic is what I'd call it, bloody ironic."

I could see that in some perverse way the destruction and carnage that Ferdinand had experienced in Kosovo had never left him, and probably never would. How he really did believe in his own twisted mind, that working for the Serbs in Bosnia was nothing more than an exercise.

"When I came back to England, I didn't really know what the hell I was doing, except getting drunk and doing a little coke more often than not."

"Anyway, after a while I got introduced to a local East End lad who operated a string of lap dancing clubs in Soho and was heavily into dealing drugs. It wasn't long before I had a flat and a flash car. He told me that in return for the lifestyle, I would be contacted when the occasional 'special job' had to be done, otherwise my time was my own."

Ferdinand looked at me and shrugged.

"And you fell for this guy's bullshit?" I said.

"I fell for it," said Ferdinand.

"Then you met Jasper Lockhart?"

George didn't fall into the trap; he walked into it slowly and deliberately. He looked at me and said, "Yes, I saw him soon after I'd started. He told you?"

I tried a simple lie. "No, I guessed," I said, "when I saw you in London. It was when I met Jasper Lockhart at that lap dancing club."

"That was you, was it?" said Ferdinand. "Yes, I sometimes go back there to see some of the girls. Purely for pleasure, you understand."

I knew he was lying. He had obviously been there delivering a consignment of drugs that afternoon, but I said nothing.

The brandy was helping Ferdinand to relax, so I poured him another drink.

He finally said, "It was the redhead."

I handed him the glass. "It was - the redhead," he said again. As I got up and walked up to the wheelhouse, Fiona was sat on the stowage locker talking to the girl. I stretched some of the tension and stiffness out of my body. George screamed as loud as he could over the force four that was blowing, "It was the fucking redhead, do you hear me?"

Both Fiona and the girl looked around sharply.

"OK," I said.

"Listen, she's one of the dance girls I dated when I worked in London, I keep in touch with her because she feeds me little snippets of info about her boss - who used to be my boss. I like to know what he's up to, especially as we're - were in the same line of business, so to speak."

"Tell me about how you met Robert Flackyard?" I asked him.

Ferdinand's eyes flitted around like a butterfly in flight, first in one direction and then another. He started to talk quickly. "Flackyard was a big man at the Russian Embassy in London, and a group of them used to come to the titty bars in Soho, usually once or twice a month. They spent money like it was going out of fashion, a thousand sometimes two thousand at a time. On one occasion my boss made a point of introducing the Russians to me.

The reason, very simple, I was to look after his esteemed guests personally. They all liked to snort coke, just as they liked to touch the girls who were dancing for them. Some of Flackyard's cronies paid extra to take the girls up to a private room and have sex with them. But, the only thing that Robert Flackyard was interested in was the set-ups with the clubs and of course a little cocaine now and again, for recreational purposes only."

"My break came about three months later. Flackyard came into the bar on his own without his minders, which was very rare because they followed him everywhere. He talked around the houses for hours, never getting to the point, always in riddles. Eventually, he came clean and offered me an opportunity beyond my wildest dreams."

"What did he offer you," I asked.

"He offered me the opportunity of a life time - to get back at, and get equal, with the stuck up gits in the army who had me kicked out. But most of all he offered me Oliver Hawkworth on a plate. The man I most hated and still hate to this very day."

George poured himself another brandy from the bottle I'd brought down from the saloon. He picked up his drink and sipped at it. "You're probably wondering what the catch was with Flackyard. Well, there wasn't one, all he wanted from me was my help in setting up a string of titty bars along the south coast."

"Did you plant the bomb that killed my friend Charlie McIntyre?" I asked.

"Kill him? I couldn't have killed him." He drank some more. "You can't imagine a mountaineer cutting the rope of another mountaineer, could you?"

"Well, it's like that. I had a lot of respect for Charlie, he was undoubtedly the best explosives expert on the open market as well as a damn good diver."

"I didn't mean to insult you George, but I had to

ask."

"It was Rumple," George said, ever so quietly that I almost didn't hear him say it.

He poured himself another brandy, shouted up to the girl to cut the engine revs, and told me that we were just wasting fuel. We sat in silence for some time, looking out to sea. Somehow I knew what George had told me was all true.

Chapter 31

Ferdinand and I sat on the rear deck of the "Star Dust" in silence for some time. When I finally said it, I tried to make it sound as casual as you like. "So were you given Constantine's list by Flackyard at the very outset, were you, George?"

"You must be joking; Flackyard would never give anyone that list."

"So how did you get the names from it?"

"You make me laugh," said Ferdinand. I found that difficult to believe.

"Don't you realise even now, that we have all been completely outsmarted by a man who is cleverer than all of us put together?"

"Go on," I said.

"One man and one man only has access to the list, to the only copy that is in existence. One man went to a lot of trouble to get it and even more to putting it somewhere only he can get to it." He paused, after a long silence he said, "The list is stored on a CD inside a watertight canister made to look like a lobster pot on the sea bed. To retrieve the pot you have to know roughly where it's located, but because of the tidal currents it moves around."

"That equipment in the aluminium case over there," he pointed to the case laying on the lower deck, "well, that underwater sonar 'calls' the lobster pot to the surface by remotely detonating and inflating the pot's tiny onboard ballast tanks. But you have to be virtually on top of it before the sonar can send a strong enough signal."

"And that's what you were trying to do just now."

"I stole that equipment from Flackyard's house. It's a portable unit designed for close range locating. Flackyard has the real thing in his study."

"He sits there every evening before dinner and gloats because he knows exactly where the list is at all times. All he has to do is bring up a local coastal chart on his computer screen; the homing device he had fitted to the pot interacts with the specially designed software, and bingo the computer does the rest." Ferdinand's voice went very quiet.

"He'd tricked me again." He looked up at me sharply. "It's not there in that cove, it's moved to another location!"

I nodded. "Tell me about Hawkworth," I said.

"Hawkworth was only one," George went on, "Flackyard forced a lot of people on the list to invest money in his businesses or ensure that lucrative Government development contracts were his for the taking."

"But you soon got the idea," I supplemented, "you told Hawkworth to arrange a supply line of raw opium so that your little partnership with Caplin would flourish."

"It wasn't hard to guess, I suppose." Ferdinand nodded.

I said, "What did Flackyard do with the money?"

There was no reply. I said, "Has it gone to finance extreme right wing movements? Has it gone to finance present-day fascist groups – is he part of an organisation they call the New World Order?"

Ferdinand closed his eyes, "Yes," he said. "I'm still a believer in the cause."

"Robert Flackyard is a great man, but like many that are truly great he has some childish weaknesses that will most certainly bring him down off that pedestal one day. Of that you can be sure." His eyes were still closed.

The girl's voice from the wheelhouse sounded above the beat of the sea.

We were rounding Old Harry Rocks.

"I'll come up." As I said it there was a thump like a heavy hammer being swung against the hull.

"A piece of flotsam," Ferdinand shouted up at me. The girl had brought the throttle back to half speed. Again there was a thump and a third immediately after. The girl coughed and then slumped, falling sideways off the stool. I caught her. She was limp as she slid to the floor. The front of my shirt was soaked in blood.

Ferdinand, Fiona and I all stayed motionless; Ferdinand still tied to the boat and the girl at my feet.

As we processed the possibilities through our brains. I was thinking of Flackyard, but Ferdinand had a more practical slant. He knew the person concerned.

"It's Harry Caplin," he said. The boat purred gently towards the shore.

"Where?" I said.

"Firing his hunting rifle from the cliff-top if I know him," said Ferdinand.

There were two more thumps and now listening for it, I heard the gun crack a long way away. The deck was slippery with the girl's blood.

Ferdinand had broken out in a sweat, and his eyes were nervous, flitting around trying to see the invisible sniper. "If we go up to the wheelhouse we get shot. If we stay down here the boat heaves itself on to the rocks around the point at Old Harry, and we will drown." The cruiser lurched against the swell.

"Can we get to the rudder control without going across the deck?"

"It would take too long, in this sort of sea we have to do something quick."

Without the girl at the helm the boat was slopping and slipping beam-on to the sea. It was a big fibreglass and plywood craft. I imagined it hitting the rocks and changing to shredded wheat at one swipe. The girl had regained consciousness, crying out with the searing pain from her punctured lung.

Fiona knelt down and took off her jacket. She covered the girls upper body and then said to me.

"Jake, throw me over that life jacket. I want to prop her head up into a more comfortable position."

Ferdinand had clambered up the steps from the dive platform and was screaming at me to untie him.

This done, he snaked his way towards the saloon on his belly, reappearing a few seconds later with the one-inch thick; round aluminium tabletop from the main cabin in his arms. How he had managed to lift it with so much brandy inside him, I have no idea. But he had summoned the strength to heave it up the four steps without getting his head shot off, letting it thump heavily onto the floor of wheelhouse and then staying low using it as a shield to get onto the bridge. He rolled it forward and I heard a great echoing clang as one of Harry Caplin's bullets glanced off the metal. Ferdinand was lying full-length on the deck by now, with the lowest part of the boat's wheel in his hand. He spun it round and the boat began to respond.

Through the port windscreen I could see the lethal looking rocks. They were very close, and after each great wave the water ran off the bared and jagged fangs in great rivers that ended their journey back into the sea, creating foaming spume everywhere.

The boat was well into the turn now. I shouted to Ferdinand to come back down; but he yelled, "Do you want to go round and round in a bloody circle?"

He stayed where he was. Again there was a slam of metal hitting metal. The large piece of flat table top came thumping down steps to where I was crouched.

As soon as we were round far enough Ferdinand jammed a pole hook into the wheel. He began to crawl back, but he had left it too late. The change of course that had reprieved the cruiser, sentenced George to almost certain death. With nothing left to protect or shield him, Caplin pumped four rounds into him in quick succession; but with those Zeiss x 8 telescopic sights, one would have done the job.

Fiona shouted something from the other side of the wheelhouse, but with the howling wind, and sea spray now coming through the smashed windscreens, her words were drowned out. All I got was her mouth moving and her right arm waving frantically up and down.

In my crouched position, I had no way of knowing if Harry Caplin was still up on the cliff top. But I soon got my answer as I cautiously went to stand up.

Caplin fired two rounds in quick succession. Both only just missed me, whizzing past my head and ending their journey in the main control console.

The bastards trying to kill us all, I thought, as the instruments disintegrated as the bullets smashed through the flimsy plastic.

I flattened myself against the wet deck and crawled towards Fiona and the unconscious girl. As I got nearer to them, another round slammed into the bulkhead just above me.

"He's trying to disable the Star Dust and kill us into the bargain." Fiona shouted.

"I know, just stay down!" I replied.

Fiona came closer to where I was spread-eagled on my stomach.

"Jake, have you got your mobile phone on you?"

"Yes, why?"

"Give it to me. Quickly." Fiona said.

I handed the phone to her and she immediately started to dial a number.

"Who are you calling?"

The local police. I'm going to ask them to put up a helicopter. It'll be the only chance we have of getting to that psychopath Caplin up on the cliff top.

If they're quick enough they'll catch the bastard red handed.

The next moment. We could hear the thrashing of rotor blades almost above us.

"Surely the police can't have got here that fast." I said.

"It's not the police, look." Fiona pointed to the stern of the boat. It was Harry Caplin at the controls of his own helicopter. He dropped down and hovered about twenty feet above the ocean. Knowing that we could see him, he looked straight toward Fiona and me. The boat's radio crackled, and then Harry's voice came over the loud speaker.

"You should've listened to the little lady, Ace. Letting me go was a big mistake. Anyways, I've got to go now, before the boys in blue arrive. Like I said before, Ace. You have a nice life, now."

He then mock-saluted us before banking the helicopter to the right and rising up into the air. A minute later the police helicopter arrived on the scene.

As we limped back to the shallow water of Studland Bay, Fiona came and stood by my side, she put her hand on my shoulder. Nothing needed to be said. But, we both knew what I'd done by letting Caplin go.

"Your time will come, Harry. Make no mistake about that." I said quietly to myself.

Chapter 32

A dozen spent 7mm-cartridge shells on the cliff-top were the only trace of Harry Caplin by the time we had anchored the Star Dust just off Studland beach. The weather had dragged the cloud base and the barometer reading well down.

I used my mobile phone to call an ambulance, and LJ in London. The girl needed a paramedic quickly. LJ, answered immediately, and I proceeded to give him a brief update of the situation in Dorset. He told me to stay put, and that he would arrange for a local contact to pick me up within the hour. I broke the connection. This would just give me enough time to make my way along the coastal path to Old Harry. When I reached the top of the slope that led up to the cliff-top, I looked back down at the cruiser using my binoculars, the girl was still where I'd laid her with eyes unseeing and her mind in neutral; she was holding George Ferdinand's hand very tightly. She wouldn't let go.

Fiona stayed on the boat and liased with the police. She took the death of George Thomas Ferlind in her stride and wrote it into her report smoothly enough to allow me to escape entanglement and any awkward questions.

After what George had told me, a lot of the unrelated ends began to tie themselves together. Not all of them did, of course, but that was too much to expect. There would always be those inexplicable actions by unpredictable people, but the motives began to show. I knew, for instance, what we would find up at Flackyard's house, but I went anyway.

I told the driver to drop me off around the corner,

entering through the old rusty gate at the side of the house. Inside the furniture was shrouded and my footfalls echoed and creaked round the bookless shelves. The big chandeliers were also covered to protect them. I went downstairs to the cellars, searching for the sort of room that I knew must be there. At the far end of the wide passageway I found what I was looking for. I studied the square shaped panel on the wall for a moment; it had a digital keypad in the centre and a credit card size slot at the top. I knew from experience that only by entering the correct entry number once and inserting a card that matched would anyone be able to open such a heavy oak door. It was just my bad luck that this type of locking system invariably came with automatic lock-down steel shutters that seal all windows and doors in a matter of seconds.

I turned the polished brass handle anyway. It moved easily in my hand.

Pushing gently, the heavy oak door moved silently on its hinges. It was a cold room, painted white. From the low ceilings hung long fluorescent lights on chains. Under these were lines of stainless steel benches. Walking up and down the lines of benches it soon became apparent that this had been a very well equipped workshop and storage area.

In their haste to leave, Flackyard's people had not only neglected to activate the alarm systems, but a lot of equipment had been left behind also.

This wasn't any make shift facility. It was a large air-conditioned strong room of the type that organised crime syndicates build instead of paying corporation tax.

I moved along the benches, looking at the machines and array of electronic calibration equipment. I examined the complex array of ammunition. Some of the bullets looked like sophisticated hollow heads containing, I'd no doubt, various volatile liquids. I didn't, however, find Mr

Robert Flackyard, because he had been gone for some time.

* * *

I called LJ from my mobile phone. I advised him that Jasper Lockhart should be kept under surveillance. Use Vince Sharp and his many gadgets, I suggested. LJ protested that he wouldn't make a very good watcher, but I reminded him that Vince had asked many times for fieldwork of this type and that he was the best in the business at eavesdropping. Anyway, we all have to learn at sometime. "Suppose Lockhart tries to leave the country?" LJ said.

"I doubt if he will, but if he does try, simply call in a favour and get the police to arrest him," I said patiently.

"On what charge?" LJ asked.

"Try soliciting," I said, and hung up irritably.

Chapter 33

I stepped into the cool air-conditioned environment of Ferran & Cardini. The lift descended to the department quickly and silently. Tatiana was waiting for me as the doors slid back with a heavy looking briefcase.

It looked like the beginning of a week of hard work; we had a meeting with the various people involved with the new European Network. It went as all initial meetings go; some individuals requiring definitions, and others wanting copies of memos that had long since been put through the shredder.

LJ and I seemed to make a reasonably good team; I turned major objections into minor objections and LJ's speciality was ironing out the minor objections. As Ferran & Cardini were a commercial profit-making organisation, I thought that the discussions were successful enough but I could see that Clive Bingham-Carter from MI6 was going to cause a few problems for us. He insisted upon all kinds of procedural rigmarole, hoping that LJ would slip up or get annoyed, or both. But LJ had been weaned on this sort of thing. He let Bingham-Carter talk himself to a standstill and then paused a long time before saying, "Oh yes?" as though he wasn't sure that Bingham-Carter had made his point. Then LJ made his point all over again in careful measured syntax as though speaking to a small child. LJ would rather split a hair on the back of his neck than an infinitive.

* * *

Roberts was a new, young and intelligent graduate

from Cambridge that the Partners had borrowed from MI5, in my absence. He was a tall, good looking twenty six year old who wore tailored suits, went to see plays in small theatres and was apt to use long words where short ones would do. He was sitting at my desk when I entered my office using my computer terminal. I asked him what he thought he was doing. Flushing with embarrassment he stood up and quickly introduced himself. He apologised profusely for being there and informed me that he had been assigned to work for me, for the time being by Mr Levenson-Jones. I put him to work at a vacant computer terminal in the main office; I still wanted to find out more about Oliver Hawkworth and his business dealings. Hawkworth had the best lawyers to weave an intricate web of companies, within companies, within holding companies. It would be a long task.

On Thursday morning Jasper Lockhart phoned from a public call box. Tats took the call and said that I would meet him at the Kensington address that Lockhart gave her at 9.30pm.

I was busy all that afternoon. At 8.00 pm I shut down the terminal on my desk and put my laptop into its case. I'd completed a superficial report of the assignment in Dorset, marking the Poseidon file "closed" and submitted it to LJ for initialling. Using his gold fountain pen he initialled each page without comment then gave the file to Zara, but his eyes never left mine.

* * *

Exotic cars lined both sides of the cobbled street in that part of Kensington.

Number 21 Charlotte Mews had a pearl blue Jaguar convertible parked outside with two men in short sleeved shirts and jeans leaning up against it drinking cold beer out of bottles. I tapped the heavy lion head doorknocker against its polished brass back plate and an attractive young woman wearing a French maid's outfit and mask covering her eyes opened the door. "Please, come in – enjoy," she said. Her voice sounded familiar, although she was attempting a very bad French accent.

"Dancing to the left, booze and smokers straight on and out onto the terrace." She patted me lightly on the arse before disappearing into the packed room of dancers.

There was a dense scrum of smokers and drinkers around the rear of the house; men with gelled hair sticking up in all directions and girls talking about their latest man and how much he was worth. In the corner there was a serious tequila-drinking contest under way and a man attempting to drink a yard of ale.

I reached the big table at the far end. Behind it was a very large man wearing an ill fitting dinner suit and a foul coloured dickey bow.

He said, "There's only gin, vodka, beer and what looks like…" He shook the bottle of cream liquid viciously, "… Bailey's." He held it up to what light there was, and said. "Bailey's" again. A girl with a long cigarette holder and wearing a twenties style outfit said, "I really would recommend my surgeon, he's done wonders for my tits."

I took my drink and wandered off through a doorway into a small but very well equipped fitted kitchen. A girl wearing a cat suit, complete with long tail and painted whiskers on her face, was eating canapés and talking on her mobile phone. I turned around. The girl who liked her tits was now talking about lipo-suction. Nowhere did I see Jasper Lockhart. It was just as crowded outside on the terrace except for a small octagonal summerhouse at the far end of the walled garden.

Inside were three people all dressed in black. The soft music came from a CD player and the gentle fug of reefer smoke drifted around the small dimly lit room. They all turned their heads slowly as I stepped into the open doorway.

One removed its dark glasses. "Jake Dillon, you old rogue, you came after all. Well, don't just stand there, come in. Shut the bloody door, will you, you're letting all this wonderfully mellow air get away."

Jasper Lockhart dismissed his two nubile girl friends, got up and shook my hand vigorously.

"Great to see you, pal," he said in a slurred voice.

"Great party, don't you think?" One of them said as they left.

"Fascinating," I said. He shook his head a couple of times in an attempt to sober up, getting up and throwing open the door to the wooden building he took great lungfulls of fresh air, which seemed to make him feel worse and turned him a strange tint of green. After he had been to the bathroom Jasper Lockhart wanted a word with me. He went out to his car with uncertain steps.

The girl in the French maid's outfit and mask was holding the shoulders of another girl who was being spectacularly ill into a flowerbed.

Chapter 34

"Do you know what?" said Jasper Lockhart once we were seated in his car.

He was looking around the dashboard and under the seats anxiously. I asked what he was looking for. "Listening bugs, old son," he said, switching on the radio.

"What's the problem?" I asked.

"I'm being followed, that's what the problem is," he said.

"Really?" I said.

"Absolutely and without a shadow of a doubt, although I wasn't sure until today. That's when I decided to phone you."

"I don't know why you phoned me," I said. "What can I do?" I paused. "It's gone too far for me to get involved, Jasper."

"Too far?" said Jasper Lockhart. "What's gone too far?"

"Look, I don't really know too much about it," I said, like I'd said too much already.

"You mean the business down in Dorset, don't you? All that stuff with George and that chap Robert Flackyard?"

"What do you think?" I said. "You've been dabbling in some pretty heavy stuff. Can't Hawkworth help you?"

"He says he can't get involved. What's going to happen now?"

I tapped him on the shoulder and said, "You know I could get into some seriously deep shit for just talking to you."

Jasper Lockhart said, "Yeah," about four times.

After what I considered to be an appropriate length of silence I said, "It was because you tried to con me that started to make things drop into place you know," I said casually. "When you became part of an official MI5 enquiry," I dropped in for good measure.

Jasper Lockhart repeated the word five a few times, changing it from a statement to an interrogative. "What you mean is that they'll come for me during the night?"

"Well," I said, "that's a little melodramatic, this is England after all. Things like that only happen in films and spy books, don't they? No. These guys are good, I mean really good. Your death will almost certainly look like a traffic accident or something along those lines."

"You are joking, I hope." Jasper Lockhart's voice came like an echo of long ago and he leaned heavily against the driver's door. He had passed out. The girl with the French maid's outfit left her friend and asked if she could help.

"My friend isn't feeling well," I told her. "It's probably just too much to drink."

"Perhaps a glass of water would help." It took her a long time to push her way through to the kitchen. In the meantime Jasper Lockhart shook his head and breathed heavily. "I'm sorry," he said, "you probably think I'm a complete prat."

"Something like that, but don't worry about it, we've known each other far too long for it to be a problem," I said, "I know exactly how you feel." I knew all to well.

"You're all right, you know that, Jake," he said. "But what should I do, go to the police, make a statement and try to bargain my way out of this mess? Hell, I'm just small fry. Those fuckers Hawkworth and Flackyard are the ones." He closed his eyes at the thought.

I was about to say that a statement at the appropriate

time would be sensible, when the French maid came back with a jug of water.

"There aren't any glasses left in the kitchen," she said, thankfully without the French accent.

She offered the water to Jasper Lockhart, who said, "She's one of them," in a shrill, excitable voice and lost consciousness again.

"Is the really big guy with the tux, Australian bush hat and the foul coloured dickey bow still serving at the bar?" I asked.

"Yes," said Frenchy, adding. "He says that this is the driest do he's ever been to."

"Would you do me an immense favour and take him this note, oh and tell him that he can go home now."

"OK," she said and went back inside to the party.

A minute later Vince Sharp came through the doorway. His seventeen stone frame waddled over to the Jaguar. "Looks like our baby will be out for the count, do you want a hand getting him to bed?" Vince asked.

"No, you get off, I'll get his friends to put him to bed. I'll see you tomorrow."

"Oh and Vince, please take off the bow tie, it's making me feel very sick."

Chapter 35

If you ever get clear away from a dangerous or difficult situation by abandoning a large number of your personal possessions, you may feel a compelling need of certain things you have left behind, like your seventy-foot luxury power cruiser. Don't send for them, because that's how Robert Flackyard was traced.

I asked Zara for a box file and wrote "Fulcrum" on the front. Into that I put copies of Jasper Lockhart's bank statements and his written statement that he had made the day after the party. A precaution in the event that he or possibly I met with an unfortunate accident.

I secured the file with the firm's official seal and locked it into the top drawer of my desk. So far it had no file number and had not been entered onto the firm's computerised system. It was my little secret, for now.

Vince Sharp had left a file on my desk, so I flicked open the front cover.

The report was thorough, with satellite images to support the maps laid out before me. Flackyard's yacht was moving south and looked as though it had made good time, sailing through the Bay of Biscay and the Gulf of Cadiz. I wondered - was she heading for the Strait of Gibraltar and on into the Mediterranean or would she sail on down to the coast of Africa?

That evening, LJ called me into his office for a drink. He had been harassed to hell and back, organising the administrative protocol for the New Network, so much so that I'd hardly seen him all week. I knew that Bingham-Carter was still making things difficult for us. Bingham-Carter, mid 40s, divorced twice, propped up the corner of the bar at his club, twenty-four hours a day. What he was giving up in food he was gaining in influence. Bingham-Carter was trying to get certain Foreign Office people to assert their considerable power on the Partners of Ferran & Cardini. His motive was quite clearly to get control of the New Network for M16, and more importantly for himself. LJ said that, at the meeting I had missed, he had taken the liberty of putting me up as convening chairman of the field-training group.

I told him that I might be away for a few days. LJ said he thought that might be the case. He blew his nose loudly and smiled dryly from behind his big handkerchief. "I'll convene the meeting and you delegate your vote to me."

"It will be all right."

"Thank you, that would help me enormously," I said, and drank to his success. LJ came from behind his desk and stood in front of the large portrait of Winston Churchill. Taking hold of a corner he gently raised it and then stepped back to satisfy himself that it was straight.

"Did you check with Interpol about Harry Caplin?" I asked him.

LJ gave a histrionic sigh. "Don't you ever give up?" he said. "You are quite impossible, Caplin has never been, and is not our concern. Miss Price has been assigned, I am told, to the team searching for Caplin and Flackyard, somewhere in southern Europe." We stared at each other for a minute or so.

"Oh, very well, I'll see if I can find out where they are." He closed his eyes, gulped down his claret and leaned back in his chair like a worn-out roll of carpet. He said, "That liaison officer from Scotland Yard - what's he called, Jefferson - was on the phone today. He said they can't keep Jasper Lockhart locked up and available for questioning unless they're considering charges."

"I'll clear that in a couple of days," I said. "He'll

make no complaint; he wants to be kept in custody – he feels safe there."

LJ said, "Look, I realise it's not yet quite over, but I'm feeling a certain amount of pressure from upstairs in respect of this Poseidon business in Dorset."

"No! You look," I said, "I didn't ask you to hold the door open. But don't start closing it now that I'm half-way through."

LJ got up and paced the office, his hands clasped behind his back as he walked up and down the room. "Careful not to slam it on my fingers," he told me, "there's a good boy. Oh, I know that you have a thousand reasons for not slipping up, but remember what the man who fell off of the high building said to a resident on the seventeenth floor as he fell past him. So far so good." LJ smiled blandly.

"Thank you for those kind words of encouragement," I said.

LJ walked across to his map cupboard, and his secret stash of alcohol. He spoke over his shoulder. "There are certain things which if I know about I must act upon. As it is I'm happy enough to leave them. But if you get it wrong I'll tear you to shreds and anyone you try to protect will be torn up with you."

"What about another drink?" I said.

"Well, old son, it's a jolly good thing you like sangria," replied LJ self-consciously.

LJ thought I was heading for the land of flamenco dancers and sherry.

Chapter 36

As a king watches over his kingdom, the stunning Boquer mountain range overlords the port of Pollensa at the northernmost tip of the island of Mallorca.

Along the streets, which lie between pastel coloured buildings, a shabby old mongrel, its muzzle grey with age, yawns scratching behind its ear while it lies in the shade of a doorway, taking pleasure from the cool sea breeze.

Tourists of all ages casually stroll along the waterside pine walk; the aroma of mouth-watering local fish dishes waft out from the many fine restaurants along the tree-lined natural harbour. People sit, laughing and drinking, letting the burden of modern life float away while they absorb the mellow atmosphere. Children play tirelessly on the beach and splash around in the crystal clear water of the bay.

Café Maritimo is a bright, vibrant, espresso temple. Cups clatter, machines hiss and the young waiters move with ease across the white marble floor. A young English couple with a baby, argue about why he stayed out all night partying. The large television screen inside is showing a football match, young men and women stand around drinking, suddenly jumping up excitedly and cheering when a goal is scored. From the supermercado along the street there is a continual flash of red neon and an advertisement for San Miguel beer floats in mid air above the door.

I sat near the front of the café, outside, where I could see the street and the harbour. I ordered some hot chocolate, and watched a tall African man in his late twenties, dressed in a shabby dinner suit, perform magic tricks for the passers-by. I sipped the sweet cinnamon chocolate for which the café is famous. The magician man's box of props had stickers all over it from many different countries; presumably places he had performed in.

He delved amongst the silk scarves and playing cards and offered the crowd that had gathered one last trick, which was to conjure up half a dozen white doves from apparently nowhere. The children who were sat in a small half circle at the front of the crowd clapped with zealous amazement, and sheer joy as the birds appeared and fluttered above their heads. At the end of the show, their parents were press-ganged into digging deep into their pockets for some coins to throw into the magician's top hat.

A young officer of the Spanish Navy wearing an immaculate white uniform, got up from his table to the side of me, and went over to the magician. After some haggling, payment was given in advance and then the tall slim African sauntered over to where the officer and his girlfriend were sitting. He started to perform card tricks, much to the amusement of the officer, and somewhat to the embarrassment of the young raven-haired woman. It was 7.30pm. I looked at the menu. I was worried in case something might have gone wrong. With the stakes this high, it would be a disaster if anything went astray.

After their private show, the magician bowed to the young couple and left them and moved amongst the other people in the Café, showing off his talent.

And then came to sit opposite me at my table. Smiling, he politely asked, in perfect English, if I'd like to see a trick or two.

"Why not?" I said.

He sifted through his box again, pulling out three plain brown envelopes.

He placed them on the shiny metallic surface in

front of me. "What you've got to do is simply pick the correct envelope. Inside one of them is a ten Euro note," he said in a deep, cultured voice, gesturing with a sweep of his up turned palm over the envelopes.

"How do I know which is the correct one?" I asked.

"You don't," he replied. "But if you choose wisely you will be a richer man," he added.

I could easily have said no to this childish challenge, but instead I said, "OK," and after a moment tapped the middle envelope with my forefinger.

The magician put the other two envelopes back into his box.

I picked up the envelope and tore it open. Inside was a ten Euro note and with it a small piece of paper folded in two. I left the paper inside and pulled out the money.

"You have chosen wisely, my friend, use your new found wealth carefully," he said, beaming a dazzling white smile at me. He closed his box of tricks, and was gone, as quickly as he had arrived. I went to the toilet and read the note. On the small folded piece of paper it simply read, "Calle de Jaime and Avenida del Pinar. Corner 8.20pm." Both the arguing couple and the navy officer and his girlfriend were gone by the time I returned to my table.

The on shore wind coming off the bay whistled down the Avenida del Pinar and the night was suddenly cold, the way it sometimes goes in the Balearics.

A new Toyota land cruiser 4x4 rolled down on me like the day of judgement, all headlights and chrome bull bars. I got in and sank into the black leather upholstery; the seat wrapped around me as the large vehicle wound its way south through small streets towards the residential area overlooking the harbour and the Bay of Pollensa.

Cats sat around with nothing to do and stared

insolently back into the headlight beams. The driver parked the 4x4 with meticulous care and killed the lights. He opened a wrought iron gate for me and took me up to a first floor room overlooking the front of the villa. Someone was already in the room, silhouetted in the narrow rectangle of window studying the harbour berths opposite with an enormous pair of binoculars fixed onto a tripod. The black clothed-figure moved to one side.

On the far side of the marina a party was in full flow on board a large yacht.

Men in swim shorts and girls in bikini bottoms were lounging around on the top and rear decks drinking and laughing, while others were diving and jumping into the water. A small group of men were singing lewd rugby songs, smoking, drinking and then singing loudly again. I applied my eyes to the soft rubber eyepieces of the binoculars. They were trained on the main cabin windows of a seventy five-foot luxury cruiser berthed next to the party boat.

The small Armourlite logo in the bottom left hand corner of each window, denoting that one-inch thick blast proof glass surrounded the main cabin area, was just discernible with the powerful lenses. The scene beyond was bright and clear. The 4x4 had been parked carefully with good reason. The Toyota had more spotlights, fog lights and lens work than a fly's eye.

Now I realised that the three large spotlights on the chrome bull bar at the front were still switched on. Through the night sight infrared binoculars I saw three men opening a number of wooden crates and taking out what looked like aluminium boxes about the size of a suitcase. Polyfoam packing littered the floor. Into my ear a feminine and familiar voice said, "They must be nearly finished. They've been at it for nearly an hour." It was Fiona Price. Working with the crime squad on the island.

"They're not going to leave those in there," I said.

It wasn't feasible on board the cruiser, or was it? I moved aside for Fiona to resume her observation.

"What brings you to Mallorca, stud, I thought you had been warned off big time?"

"I have, and between you and me, I'll probably get the sack when the Partners find out. But what the hell, this son of a bitch Flackyard has got to be stopped. Otherwise he's going to walk away, and start up all over again somewhere else," I replied. "So tell me, who does this villa belong to?" I asked.

"A friend of my father owns it; he's in Australia for six months."

"When did you get here," I asked her casually.

"About ten hours ago I was sent out here after Interpol emailed my boss with a positive identity match for Robert Flackyard. Would you believe it, he was caught on a CCTV when he arrogantly went into a bank to change some traveller's cheques? We liased with the local police department in Palma who sent out an internal bulletin to local officers all over the Island with Flackyard and Caplin's photographs on the front page. The next thing we get is another email, this time from the police here in Pollensa, giving us the address of Flackyard's private villa. Like your Vince Sharp, we've been tracking Flackyard's yacht all the way from England until it docked in the early hours of yesterday morning right over there."

"Who are the hired help?" I asked.

"Two along for the ride, Jason Stewart, he's a DC with the Met and an absolute genius with the surveillance stuff. As well as Antonio Carreras he's with the local plain clothes squad here on the island..." She nodded her head towards the boat, which held Flackyard and his aluminium suitcases.

"Perhaps your young DC would like to make us all some strong coffee," I suggested.

"Sure," said Fiona.

"I have a feeling that we're in for a long wait," I said.

After a lifetime of travelling around, one tries to be prepared for transient discomfort. A good quality jacket will always keep you warm on the coldest of nights, and a pair of soft nubuck shoes always go into the hand luggage, as they can be worn for either comfort or running, should the need arise. I had both of these things - at my apartment in London.

Fiona and I took one hour each at the binoculars and Stewart took the Toyota to the other end of the marina to cover the side door. I don't know what he was expected to do if they went out that way, but there he was.

At 3.30am in the morning, or what I call night, Fiona woke me.

"Jake, wake up. A big white van has just pulled up at the entrance gates to the marina berths," she said. By the time I had got to the binoculars they were moving the aluminium boxes off of Flackyard's boat, down the pontoon towards the van.

"Do you have a gun with you?" I asked Fiona.

"No, I don't," she said. "I hadn't considered the need for one, or the possibility that Flackyard would move the merchandise elsewhere."

Half an hour later and with the van sagging on its rear springs, the two burly looking men locked the back doors and drove away. We stayed a safe distance behind them as we followed the two men through the Mallorcan countryside, daylight fast approaching over our shoulder. It wasn't a long drive to the small airfield.

* * *

As another Mallorcan dawn rose across the horizon, the tired night sky faded into the hazy pink watercolour of early morning. In the distance the twin engines of a Cessna aeroplane turned its nose south southwest, making its way unhindered towards the horizon.

"A Cessna." I thought of Flackyard's personal profile; it had to be a Cessna. The three of us watched from the grass runway because none of the four charter planes were available at this early hour. Jason Stewart beat on the door of the padlocked offices, using the 'f' word three or four times, but it got us no nearer to what was in side those cases that were now at three thousand feet and still climbing. It was 5.24am, June 2nd.

Chapter 37

"This is an outrage against civilised behaviour, have you any idea what time it is?" I was asked in true Castilian Spanish.

A rather rotund and stout balding man in a brown habit barred my way.

"Step aside, fatty," I said; "I haven't got time for niceties."

Fiona and Stewart followed me into the cold empty, echoing hallway.

"Go and get your boss out of bed," I said, "and tell him that his presence is required downstairs urgently, and that doesn't mean in half an hour's time."

"Who shall I say is calling, sir?" said the stuffy little man in the brown habit, aggressive, but doubting.

I wrote on the back of an envelope, 'Jake Dillon. Minutes are vital.' And waited while he took it upstairs.

My treatment of a brother of the monastery of San Sebastian was causing Fiona Price and Jason Stewart physical pain and the sight of the good father in pyjamas was almost too much for them both.

We were shown into a bright airy room, quite the opposite of the hallway.

Floor to ceiling bookcases made from seasoned oak surrounded us on three sides. Every shelf was filled with books, some rare, some first editions, but all were in alphabetical order. The room was warm from the sunlight streaming through the tall elegant French doors and windows that ran along an entire elevation. Stepping out onto the wooden balcony, the cold early morning air along with a stiff breeze took my breath away. At around

400 metres above sea level the view from this magical place really is magnificent, and the mountain air even in the summer is crisp and fresh.

"Jake Dillon, what are on earth are you doing here on Mallorca?"

"Now, Father, you know that if I told you that I'd have to kill you, and I most certainly have no wish to do that to one of my oldest friends." Father Pedro Ramon Sancho came across the room and gave me a tight hug as two people who have not seen each other for some time do.

Introductions done, the tall bookcase on the far wall slid back to reveal a hidden panel with an array of colour monitors, keyboards and electronic displays full of listening and recording equipment. These are the eyes and ears of Ferran & Cardini in Europe and can watch and listen virtually anywhere and at anytime using satellites that happen to be in the right place at the right time. This has been particularly useful to the firm over the years, especially with some of the more covert activities of the department. But also when negotiating deals of a more delicate nature or avoiding international currency and stock market fluctuations, Father Pedro Ramon Sancho and his many guiding stars have shown us time and time again the true path to tread.

An American satellite was just coming into range of the coast of Spain and the Balearic Islands. "When did the plane leave the airstrip?" asked Father Pedro as he positioned himself in front of one of the flat screen monitors.

"It was 5.15am. No more the twenty minutes ago," I replied quickly. "If we assume it has an airspeed of 150m.p.h. and stays on that south-south-west heading, we'd expect it to be half way between here and Morocco. Wouldn't you say, Father?"

There was a long silence while Father Pedro,

looking intently at the monitor watched the satellite rotate its onboard spy camera and give us a bird's eye view of the Spanish coast line from Barcelona right down to Gibraltar. The North African coast showed clearly at the bottom of the screen. Father Pedro typed in a number of command sequences. An overlay of all the light aircraft flight plans for the region now covered the screen, and one of these thin lines showed darker than the rest.

"The dark line is presumably our Cessna?" I said over his shoulder.

"Possibly, but at this stage it's difficult to be positive, Jake. I have given the computer all of the information to hand. That is to say, the airstrip where it took off from, the time that it departed and of course the heading that it left on. Now, what we have here is the official history overlay of all light aircraft movement in the area for around that time. Even if your man hadn't filed a flight path, it would still show up here, as this shows everything that has been and is in the air up to this point in time. Give me a moment and I will have the real time imaging direct from the mainframe of air traffic control at Palma International Airport. Unofficially, of course."

"Of course, father," I agreed, nodding soberly

The lines moved around the screen. Some altered to new headings while some disappeared completely as they left the Palma control zone.

"The line that is still showing darker than the others, I would say, is most likely to be our Cessna. It fits the profile almost exactly. But wait a minute, it's changing course." The small blip was turning, the Father typed more commands, and this time most of the lines disappeared, leaving just half a dozen all heading in roughly the same direction.

"Look here Jake, this is very interesting. Our Cessna has changed course towards the Spanish mainland. It looks like they're heading into the Seville air traffic control zone. This may get tricky if they keep on this heading. We may even lose them in the thick of all the commercial air traffic in that area."

"Sorry Father, but that's not one of the options. Get the satellite image enlarged over that region," I said patiently.

"Now, merge the flight path of the Cessna on your screen with the satellite image on this screen." He quickly typed in the command. The dark line now showed on the live satellite image.

"So we should be able to pinpoint the Cessna's position just as long as the satellite stays within range."

"That is correct Jake, but I can do better than that. Watch, learn and be amazed, my old friend."

The good Father tapped away at his keyboard, until the image that filled the screen was that of a solitary twin engine aircraft, high above the cloud level and travelling along the dark superimposed flight path. "The satellite will track the plane for as long as it is in range," he said. "I'd say that we have thirty minutes, maximum," he added.

We were brought freshly baked croissants and coffee. The manner of the rotund monk who had let us in hadn't changed, he was still aggressive and doubting. We all waited in silence as the Father did his stuff; the small plane eventually changed course. The Cessna was one of the larger twin engine planes, with a forty-foot wingspan. It was apparent that it was 'coasting' on a pre-determined course, away from the main commercial routes.

"I would say, Jake, that given the flight path, the aircraft is on auto-pilot," said Father Pedro.

"What do you think he's going to do?" I asked.

It was Jason Stewart who answered. "I'd say that he's probably 'coasting', he'll continue on that bearing until he reaches the coast. Then he'll drift along the coast until he recognises Marbella. Then the pilot will set himself a new course, using wind direction and velocity according to how far he's off his original course. That is quite an old plane by today's standards and he probably has only very basic navigational aids, you see."

"Will he cross the coast at Marbella?"

"No, he'll go for maximum cover. It will more than likely be a little bit east of Malaga."

"Jake, we're just about to lose the satellite, it will be out of range in two minutes. But we'll still be able to track the Cessna by using the link with the air traffic control system,"

"OK, Father. You've been more than helpful and I'm sorry for dragging you out of bed, but your job isn't quite finished yet. I must know where that plane lands. Let the computer continue to plot its course and call me on my mobile phone immediately it touches down with the location. We're going back to that airstrip to question anyone who can or will tell us where Flackyard is heading and to find a plane fast enough to get us to wherever that Cessna is going."

In the meantime Fiona had slipped out and had brought the 4x4 round to the side entrance of the monastery.

Chapter 38

Marrakech, the old pink city with its narrow streets, lies coiled in the shadow of the High Atlas Mountains like a viper on a bed of rumpled hessian. By June the tourist season is in full swing, although this fantastic city is best-visited early summertime when the heat is still bearable. In the bars of the big white hotels of the Ville Nouvelle district, drinkers steadily ruin their livers, and wallets get a hammering in the souvenir shops of the Medina, the heart and soul of this mystical city.

In the afternoon heat the bustling square of the Djemaa is crowded with people who seek entertainment; they gather round the many storytellers, acrobats and musicians. American and European tourists stroll around the Koutoubia mosque, visible from practically anywhere in Marrakech.

The call to prayer ricochets down the tortuous labyrinthine alleys of the old Arab quarter, quivering through the lemon and orange groves and out across the dusty walled town. Overhead, interwoven matting squeezes sunrays like orange pips and transforms the dried mud into dazzling patterns. Wispy tentacles of smoke rise through the dusty air from small fires, giving the beams of sunlight tangible dimensions. Sliced kidney crackles in aromatic cedar smoke. Men from all over congregate here, those with black-enamel faces from Timbuktu crowd together with light-skinned Berbers and ruddy-faced men from Fez in the narrow thoroughfares.

Outside the riad where we had settled the crowds moved back as an old black Mercedes saloon came to a halt. It had darkened privacy windows.

The occupants got out of the vehicle and knocked hard on the heavy wooden door.

No sooner had our gracious host's manservant announced "A gentleman to see you" than he was unceremoniously brushed aside by a short burst of Arabic.

The three men entered the riad's courtyard and through double doors to the palatial room beyond.

Two of them were dressed in black suits and very dark sunglasses. The third man wore a white linen suit and soft red fez over a round brown face.

His moustache, although sad, was well cared for, and a large nose drove a wedge between his small eyes. He tapped the nose with a silver-topped cane. In fact, as he stood before us, he looked like something dreamed up by Hollywood. He spoke:

"My name is Hassan, Youssef Hassan of the Moroccan Internal Affairs Bureau. I would like to welcome you and your friends to our beautiful country. The fruit is succulent and plump on the trees. The date is moist and the snow is still crisp and firm on the top of our mountain slopes. We hope you will stay long enough to take advantage of the many wonders of our land."

"Yes," I said. I watched his two colleagues. One opened the fly screen and spat into the street, the other riffled through my papers, which lay on the table. I'd had dealings with Hassan and his department on a previous assignment. He was not a man to mess with.

"May I ask - Mr Dillon, what is the purpose of your visit is here in Marrakech on this particular occasion? Of course you must consider yourselves the guests of my department. Whatever you wish, it will be arranged and naturally we hope you will have a most pleasurable stay in our country."

"You know what we European capitalists are like, Hassan, all work, work, work."

"Without capitalism, Mr Dillon, I would most

certainly be out of a job," he said while snorting a laugh down his nose.

One of Hassan's sidekicks was looking through the wardrobe and the other was polishing his shoe with a handkerchief. Overhead I heard the whine of a jet engine.

"Yes," I said.

"I am, of course, fully aware why you and your friends are here. You are, how do you say, on the trail of the multi millionaire entrepreneur playboy Mr Robert Flackyard. Am I correct?"

"You are very well informed, Hassan, and you are quite right, we are keen to have a little chat with Mr Flackyard." I said.

"So, as with anyone who breaks the law, my country is most enthusiastic that the criminal is apprehensive."

"I know exactly what you mean." I said, smiling to myself.

Hassan turned and walked up to Fiona, "I am told by your superior, Miss Price, that you intend to make the arrest of this person and any associates that may be with him here in Marrakech, is this true?"

Fiona was quick to say, "No, that is not true, Mr Hassan, but you are right, it is Robert Flackyard that we have followed to Marrakech. We're hoping that he can help us with our enquiries, that's all. I am currently investigating an associate of Mr Flackyard, a Mr Harry Caplin, and American. It is this gentleman that we wish to apprehend, Mr Hassan."

"Ah, those famous English words of Scotland Yard, 'able to assist those in their enquiries,'" Hussan, said it again for practice. He stopped twirling his cane for a moment. He leaned close and said. "Then before you make your arrest, you tell me because it may not be permitted."

"We'll certainly tell you, Hassan," I said, "but Miss Price and Mr Stewart are here under special license and by the kind permission of your Government."

"They will be very unhappy if you do not permit."

Hassan looked perplexed, to say the least.

"So," he said, "we shall liase again soon."

"OK," I said.

"Meanwhile," said Hassan, "I have transported your colleague from the airport. Your colleague Mr Vincent Sharp."

Hassan shouted some Arabic, and one of the black suited policemen drew a pistol. Hassan bellowed very loudly using one or two very rude Anglo-Saxon words. The young man put away the gun with a shamefaced expression and went downstairs to get Vince out of the dusty black Mercedes.

"Your friend is a specialist for the lady investigator?" he said, tapping his nose with the silver tip of the cane once again.

"Yes," I said.

"I think I am recognising his face, your friend."

Vince came through the door wearing his Australian bush hat, a billowing bush shirt, as big as a tent covering his seventeen stone hulk, and trousers with dirt and dust all over them.

"Then I shall leave you in peace," said Hassan.

"Allah goes with you," I said.

"See you around," said Hassan; he tucked a smile under his sad moustache.

The Mercedes hooted its way up the narrow street.

Chapter 39

As Hassan had said, it was a country full of wonders. That evening we went to the Medina, searching out cafés to drink sweet tea and sample some of the local food. We sat outside wrapping skewered meat, sizzling hot from the spit, into rich coarse bread and discussed the various options open to us.

Vince went through a plan that he thought could be simply put into action the following day and roughly sketched the layout of Flackyard's house here in Marrakech. The crowds had thickened, and the lines of food stall vendors and cooks advertised their skills like chanting auctioneers to those seeking sustenance.

Vince explained at length that his plan would require precise timing, and a head for heights. Storytellers and musicians had arrived, while fortune-tellers revealed the secrets of one's destiny for the price of a cooked meal.

Acrobats, contortionists and clowns entertained the crowds. Snake charmers, dancers and boxers performed for gathering knots of passers-by. But amidst the cacophony of noise and the rising tide of odours, sweet and foul, to assail the nostrils of the medieval town square, our beds and the need for sleep beckoned.

The next day Fiona and I visited Robert Flackyard.

He wasn't a cheerful criminal like Harry Caplin, or a sad fanatic like George Ferdinand. Here was a man who had a special kind of manipulative and devious brain. An intellect that had no bounds, and a conscience that did not exist.

Flackyard's residence was a traditional Riad, in

the old Arab quarter of Marrakech. The narrow lane that led to it was barely five feet wide between the other ancient dwellings that pressed in on both sides. We entered through a mysterious door set in the age-worn and blank white wall. Once inside the hidden courtyard, high wrought iron gates made shadow pictures on the hot tiles. A small red and yellow songbird high on the wall sang a short cadenza about how it wanted to escape from its tiny bare wooden cage.

Inside was cool and calm. Flackyard sat cross-legged on a fine antique carpet reading a copy of the Times newspaper. Other carpets lined the walls and behind them bright-coloured tile work shone with complex Arabic calligraphy. Here and there were large leather Berber cushions and through the dark doorway, just visible at the end of the corridor, a cool green patio; the slim leaves turning to silver swords as the breeze moved them under the hot sun.

Flackyard's features were different, thinner, but he wasn't thinner; he wasn't even different, when I had seen him before he was the part of a wealthy English playboy. But here, in this place he no longer had to portray himself to the world.

"Mr Dillon, Miss Price," he said, continuing to study his newspaper. "Your letter, Miss Price said, 'investigating'"

His voice was booming in the sparsely furnished room.

"Investigating what, exactly?"

"Class A drug manufacturing and distribution in Sandbanks, Mr Flackyard," Fiona told him.

He laughed a course spiteful laugh that was rich with gold.

"Ah, so that's it," he said. His eyes stayed completely calm and still.

"Miss Price works for the Government, Flackyard.

She's assisting Scotland Yard which is involved with an ongoing European investigation in conjunction with Interpol," I said, with the hint of a sneer, "into serious criminals, just like you and Caplin. The arrests so far have been impressive to say the least."

"So what, Mr Dillon – you wouldn't dare try…"

It was my turn to laugh.

"They sound like famous last words," Fiona said.

He shrugged. "What a ridiculous notion, it will be quite impossible to connect me to any illegal activities in any way, Miss Price."

Over Flackyard's shoulder I could see through the window across the patio.

The red and yellow bird was singing. Over the edge of the flat roof came a foot, slowly, waving from side to side looking for a foothold.

"Tell me, Miss Price, who is behind this outrage?" His voice had become hard with a razor sharp edge. "Perhaps it's the Partners of Ferran & Cardini."

"Have they forgotten about the arrangement I have with them regarding a certain currency transaction. After all I'm the only person who can make that possible."

"At Hawkworth's suggestion?" I asked.

Flackyard shrugged. "The fool has it all wrong. He just wouldn't leave it to me to sort out. He always has to interfere."

"I know exactly what he's like," I said.

Fiona, seeing the dangling foot, said. "Please forgive me, Mr Flackyard, but I've not had anything to drink since breakfast, is there any chance of some coffee? I just love the way in which they make their coffee here."

Flackyard clapped his hands twice, the door that we had been shown in through opened, and a servant entered immediately. "Please arrange refreshments for our guests. Of course, I have friends both here, and in England who are very powerful, you know," he added.

"By here you mean Hassan?" I said.

The servant brought a big brass bowl and an ornamental kettle. He set the bowl at Fiona's feet and poured water over her hands slowly and efficiently, then he repeated the process with me. It is still the Muslim custom before food is eaten. I hoped the servant wouldn't turn to Flackyard too quickly. I washed my hands slowly and efficiently. The figure that I had seen on the roof was now suspended from the parapet by both hands.

"Actually, Hassan came to see us yesterday shortly after we arrived," I said casually, trying not to look out of the window. The feet came a few inches lower.

"But, as I told him, I'm here purely as an observer, it's Miss Price who comes here on behalf of the British Authorities. There are few governments that will hinder her, either." The feet sought and found the grille of the first floor window.

"Really," said Flackyard. "How fascinating."

"Absolutely," I said. Flackyard smiled. I finished my hand washing as DC Jason Stewart disappeared through the window above. The servant took the brass hand washing bowl over to Flackyard.

"You are an intelligent man," I said to Flackyard. "You must have known what Caplin and Ferdinand were up to at the house in Sandbanks."

Flackyard nodded.

I said, "So tell me, what were your impressions of Harry Caplin - and of George Ferdinand?"

Flackyard removed his simple but expensive gold wire spectacles, rubbing the bridge of his nose with forefinger and thumb. "Harry Caplin, well let me see, he's witty, physically a little over-aware of himself. Naturally charming in a brash and brutishly unsophisticated way."

"His business?"

"Managed with great care." Flackyard answered immediately, and then paused. "He obeyed what I imagine are the basic rules of the drug trade."

"Really," I said, "What are they?"

"Nations the world over have to be seen to take a hard line against the illegal trading of drugs. But in reality they're all guilty of being two faced about the narcotics industry," he said, adding. "Few law enforcement agencies ever get to arrest those individuals who purchase drugs and then export them to another country. The rules are very simple, Mr Dillon: The first is that you should never sell them in the same country that you buy. Secondly, one should never process in the country where you sell. And the third rule, is to never sell in the country of which you are a citizen."

Given these rules, my thoughts were with Harry Caplin. Fiona was right, he'd fed me a complete pile of bullshit that night in his cellar. The worse thing about it was that I'd fallen for it all. He wasn't using the under belly of the cross channel ferry to bring the raw material in. He was exporting pure heroin over to France.

"Personality?"

"He was to my mind an idealist gone sour," said Flackyard. "To be an idealist in this day and age, it is as well not to be born in America. Men like Caplin go through life acting like criminals, but deceive themselves into believing that they are being persecuted for their ideals."

"What about Ferdinand?" I asked,

Flackyard smiled. "I'm tempted to say that men like George go through life acting like idealists but find themselves treated like criminals; but it would not be exactly true. George was a patriot, and he fell apart when the one thing he loved more than anything else in the world cast him out of the fold, for one indiscretion. Of course I'm referring to his army career and his subsequent court martial and dishonourable discharge. Anything that he finally became was due to the environment through which he passed. He was neither good nor bad; his misfortunes have always been due to the fact that he was always prepared to listen to the other side of the argument. Not a very grievous fault, I would say."

I agreed.

Flackyard said, "And now you want to know why I did nothing to stop these two men plying their disgusting trade. That is why you have followed me, or rather followed my boat."

I nodded.

He said, "My cruiser made extremely good time from England. But you already know that because of your satellite tracking, I've no doubt."

"Unfortunately I knew that a boat of that size would cause a little excitement when it docked, and that's why I chose Puerto Pollensa. It's an area used to seeing luxury craft of that size. But I'd not taken in to account having Miss Price hot on my heels."

Fiona bowed her head.

He said, "I knew that there was a risk of it, but…" He shrugged his shoulders.

"I require the articles in the crates to enable me to fulfil certain obligations."

"What is it that you really want, Mr Dillon? No, please do not answer. Let me guess what it is, and why you have followed me across Europe - Constantine's List?"

"Ah, Constantine's List. Well there's no denying it Flackyard, a lot of very important people would sleep a whole lot better at night if that list were not in existence. But, I'm not so sure now; perhaps there is a much bigger picture to consider?"

I paused. "You say the cases you had unloaded from your boat will enable you to fulfil certain obligations. what are those obligations, Flackyard?"

I paused while I took out of my jacket pocket a folded sheet of paper.

"Yesterday I sent London a number of images taken of those crates on board your boat. They show them being opened and examined by you and your two associates." I paused, just long enough to allow a little more tension to build up, and then added.

"I received a reply by email this morning. Let me read you their findings..."

"...no let's skip to the interesting bit - here we are, says... *'Image 2 received shows military equipment being examined. These weapons are of the laser-guided tank busting type. However it must be stressed that without further evidence to corroborate this, it can only be speculation, although this is based on an in-depth knowledge of this particular type of weapon. Image 4, an exposed crate with packing material removed. Digitally enlarged by four hundred per cent we find that it is without doubt holding automatic machine pistols and ammunition, and image 5, open case, unconfirmed - packages are similar to those used for transporting plastic explosives'"*

I carefully folded the paper, and placed it inside my jacket, taking great care not to let him see the message.

"You come to the point very quickly," said Flackyard. He smiled a great self-satisfied smile and then added, "The military aspects do not interest me at all. The financial investment represented in those crates however is considerable and involves the type of people who you cannot even begin to imagine. Not even in your wildest dreams. So I congratulate your analysts back in London for spotting the weapons. How careless of my associates and me to leave them on show like that. But no matter how interesting this may all be, your digital photographs can be manipulated and changed, so they are completely inadmissible in any court anywhere. This you both know only too well. I will, needless to say, refute most strenuously through my team of lawyers any insinuation or accusation that I am, or my companies are, involved with illegal drug or arms trading." He closed his eyes, rotating his neck back and forth, side to side, in an attempt to relieve his tension.

The servant had brought sweet pancakes with almonds and sugar inside.

He placed them in between the three of us, and Flackyard tucked into the plateful. I was wondering how to handle the next part while keeping an eye open for DC Stewart's exit.

Flackyard leaned towards me. "You've come a long way to see me," he said. Flackyard chewed into a honey cake. "I appreciate that, and I'm duly flattered. I'm given to understand in fact, that your peers, Mr Dillon, hold you in high regard. Well, whether you come here offering good or threatening ill does not change the compliment you pay me. I shall however give you a piece of advice to take back to your superiors: To meddle in my business is an extremely hazardous pastime." I thought of taking that message back with me. I imagined walking into LJ's office and saying to him, Flackyard wants you to know that meddling in his business will be extremely bad for your health.

He continued to eat the honey cake, and when he'd finished he dabbed the corners of his mouth with a silk napkin. Looking up, he spoke at both of us.

"It has taken over twenty years to form my connections at the highest level."

"I'm not talking about the here today, gone tomorrow politicians. They are two a penny, and very easy to bribe. No I'm talking about the real people who matter, and who actually run the British Government. People who are able to influence and manipulate easily, because of who or what they are, people like me who see what is happening to our great country." His eyes became almost unfocused as he stared in to nowhere.

"By people, you mean other fascists," Fiona said with rancour.

"The people I'm talking about Miss Price, are those who actually run the country. People with culture and taste, not jumped up trade unionists or rabble-rousers. These are men of breeding who have power running through their veins." Flackyard was looking beyond Fiona in a fixed way. I dared not look round. His sharp, bony fingers were interlocked in front of him and his words were laden with spittle. "You dare to call me a fascist..."

"No," Fiona said nervously, "I called you nothing of the kind."

He hadn't waited for a reply. "Perhaps I am," he shouted, "perhaps I am a fascist! If you think that people like me are fascists, then I'm proud to be what I am."

Two servants were hovering at the door. These were twice the size of the scrawny one that had served us the pancakes! I noticed that these were well over six foot seven of toned oiled muscle dressed entirely in black robes.

"Seize them," Flackyard suddenly commanded.

The two burly servants moved the short distance from where they had been standing, with lightening speed, and pulled us roughly up from the floor.

"Take them down to the cellar," he shouted. "Tie them up and make them very uncomfortable. Perhaps I'll give you six lashes each. Maybe it will teach you to enter my home with a little more respect, and fewer accusations."

His mouth was a foaming mousse of anger.

I said gently, "You're an intelligent man of culture, and you know as well as I do that imprisoning us will serve no useful purpose. It will only calm the anger you feel now. You're not a barbarian."

Flackyard stretched himself to a regal height. "I

will take your message back to those concerned, but I can only do that if we're allowed to leave here unharmed," I coaxed. He looked through me for a moment or so and then gradually brought me into close focus.

He said, "And it's only because of this that you shall leave here unharmed, Mr Dillon." He was speaking a little more quietly now. I caught the scrawny servant's eye and he gave a slight twitch of the shoulders that may have been a shrug.

After being released from the grip of the black robed manservants, Flackyard came over and shook my hand gravely. He said, "I apologise for my sudden outburst. It is unforgivable that I lost my temper. Please accept my sincere regrets at such behaviour. Perhaps it would be possible for me to see the message that your London office sent you?"

"The message? I'm afraid not. But you can have a look at this if you like." I pulled out from my inside jacket pocket the folded piece of paper that I'd used earlier and handed it to Flackyard.

He took it from me and walked away to the other side of the room, unfolding the small square of paper as he went. As he turned to face me, I saw the fire in his eyes flare, but the self-control was securely in place as he came and handed it back, folded once again. Without another word, we were shown out into the brilliant sunshine of Marrakech.

"What was that all about," asked Fiona.

I handed her the folded piece of paper as we walked back down the narrow side street towards our hire car.

"But - it's blank?"

Chapter 40

"Delicious," said Vince, "absolutely melts in your mouth."

It was perfectly true. The pastries and cakes in the little café were superb and among the some of the best I've ever tasted.

"Did DC Stewart get it?" I asked quietly.

"Oh yes," said Vince. He tapped the leather rucksack on his lap.

"Went like a dream. Just like I said it would. An astonishingly simple thing to get into. The people who make shoddy safes like that really should be locked up. It only took young Stewart forty-five seconds to open it up! But, although this must seem immodest, he did have the benefit of me talking him through the whole process with the bluetooth earpiece I gave him. This obviously made the whole job much easier, and of course we also had the added bonus of being able to use the Black Widow."

"Black Widow, what's that?" asked Fiona, leaning forward and lowering her voice to just above a whisper.

Vince lowered his voice conspiratorially. "The Black Widow, my dear, is a real piece of hi-tech gadgetry. Only got it last week through a chap I know in Brighton. Who, thinking about it, is a very strange and definitely unsavoury character with almost white hair and very red eyes, but he does know his stuff." Vince always got excited when he was talking about gadgets, especially those that were illegal.

"This Fiona." He held up a black flat box-like object about six inches square, "is the latest professional's delight, direct from America. It uses X-ray images and magnetic impulse energy to re-align the tumblers, all you have to do is stick it straight onto the front of the safe. The rest, as they say, is history." He took another fresh seed cake and devoured half of it in one mouthful.

"You did make the call?" I asked.

"Of course I did, I used the public phone in a near by hotel and dialled the boss's unofficial direct line, like you wanted. LJ picked it up almost immediately as luck would have it. I told him that the meeting had gone as expected with no hitches and that we would be moving to another location imminently. Advised that the target 'Hudson' has been approached with success in Marrakech, and should be eliminated from the picture as soon as was physically possible. LJ confirmed that he understood what had to be done and hung up." He smiled, "Do you think that Hussan will think Hudson means Hussan when he intercepts the call?"

"Only unless he's more stupid than I think he is." I replied.

"I know for a fact that his department is in charge of call monitoring. That means every call made from a public telephone is routed through a central computer system."

"This is programmed to do the work of a thousand people. He'll get the message alright, but he'll never be able to trace where the call was made to."

Vince chuckled in between mouthfuls of honey cake. He'd taken an unreasonable dislike to Hassan and loved the idea of him looking for a non-existent assassin.

"So, how did it go with Flackyard?" asked Vince. "And why are you constantly looking at your watch, Jake? You weren't followed here, were you?"

"No. Stewart is due to collect you in five minutes," I said; it was 1.55 p.m.

"Well I'm sure he'll get here as quickly as he can given the traffic out there."

"Anyway you won't get him here any quicker by interrogating the watch every few seconds. Tell me about your chat with our friend the gunrunner. And please have a honey cake. You are absolutely positive that you weren't followed?"

"Vince for the last time, we weren't followed." I took a honey cake and told Vince about our conversation with Flackyard. "But that's not true," Vince told me at various places in the narrative.

"How do you know it's not true? Either you want me to adapt the conversation, for your entertainment or not." I jested.

"Best liar I know, you are," said Vince with a friendly grin.

"And so he really is connected at the highest level of Government. But he's saying that these influential back room Government boys are all fascists."

"I think that's only the tip of the iceberg, Vince. It's not only the British Government who have been infiltrated over many years but the French, Italian and Germans, along with all the others no doubt and I think it's a lot more sinister than just fascism."

"So if it's not just fascism – what is it?" asked Vince, like he hadn't been running his fat sausage-like fingers through secrets for many years when he was with MI6.

"Look I know this is going to sound a little weird, but it's something that Flackyard said when I had my cosy fireside chat with him at his house in Dorset. While we were talking he made a throw away comment about belonging to a secret society, I think he said something like the New World Order, or something very similar anyway."

Vince spoke as he wiped his mouth with his handkerchief, "Jake, let me tell you, that stuff about a New World Order is not fiction, you know. He's not invented it and seriously, it really does exist. Those who have studied this say it's a conspiracy that originated from an ancient order started in Bavaria in 1755 called the Illuminati. Both Five and Six know all about these guys. If you want my advice I'd leave well alone if I were you, my friend."

"Well I'm not you, Vince, and if I want your advice – I'll give it to you." Although looking a little put out Vince asked, "So what about this report you had back from London of the images you sent. I liked that. What did the message really say?"

I took the folded piece of paper from my inside jacket pocket and handed it to him.

I watched his expression as he unfolded the white A4 sheet.

"It's blank! You crafty bastard," he said.

Jason Stewart pulled up in a cloud of dust at the end of the narrow street. I helped Vince carry his luggage to the car. He squeezed his seventeen stone frame into the front seat of the small saloon. Winding the window down he said, "I'd love to see the face of that Hassan."

"That's exactly what I'm trying to avoid," I said. "I'll see you when we get back to England."

In the café, I opened the leather rucksack that Vince had left for me. Fiona and I looked at the small digital transmitter that could recall the underwater lobster pot. I made a mental note to look up as much information on the Illuminati, when I returned to London

Chapter 41

The long flexible blades of the Sea-king helicopter cut the air above our heads. I tapped the pilot on the arm. "Just one more sweep," I said, "then we'll return to base and try again tomorrow." He nodded.

We dropped towards the heavy sea and I watched the wave-tops, flattened by the downward draught of air from the rotor blades.

"OK, Chief," I shouted over my shoulder. Chief Petty Officer Redfern of the Air-Sea Rescue watch at Portland in Dorset leaned through the door and watched the ocean top.

"Keep her steady, back a bit." Redfern spoke to the pilot through the microphone in his helmet. The pilot obediently brought the helicopter along a reciprocal course.

"Just a floating piece of wood," Redfern's voice came over the intercom.

We moved on to the next square of the search area. Three miles away on the starboard side I could see the English coast around Kimmeridge and Dancing Ledge. Through the grey sea ran black veins as the light fell across the contours of the water. "Too dark now," I said, and Vince switched off the transmitter. The interior of the cabin glowed with the green light of the instrument panel.

It was two long days before our effort was rewarded. We had hours of 'forward a bit' over foam-lashed pieces of flotsam and sliding over for a closer look, only to find a shoal of fish, their scales shimmering in the sunlight just below the surface of the water.

When we made contact, the radio transmitter set on Vince's knees – the one we had stolen from Flackyard's safe in Marrakech – gave a high pitched 'pulse' of response. The pilot held us steady. The wave-crests were inches under us. 'Beep beep': it was emitting a signal to us. Vince was talking over the intercom and I grabbed the diver's rubber-clad arm and tried to go through his instructions all over again in thirty seconds flat.

Redfern tapped my arm and said, "It'll be OK," then like a pantomime genie he disappeared. Hands crossed, face lowered, he hit the water with a splash. Only now did I see the target that he had dived towards.

The specially adapted lobster pot was floating amid the waves, green vegetation from the seabed covering most of it. C.P.O. Redfern had the cable lashed around the large brown cage within a minute. The winch operator began to haul it up and brought it splashing and dripping into the cabin of the helicopter. A number of small crabs and seaweed spilled out onto the floor as it rolled around the cramped cabin.

LJ had done his stuff with the top brass. When the helicopter got back to base everything was ready and waiting – even a ration of rum for the still wet C.P.O. Redfern. Vince and I were housed in one of the Air-Sea Rescue workshops with the inner cylinder laid out on the bench when the Station Commander came in to ask if there was anything more we required.

Four bolts had to be cut off, but that was only to be expected after being submerged for prolonged periods of time in salt water. The light alloy panel came free to reveal a large compartment and gave access to two small ballast tanks the propulsion motors and the remote control circuitry.

Vince took a closer look around the compartment using a fibre optic camera linked up to his laptop so as to make sure that the cylinder wasn't booby-trapped.

"Very interesting," he said. "Bloody clever, this," he added.

"What is it?" I asked impatiently.

"It looks like whoever designed this cylinder decided to build in a nasty little explosive device, I'd say just enough to blow the front of your face and hands off, but not enough to kill you. Obviously anyone tampering with it, and who didn't know the correct procedure for dismantling the thing. Would I'm afraid get a very nasty surprise."

"Can you deactivate it?" I asked.

"Give me two minutes, after which I'll either be lying in a pool of blood on the floor or wiping the sweat off of my brow and supping a large glass of that rum over there," said Vince with a thin smile.

He rendered it safe within minutes.

"Well, that was easier than I'd expected." Vince held up the flat piece of plastic.

"What we have here, mate, looks like a common or garden processor chip."

"For your laymen's mind, that means that it has been programmed with a number of prearranged instructions. Nothing unusual about that, I hear you say, but then this little chap here," he pointed to a part of the microprocessor.

"I've only seen this once before, and that was on-board a Russian nuclear missile." He saw the look on my face. "Oh don't worry, it's nothing sinister – well, not now anyway, all it does is allow it to think for itself once activated."

"But what the hell is it doing in a lobster pot? Anyway, what they've done by the looks of it, is configure it so that every twenty-four hours it would relay a simple message to the motors and ballast tanks to take it to the surface."

"Then once on the top it would transmit a signal,

now the signal is unique to this processor only. When it's sent its message it simply refills its ballast tanks and then sinks to the bottom again." He continued to prod around inside the compartment for another ten minutes before proclaiming it absolutely safe.

"So every twenty four hours this metal cylinder had surfaced inside the lobster pot and its unique signal had told Flackyard that it was still "alive and well" as well as giving its exact position, before returning to the bottom," I said.

"Spot on, old son."

So George Ferdinand had tried to 'home in' on the signal, but failed to spot it before it descended to the seabed again.

Harry Caplin knew that his boat had travelled ten miles on each of Flackyard's trips.

"Down the coast" he had said.

I reached inside to where a small circular cover was; I could only just get a finger hold to twist the quarter turn required to release it. Once open I found the compact mini-disc stored in an aluminium case, along with two envelopes inside one of those seal-top document bags. Before we opened the CD, we sent for a large jug of coffee and anything that could be rummaged up to eat.

Vince held up the compact mini-disc in one hand and his well earned tumbler of rum in the other, "Based on the trouble we've had finding it, I think this is going to be a tough one to get into!"

I agreed. The man, who had successfully concealed Constantine's List for many years, had not wanted anyone except himself to view its contents.

This was going to take a long time.

Chapter 42

Perhaps I was expecting the typical type of letters inside the cylinder. I spread both of them out on the tabletop. One was type written on official Whitehall headed paper. The other was hand written on a heavy embossed woven paper. But, why were they in the cylinder together?

I shook the small bag of silica gel crystals that had helped keep the documents dry, and threw it into the waste bin. After examining both letters under the bright light of a desk lamp for watermarks or anything unusual, I read the typed letter from Whitehall. It had been sent to a Russian diplomatic attaché in the commercial department of the London Embassy. His name was Alexandr Vladimirovich Donskoy. It read.

Thursday 7th October 1998
Dear Alex, I shall ask you to destroy this the moment that you have read it.

Tell Uzbekistan that they will have to supply anything from the factory that you ask. Remind them that it wasn't the Chinese that have supported them financially for the last nine months.

I want the production increased by twenty per cent by the end of the month or I will sell the whole plant. Would your people in Moscow be interested in buying the place? I will leave this with you. Should you be interested, the usual rate will apply. I think the investors here are beginning to realise which way the wind has blown with the bureaucrats and are already becoming restless. You can mark my words that should your fellows actually come into conflict with the hard line fundamentalists, the British will not be long in understanding what must be done.

I am in the process of forming a think-tank group of like-minded people, who see eye to eye with me on certain points regarding this volatile region, so that when the time is right we will be in a position to do something about it.

Your intelligence people are right about the British Prime Minister. Because of his stance on the Iraq war, he won't survive in office much past this term, if indeed he lasts that long. The weenies in London are already speculating and about to welcome his successor to Downing Street with open arms.

If the worst does happen, then we can expect to have a backlash from Government towards this region of the Middle East and Asia. Demand for farm machinery though, will go through the roof!

Burn this now,
Yours, Oliver

Before reading the other letter, I thought back to my meeting with Adrian Vass at the Central Archive Depository and the subsequent fireside chat that I'd had with the Right Honourable Oliver Hawkworth MP.

Wednesday 27th October 1998
Dear Robert, What a pleasure it was to see you here in London last week. We really must get together more often and not only when there is a trade conference in town! I will come straight to the point, as we are both busy men. The present owners are about to shut down the factory in Uzbekistan, so I am reliably informed. I advise that you instruct our associates in Georgia to take over total control immediately, by force if necessary. Please call me on my number to confirm.

This would of course be a private matter between us and I feel it would be for the best in the long term. The usual procedures apply. I also have pleasure in passing on to you a gift from your Uncle Constantine, who sends his warmest regards, and hopes that your cause benefits greatly by being the guardian of it. He asked me to tell you that he is well, and living a charmed life in the sun.

Your friend, Vladi

* * *

Why did Flackyard keep these letters on the seabed? He was definitely a blackmailer of that there was no doubt. Hawkworth had been like a puppet on the end of the puppeteer's string, 'persuaded' to ensure those valuable construction contracts came his way. Hawkworth appeared to be a traitor and was also so corrupt and in so deep that he had been 'persuaded' to involve Ferran & Cardini with the counterfeit currency that he so enticingly dangled like a carrot under the Partners' noses. He was also 'persuaded' to have me re-called from the assignment in Dorset away from Flackyard's business dealings. How many other people on Constantine's List were 'persuaded' to do things?

George Ferdinand always spoke with respect about Flackyard and straightened to attention whenever Flackyard came near to him. He answered him in the short monosyllabic tones of an army subordinate, but which army?

Like a lot of well-educated and wealthy Russians whose families had defected to the west, Flackyard was privileged and able to master accentless English from a very early age. Ferdinand knew about the cylinder and of the existence of Constantine's List. How much he really knew is difficult to decide, but he was told enough to blackmail at least one person named thercin

– Hawkworth. The one man he hated more than anyone else in the world. Ferdinand, however wasn't interested in construction contracts or anything like that. What he wanted from Hawkworth was large sums of money to finance his drug business with Harry Caplin.

Although Ferdinand went with Flackyard to check the condition of the lobster pot every fourth week, until our voyage together he had made no attempt to retrieve the cylinder from the ocean bed. Ferdinand had only a radio receiver from Flackyard, while we had stolen a transmitter, which would summon the cylinder from the seabed rather than just receive a signal from it every twenty-four hours. Ferdinand had rushed to try and get the cylinder when he discovered that Flackyard had fled the country (just as Harry Caplin guessed he would).

* * *

I pulled the file marked FULCRUM - a pivot about which a lever turns. I placed the two letters and the mini-disk containing Constantine's List and placed them inside the file, putting it and the 'POSEIDON' file on LJ's highly polished maple desk along with a small mountain of other files all waiting for his signature.

"So this is the lot?" LJ asked. He sniffed contemplatively.

"Yes, this is everything relating to the 'Poseidon' assignment. I'd guess that most of the people on Constantine's List have in some way donated large sums of money to Robert Flackyard at one time or another."

"Good work," said LJ, "I always knew you would be able to cope."

"Well, so good of you to think so" I said sarcastically, "especially when you wanted to close down the whole assignment mid term!"

LJ got up and started to pace around his office,

which can get to be very irritating.

"And what's more," I said, "you knew from the outset that Fiona Price was employed by a special Government department or whatever it is, and you thought it best not to tell me."

"Yes," said LJ blandly, "but she was pushed upon us from above and I had no wish to inhibit intercourse among the group." We looked blankly at each other for just a moment or two. "Social," LJ added!

"Of course," I agreed. LJ took out a cigar and lit it.

"Tell me – when will Flackyard and Hawkworth be arrested?" I asked.

"Arrested?" said LJ. "What an extraordinary question old son; what on earth gave you the notion that they would they be arrested. Surely you've been in this business long enough to know better?"

"Yes, but they should be arrested because they're both involved up to their necks in, let's see, international arms trading, drug trafficking, and possibly the murder of Charlie McIntyre. That's just for starters. It just so happens that one is a Parliamentary Cabinet Minister." I said it with as much patience as possible, even though I knew that LJ was deliberately leading me on.

LJ said, "You surely can't imagine, old son, that they can possibly put everyone who answers to that description in jail - can you? Hell, where on earth would we ever find room for them all, and besides, where would we get another Civil Service from?" He gave a sardonic smile and patted the pile of documents.

"Don't look so indignant, old son, you know I'm only pulling your leg. These two are most certainly going to get what's coming to them. Have no doubt about that. As a matter of fact," LJ glanced at his wristwatch, "Robert Flackyard should have already been picked up in Marrakech by Hassan. Who has personally seen to it that he is to be held in one of their finest prisons, until our boys from Scotland Yard arrive."

"They'll then sort out the paperwork and bring him back to the UK for questioning. Of course he'll immediately face a number of charges relating to aiding and abetting the drugs operation in Dorset, as well as those relating to illegal arms dealing. Forensics are hoping to be able to match weapons that were carelessly left behind at Flackyard's residence in Canford Cliffs, with those found by Hassan in the cellar of Flackyard's Riad in Marrakech. I'd say, that any judge worth his salt, will certainly be able to lock him up and throw away the key for a very long time."

"And Hawkworth?" I asked

"Hawkworth. MI5 want to have a little chat with that gentleman. After which they'll decide whether to simply lock him up somewhere remote or hand him over to the police and make him a public domain. Either way, he'll be finished. Personally I like the latter option, its far more messy and the ultimate end for someone like him. Thankfully, gone are the days, when the establishment simply turned a blind eye to keep everything quite and brushed under the carpet, so to speak. No, I wouldn't want to be in Hawkworth's shoes at this present time. Not for all the tea in China."

He got up and went over to the large filing cabinet in the corner of his office. Opening the top drawer he produced an even more enormous file full of documents. Across the front it said "SIS - SPECIAL INVESTIGATION", and was bulging with months of work that LJ had never even thought necessary to mention to me. "If you're to stay with Ferran & Cardini, and in particular my department, dear boy, you must understand your role," he said this in his smug voice. "We didn't send you down to Dorset just to go diving and have lots of fun, as you well knew. Constantine's List was always your priority. The official assignment was never to stir things up with Flackyard and Hawkworth and definitely not to discover anything illegal that was going on down there.

But given your past and that ever so annoying trait of yours for tying up loose ends, we somehow knew that you would take things just that little bit further than the brief that you had been given, and in turn provoke them into doing something, foolhardy. But I must say, it was rather sloppy of you to lose Mr Caplin, like that. We've had the drug boys crawling all over us. They're saying that you deliberately let the American get away, and that he's back in Cuba. Surrounded by bodyguards and no extradition treaty with the United States. Anyway, the Partners want to kick you out on your ear, but I've eventually managed to get them to see a degree of reason."

"How very magnanimous of you," I said quietly.

"What was that? Magnanimous, no, not really. Even though you are a maverick, you do actually have your uses – some of the time," he added, shuffling a large pile of papers around on his desk, before adding. "Oh, by the way, that request for two weeks paid leave has been authorised, with immediate effect, of course. Take a holiday, they say Florida is good at this time of year."

I closed the door gently as I left.

Chapter 43

The next day, I took all the material relating to the assignment down to Adrian Vass for safe keeping at the Central Archive Depository. He signed and stamped the official receipt before asking his assistant to cart it all off to the scanning suite, a quite room where a number of men and women sit methodically scanning all hard copy literature on to portable storage discs.

Afterwards the discs are brought back to Vass's office to be safely deposited in the enormous walk-in safe within his inner office, known as Fort Knox.

After thanking him for his help once again, I left his office wondering why he was always so happy and smiling, given his mundane and seemingly boring job?

As I drove through the city back to the office, I felt detached from the humdrum of life in the capital; perhaps I'd been by the seaside to long.

"Now you see what it's like where the real work is done," said LJ, and went on to make provocative remarks about lying around in the sun. LJ had convened the new training group meeting on my behalf. It was a masterstroke in his battle with Bingham-Carter at M16 for control of the new network. LJ had divided up the various agency representatives equally between Communications and Finance, with the exception of Bingham-Carter. LJ was all elbows and knees. He sat in one of his leather easy chairs and puffed clouds of cigar smoke at Winston Churchill, and said that being successful was merely a state of mind.

Roberts had spread himself all over my office again, but had taken care not to do any of my paper work. The computer monitor screen had strawberry jam on it, and my secretary had been whisked off to another department somewhere in the building while I had been on the Poseidon assignment. I kicked Roberts and his many lever arch files out, and although he protested volubly he set up office elsewhere. "Oh and by the way I'm afraid I've used all of your coffee beans, I'll try and remember to get you another bag tomorrow," he said as he left.

There were numerous emails waiting for me, according to the screen. The first one was from Fiona Price informing me that Harry Caplin had managed to get away to Cuba. Her disappointment came through loud and clear that the authorities on the island were not prepared to extradite him. How did I fancy two unofficial weeks in Florida Keys with a quick hop over to Cuba one evening?

"Um, sounds like fun but could be dangerous in more ways than one," I said, smiling.

All the others were just routine correspondence except for the last; this was from the Partners. It was to the point and very brief, confirming the two weeks leave that I was to take immediately, until the Harry Caplin escape saga had blown over. I would be contacted via email at the appropriate time. I left the building.

* * *

The weekend came and went in a flash. Tats dragged me off on Saturday to view a friend's collection of urban landscapes at a trendy art gallery in the West End. On Sunday we simply relaxed, drinking red wine and lazing around on the roof garden of my apartment, watching the boats going up and down the Thames and the world passing by.

My mobile phone rang; it was LJ working on a Sunday afternoon. After twenty minutes, I managed to hang up on him.

"Who was that?" Tats asked dreamily.

"LJ. He phoned to inform me that Oliver Hawkworth was found dead at his home in Winchester early this morning."

"Hawkworth is dead?" She exclaimed, and then added, "Was it suicide or murder?"

"The local police seem to think it was suicide. Apparently, there was note confessing to his involvement down in Dorset with Harry Caplin, and sleeping pills scattered over his desk. They also found an empty bottle of vodka on the floor."

"But you're not convinced, are you?"

"It doesn't matter what I think, does it. But I'd say it all looks a bit contrived if you ask me."

"Well, look at it like this, Jake. Hawkworth led a full, privileged and opulent life. To go to prison, simply wasn't an option for him, and by committing suicide. Well, he's saved the British tax payer an extremely large amount of money."

"Tats, that's very harsh." I said.

"Well, harsh and callous, it may be, Jake. But, all I'm saying, is that for once in his miserable life. He's actually gone and done something honourable for a change."

"Well, I suppose you've a point there." I said reclining the back on the wooden sun-lounger, and remembering that last meeting I'd had with Hawkworth.

I closed my eyes and tried to relax, soaking up the tranquillity of the rooftop garden, and enjoying the sunshine. Only the occasional sound of a car horn from the city traffic far below interrupted this.

After about five minutes I sat up and dialled Fiona's mobile number. She answered immediately.

"Jake," she said.

"Fiona, have you heard the news about Hawkworth?"

"Yes, my boss phoned me this morning. Good result if you ask me." She said matter of factly.

"Um, that's what Tats said."

"What's happening with Robert Flackyard?" Fiona asked.

"Hassan has picked him up in Marrakech and is holding him there until your lot can bring him back to the UK."

"Well that sounds promising, and what about the Rumples. Have they been tracked down yet?" She asked.

"No, they've gone to ground, and you can rest assured that's where they'll stay until things settle down. LJ seems to think that they might, have absconded with Harry Caplin to Cuba." I said a sheepishly, adding.

"And what about his consignment of opium that we've still got hidden on that German submarine in Dorset?"

"What about it? The local police will have it brought up, I suppose."

"Oh no, that can't happen. That sub has to remain a secret, Fiona. If plod go crawling all over it. Well, for a start it's location will be leaked and that will attract every amateur weekend diver down to it. Remember, there's still live torpedoes on board. No, we've got to blow the charge that I left inside the chamber."

"So, do it." Fiona said

"I can't, I'm already talking to you on my mobile. You do it."

"Okay, hang on a moment, while I go and get my phone, its in the other room."

Fiona returned a moment later with her mobile phone. "Okay, Jake. Tell me what I've got to do?"

"Press nine and then send." I said.

"Okay, I've done that, now what? Wait a minute, there's a video message coming through," I could hear Fiona lightly breathing at the other end of the phone.

"Well I'll be damned."

"What's that, Fiona?"

"You know exactly what, Jake Dillon. But I've got to admit it, this is pure techno genius."

"So you approve, then?"

"Approval given. But when did you plant the video camera in the U-boat?"

"As we were leaving, I thought it might be useful to have a method of surveillance. All I had to do was wedge it alongside one of the torpedoes in the rack. Once we were on the surface, I simply used my mobile phone to hook-up with it as and when I wanted to take a look. The best part is, that when you detonated the explosive charge in the chamber, from that point, the camera recorded everything in real time, and then converted it into a video message. This was then instantly transmitted to everyone whose number I'd programmed in."

"So who got the message, apart from you and me?"

"There were only two other numbers. One of them was LJ, and..."

"Not Harry Caplin?"

"I simply couldn't resist it. By now he'll know what we've done, and I'd really love to be a fly on the wall, wherever he is."

"So what happens now?"

"Nothing. Now that the remote detonator inside the chamber, has been blown. Those opium sacks will have been automatically disintegrated. But without doing any damage to the sub itself. I'd say that there's likely to be a few very light headed fish swimming around that U-boat right now!"

Fiona remained quite at the other end of the phone and then said. "So, Jake. Back to Harry Caplin, who's now safely back in Cuba. Thanks to you."

There was tension in her voice.

"Oh, I wouldn't say that he was that safe there, Fiona."

"Well, what would you say, Jake? After all, if it hadn't been for your Lone Ranger bravado in Dorset. I'd have had him locked up by now."

"Ouch, Don't remind me, I'm embarrassed enough already. I know what I did was a mistake, Fiona. But, I promise you that I'll put things right. All that I ask is that you don't shut the book on me just yet. Deal?"

"I suppose, but you'd better be as good as you think you are, Jake Dillon."

I broke the connection with Fiona, pondering about whether the Rumples were with Harry Caplin in Cuba, after a moment I'd made my decision.

"Tats, first thing tomorrow morning. Could you book me onto the next available British Airways flight to Florida. Oh and I'll need a 4x4 Jeep on arrival, please." I said, rotating my head from side to side in an attempt to relieve the tension in the back of my neck.

"Is that all, sir?" Tats said rolling over onto her back, stretching and yawning as she did so. "Why don't you roll over here lover boy and I'll see what can be done about relieving that tension."

"What a massage?" I said enthusiastically.

"Well sort of," she sat up and unfastened her bikini top, discarding the flimsy piece of material. "I was thinking more along the lines of a distraction."

Until the next time…

THE END

33455608R00166

Printed in Poland
by Amazon Fulfillment
Poland Sp. z o.o., Wrocław